Cover photo: Rappelling down "Ma Dalton" on the South Face of Aiguille du Midi, during the first ascent.

Topos and Maps: M. Piola

English translation: R. Vogler

English Edition distributed by: Cordee, 3a De Montfort Street, Leicester LE1 7HD, Great Britain

International book Number: ISBN 0 904405 28 1

Printed in Italy

First English edition: 1986

MICHEL PIOLA

A TOPO GUIDE TO THE ROCK CLIMBS OF THE MONT BLANC AREA

PIOLA EDITIONS

Foreword

It is with a real pleasure that I introduce to the English speaking climbers this topo guide by Michel Piola. Until now the topo method had been used for crags only. Thanks to this guidebook the rock routes of the Mont Blanc area are also depicted in such a convenient way. This is a major cultural shift as so far mountains had been described either in luxurious well-illustrated books (but not available in paperback) or in guidebooks with complete written descriptions like the Vallot.

Thousands of climbing parties are now enjoying the Mont Blanc area: how does the quest of the modern climbers of the 80s compare with that of their predecessors? Undoubtedly the lure for the Classics (Brenva, Peuterey, etc...), the Big Walls (Grandes Jorasses, Grands Charmoz) or the serious ice-routes is still very strong. However, besides these great lines, new rock routes have sprung on superb granite which can be enjoyed for the sheer pleasure of free climbing moves, and which very seldom call for aid, thanks to the use of light climbing shoes, nuts, friends and fixed bolts. And that's the goal of this topo: to describe modern rock routes as well as suggest a new and free approach to the major existing rock routes. In the past, long descents, sometimes on mixed ground, meant that one had to drag up the wall ice-axes, crampons, and boots. Today rappelling down the same route saves a lot of useless weight on the climb. The results of such a trend have become more and more obvious: aid routes being entirely free climbed, as well as amazing link-ups of even the longest routes, blowing up everyone's mind.

In the late 60s and early 70s I was a dedicated mountaineer in the Mont Blanc area, trying my best on the big walls, in summer and in winter too. Then I went on climbing, but in a quieter way, admiring those who kept pushing the frontier in the high mountains. Thus I witnessed tremendous breakthroughs in ice-climbing thanks to new technics and ice-tools, as well as more daring attitudes.

On the numerous summits around Mont Blanc, even on long or dangerous walls, free climbing standards have been pushed higher and higher. Michel Piola has been and still is one of the leading climbers of this new trend, so that no one could have done a better job at presenting these new routes. If this is the aim of Michel's topoguide, undoubtedly it will be a success.

In the near future, as more and more people go up there, climbing will lose its heroic connotations to be replaced by a joyful mood. However, those who miss the pain and commitment can still find in the whole wide world plenty of rotten icy north faces, ready to fire loads of rocks and bits of ice! As for myself, I'll be one of the first to use this great topo, even though I'll keep stacking in my bookshelf the last updatings of the Vallot guidebook.

Alessandro Gogna

ALPHABETICAL INDEX

Notice:

Topos have been drawn considering that the snow-fields are at their lowest. Thus, especially early in the season, part or all of the first pitch might be buried under the snow!

INTRODUCTION

Conquering unclimbed peaks or ridges was once the goal of mountaineers. Yesterday it was the challenge of the big walls, the technological climbs or the winter epics. But now, the climbers of today are looking more and more for the best moves on the best rock under a bright blue sky.

Therefore this craze for so-called "modern routes" is not surprising. These follow new lines up walls so far untouched because less striking or seemingly blank.

This change occurred through the even more widespread use of nuts and bolts, already drilled occasionally in the Mont Blanc area, but never systematically before the early 1980s. Most of these routes do not even lead to a summit; they boast fixed pro and abselling anchors thus resembling practice crags more and more.

However – and this isn't meant as a damper on people's enthusiasm – one should not forget that up there erosion is still at work, rocks do fall and still hurt, seracs too keep collapsing while the weather remains as whimsical as ever.

On top of that the human error may lead to very awkward situations. This guidebook wishes to describe a sample of the best rock routes in the area, which implies that the criteria for such a selection (quality of rocks, lack of major objective dangers, beauty of the moves, accurate information) are biased and might be questioned.

May the forgotten ones forgive me...

A last word: we should really try to enjoy this amazing playground outside the summer season as well, as it allows year round (or almost) great conditions thanks to its numerous micro-climates. And I bet you'll never have to wear the spare mittens which you were nonetheless wise to bring along. Have fun on the rocks!

ACKNOWLEDGEMENTS

I wish to thank all those who have helped me document this book, and in particular: Guido Azzalea, Serge Koenig, Marco Pedrini, Christophe Profit, Roland and Marc Ravanel, Stéphane Schaffter, Jean-Pierre Seydoux, Romain Vogler.

RESCUE

Look up emergency numbers next page, under "Some useful phone numbers/Rescue". All the mountain-huts usually have a telephone or an emergency portable phone (when the hutkeeper is on duty and with the exception of bivy-huts). When calling for help speed and precision regarding the information given (type of accident, topography, local conditions, type of injuries, etc...) make it a lot easier for the rescuers.

Help: standing with both arms raised/a red square/a red rocket. No help needed: standing with one arm up and one arm down.

INQUIRES

For general inquires one should ask the "Tourist Information Centers" in each area. Asking about the routes or the weather/snow conditions up in the mountain can be done at:
- Office de la Haute Montagne
  Place de l'Eglise, 74400 Chamonix
- Office du Val Vény
  Rue du Mont-Blanc, 11013 Courmayeur

These two organisations are always grateful whenever you can provide similar information in return.

SOME USEFUL PHONE NUMBERS

The area codes ( ) given here apply for the country the telephone number belongs to.
Find out about the appropriate code when calling another country.
The huts' phone numbers are given in the introductions to each area.

WEATHER

France:	a recording with 3 daily up-dates	(50)	53.03.40
Italy:	a recording with 4 daily up-dates	(011)	5.76.01
Switzerland:	a recording with 5 daily up-dates	(022)	162
	for further details contact the Geneva airport weather center	(022)	98.24.24

INQUIRES

France:	Off. du Tourisme de Chamonix	(50)	53.00.24
	Off. de la Haute Montagne de Chamonix	(50)	53.00.88
Italy:	Off. du Tourisme de Courmayeur	(0165)	84.20.60
	Off. Du Val Vény	(0165)	84.10.21
Switzerland:	Off. du Tourisme de Champex	(026)	4.12.27

RESCUE

France:	Peloton de Gendarmes de Haute Montagne (P.G.H.M.)	(50)	53.16.89
Italy:	Poste de Secours de Courmayeur	(0165)	84.24.55
Switzerland:	Gendarmerie d'Orsière	(026)	4.11.06
	Garde Aérienne Suisse de Sauvetage (REGA)	(01)	47.47.47

LIFTS

France:	Gondola of La Flégère	(50)	53.18.58
	Gondola of Le Tour	(50)	54.00.58
	Téléphérique of Grands Montets	(50)	54.00.71
	Téléphérique of Aiguille du Midi	(50)	53.30.80
	Train to Montenvers	(50)	53.12.54
Italy:	Téléphérique of Col du Géant	(0165)	8.99.25
Switzerland:	Chairlift of la Breya	(026)	4.13.44

MAPS

Maps at 1:50,000
Swiss National Maps: map 282 Martigny
map 292 Courmayeur

Maps at 1:25,000
Swiss National Maps: map 1344 Col de Balme
map 1345 Orsière
Maps from the French National Geographic Institute (IGN):
map 231 Argentière/Jorasses

ABBREVIATIONS

1st asc.: first ascent
p.a.: point(s) of aid
sup (+): superior

inf (−):   inferior
h.:   hour(s)
min.:   minute(s)
m.:   meters
R.:   belay stance
Aig.:   Aiguille
Pte: Pointe
gl.:   glacier
ref.:   hut, mountain-hut
biv.:   bivy-hut, shelter

TIMING

Approximate timing has been given only for approaches and paths to the huts.
For the routes, since people climb at such different speeds, there is no way to give even an estimated time.
All you may want to know is that almost each of these routes has been climbed in a couple of hours only, but that in each of them you also find leftovers from bivouacking parties. Only the routes where there is a great chance of bivouac are signalled in the "Gear section" with "bivouac" or "chance of bivouac". The other routes can usually be done in a day from the given starting point.

PROTECTION PLACED ON RAPPEL

A few routes were put up placing part or all of the protection on rappel (pitons and bolts).
Such routes are signalled by the caption "fixed/placed on rappel".

DIRECTION

The indications "on the right", "on the left" are to be followed in the direction of the path or route description. However the indications "right bank", "left bank" are to be taken in the orographic direction of the glacier, stream or valley.

THE CONCEPT OF THE COMPULSORY MOVE

In a route description, a move is considered compulsory and mentioned as such, when it is impossible for the climber to cheat the move by artificial means. It is often the case with blank slabs or really wide cracks (offwidths).
Moderate routes or routes following crack systems do not usually have such compulsory moves.
For instance Ao/VIa in "Nostradamus" (rated VIc all free) means that in between the sections that can be cheated by pulling on the pro (Ao), there will be one or several compulsory moves of VIa.

THE CONCEPT OF POINT OF AID AND POINT OF REST

Any use of protection for progression (piton, bolt, nut,...) is considered as a point of aid (p.a.).
Any rest on pro in the course of a free climbing attempt is considered as a point of rest.

THE CONCEPT OF A BASIC RACK

A basic rack should include all the necessary gear for an average climb, as well as some means of self-rescue, survival, first aid and orientation.
A rack should always include:

For the technical part:
- 2 ropes of 45 m. (150 feet)
- a good selection of nuts; usually 1 set of stoppers and 1 set of "friends" up to 3½ (number 4 is mentioned if needed)
- carabiners, slings, spare slings to leave on rappel anchors
- harness, abseiling device, helmet

For the approach, exit and descent:
- crampons and ice axe whenever encountering a snowfield, glacier or mixed section
- roping-up gear on any glacier

It is advisable to always check carefully check all the fixed pitons, bolts and slings.
Thus a hammer and a couple of pegs might prove useful especially early in the season.

ROUTE DESCRIPTION

Varied information is given for each route, in the following order:
- Crag, orientation and summit altitude (in meters)
  eg.: North buttress of Aiguille des Pélerins (3318 m.)
- Name of the route
  eg.: "Nostradamus"
- Overall rating
  eg.: ED
- Height of the cliff (rock part)
  eg.: 650 m.
- Hardest compulsory move
  eg.: Ao/VIa
- Date and names of the first party (1st asc.)
- General characteristics and information about the starting point
- Information on the fixed protection (fixed)
- Information on the descent route (descent)
- Information on any special gear needed (gear)

RATING SYSTEM

Free climbing:
These are the ratings most used in French speaking countries and just as severe as in any hard free climbing crag. It goes from I to V with the suffix + and − (superior and inferior) as well as a, b, c from VI to VIII.

Aid climbing:
Ao: use of one or several points of aid, without the need of etriers.
A1, A2, A3, A4, A5: sections which are usually not fixed and which require all the modern devices of aid climbing (pitons, copperheads, skyhooks, etc...).
They take into consideration the potential length of the fall, precariousiless of the rock and/or pro, commitment, strenuousness, etc...

KEY TO THE DRAWINGS

1. - MAPS

SUMMIT	HUT/BUILDING	RAILWAY
TOP OF A RIDGE	TELEPHERIQUE GONDOLA CHAIRLIFT	ROAD
MAJOR GLACIER	GOOD PATH	NORTH
CLIMBING AREA	VILLAGE	

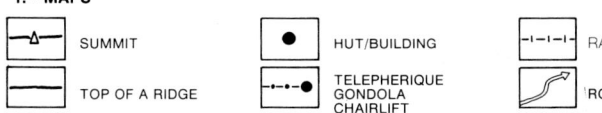

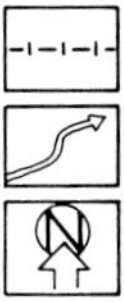

2. - TOPOS

HIKING	BULGE	MORAINE
DESCRIBED ROUTE	ALCOVE	CORNER(S)
VARIATION OR ROUTE NOT DESCRIBED	PILLAR	WATERFALL/STREAM
HIDDEN PART OF A ROUTE	FLAKE/ LOOSE BLOCK	CHANGE FROM SNOW TO ROCK
RAPPEL	CRACK(S)	CREVASSE
PENDULUM/ TENSION TRAVERSE	PARALLEL CRACKS	BERGSCHRUND
MOVING TO ANOTHER SIDE	CHIMNEY(S)	SNOWFIELD/GLACIER
COMING FROM ANOTHER SIDE	OVERHANG(S)	GRASS/ SLOPE
WRONG DIRECTION	FLAKE(S)	FOLIAGE
SLAB(S)	GULLY	TREE(S) / PINE(S)
STEEP SLAB(S)	LEDGE	ROCK GULLY

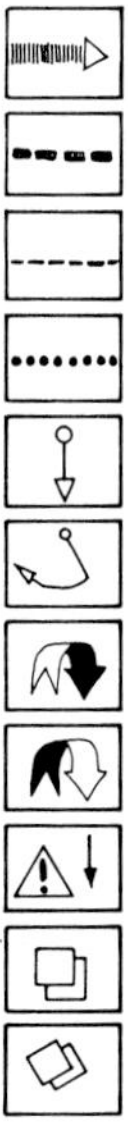

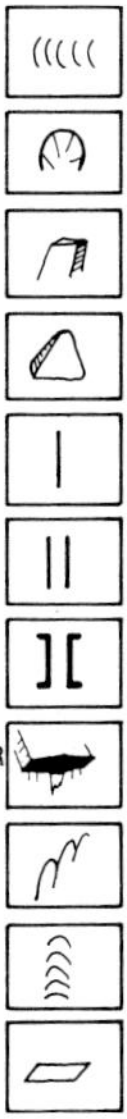

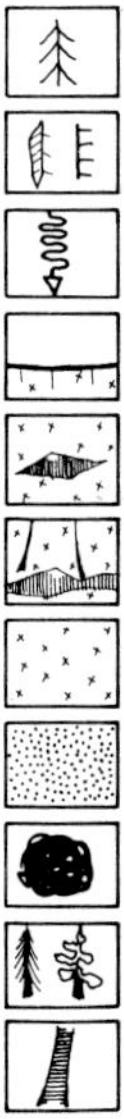

13

Overall rating:
This rating also has "superior" and "inferior" suffixes.

F: easy
PD: not so easy
AD: quite difficult
D: difficult
TD: very difficult
ED: extremely difficult
ABO: abominable!

The overall rating takes into consideration not only the technical difficulties, but also the commitment, the altitude, the run-outs, length of the route, tricky descent, etc...
In this guidebook the rating implies an all free ascent, without any points of rest.
Points of aid or aid sections are always indicated as such.

TOPO

All the information given here is the result of intense research and cross-examination of the data provided by various climbers.
In view of the next edition, any correction of further information is of course welcome.
Please forward to Maison de la Montagne in Chamonix or mail to this address:
Michel PIOLA, 237 Route d'Annecy, 1257 Croix-de-Rozon, Suisse

ECOLOGY

Serious environmental problems are being caused by overcrowding in the Mont Blanc area. Everyone should be aware of the problems, respect both from fauna and flora, and carry rubbish back to town.

THE CLIMBING AREAS OF THE MONT BLANC REGION

This region has been divided into 11 separate climbing areas. The first area which includes the crags from Chamonix to Vallorcine is not described on the drawing on the opposite page.

THE CLIMBING AREAS OF THE MONT BLANC REGION

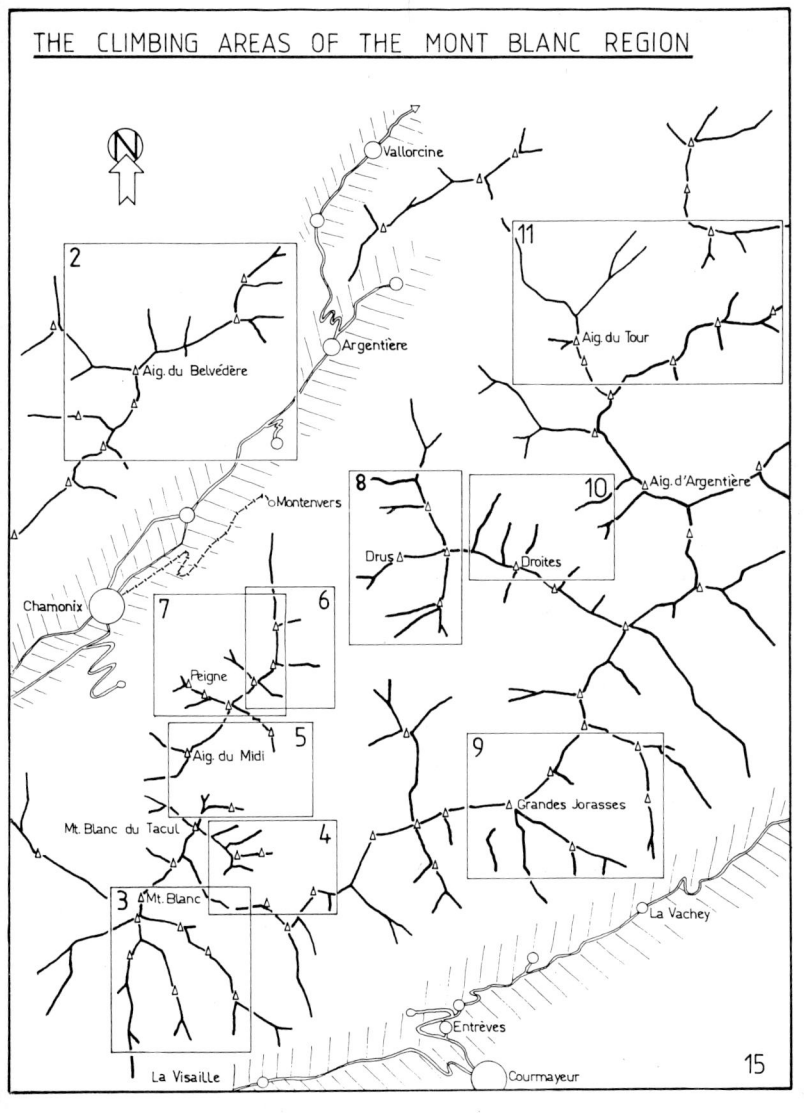

AREA n° 1

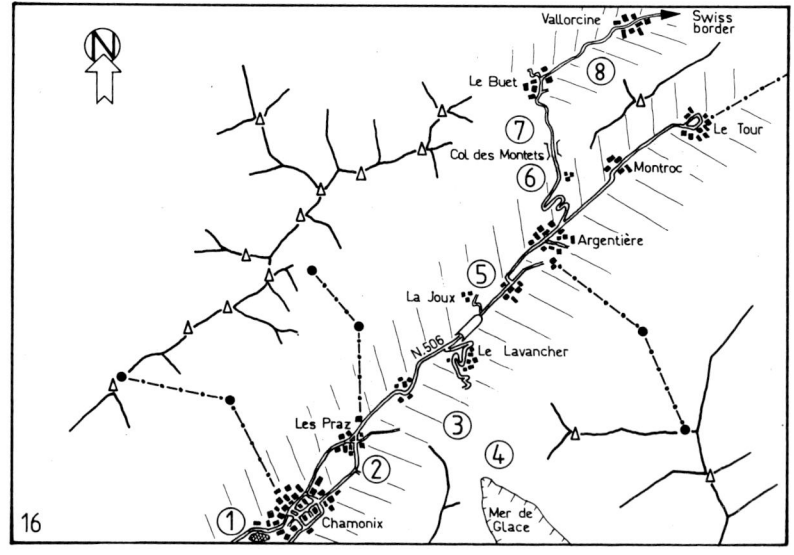

16

AREA N. 1   VALLEY OF CHAMONIX

A great number of climbing areas have appeared in the upper part of the Chamonix valley allowing off-season climbing and/or training opportunities for those with little time available.

Accommodation in the valley
In this area accommodation is alondant in the various villages: hotels, guesthouses as well as a network of well-equipped campsites.

Approaches to the different climbing areas:
1. The Gaillands
They are just above the Chamonix/Les Bossons road, by a small lake.

2. Ortha Boulder
This is a huge granite boulder. With a height of up to 20 feet it offers excellent bouldering problems. However there is no topo-description. From Chamonix, follow N. 506 towards "les Praz", and at the first big curve, turn right on a dirt road. The boulder is a bit further down, in a clearing.

3. The Arveyron Slabs
From Lavancher follow the dirt road to a small car park. Follow the trail to "Le Chapeau". Soon on the right walk down the path leading to the Arveyron viewpoint. 15 minutes to reach the 150 feet crag in the forest. One can also start from the "Téléphérique E.D.F. des Bois". (35 minutes). Not illustrated.

4. Dome of "Le Chapeau"
This is the sunniest crag of all so that you may even enjoy it in December. For the approach, same as 3, but stick to "Le Chapeau" path, and walk by a waterfall. 50 yards further a tiny track leads you down to the top of the Done, from where you abseil down to the base of the routes.

5. Slabs of La Joux
Between "Les Praz" and Argentière, leave N. 506 just after the tunnel against avalanches, and take a small road left that leads to the village of "La Joux". Follow the "Petit Balcon Sud" trail which goes right by the slabs, located in the forest just before an obvious wall against avalanches. One can also hike up straight from Grassonnet.

6. The Col des Montets boulderfield, South side
Around the Col des Montets, dozens of boulders are spread west of the road. Leave your car at the first parking lot on the right before the pass. The boulders are on the opposite side of the road. Not illustrated.

7. The Col des Montets boulderfield, North side
They are higher than those on the South. After the pass, go down a little bit towards Vallorcine. The boulders are also on the West side of the road. Not illustrated.

8. Slab of Vallorcine
This is a must for beginners. From "Le Buet", follow the signs to the crag, on a road then on a trail. There is also an approach from Vallorcine.

THE GAILLANDS - RIGHT SIDE

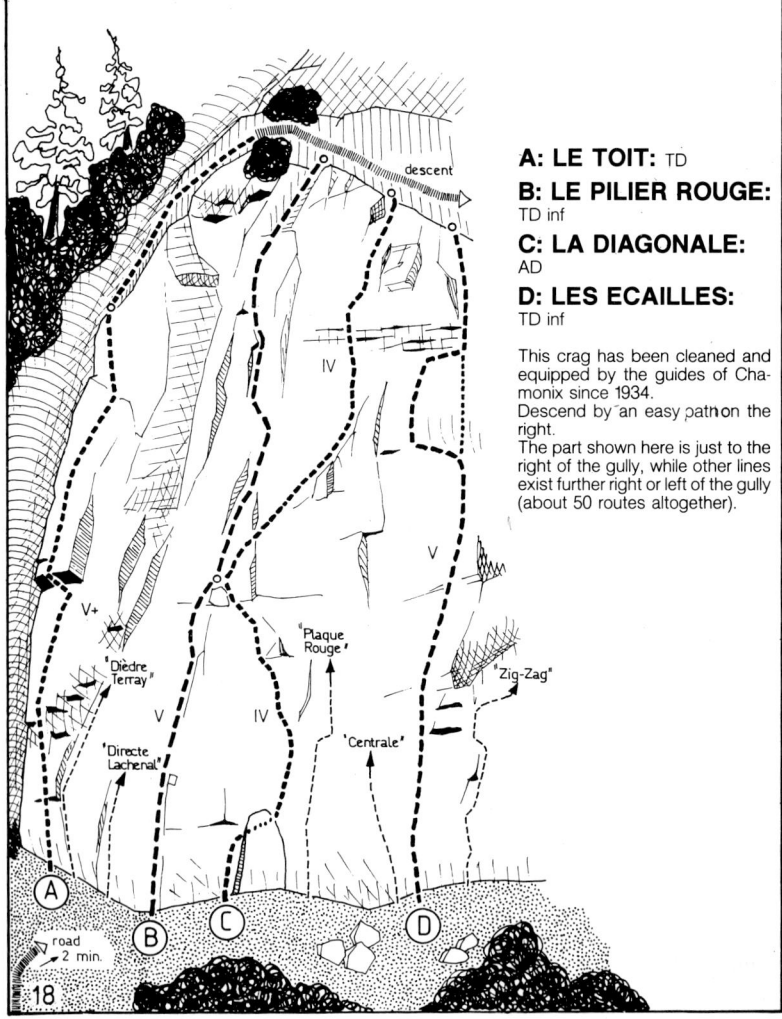

A: LE TOIT: TD

B: LE PILIER ROUGE:
TD inf

C: LA DIAGONALE:
AD

D: LES ECAILLES:
TD inf

This crag has been cleaned and equipped by the guides of Chamonix since 1934.
Descend by an easy path on the right.
The part shown here is just to the right of the gully, while other lines exist further right or left of the gully (about 50 routes altogether).

descent

IV

V

"Plaque Rouge"

"Zig-Zag"

V+

"Dièdre Terray"

V

IV

"Centrale"

"Directe Lachenal"

A

B

C

D

road
2 min.

DOME OF LE CHAPEAU - SOUTH WEST SIDE

AU GRAND DAM DE CES DAMES:

AD sup/90 m/Ao/IV sup
1st asc.: G. HOPFGARTNER/M. PIOLA in autumn 83
With bolts placed on rap. Rap down to the first tree-covered ledge. Start left. Go straight then diagonally up a slab.
fixed: pitons + 15 bolts
descent: back to the starting point...
gear: nuts are useless for once!

DOME OF LE CHAPEAU - SOUTH WEST SIDE

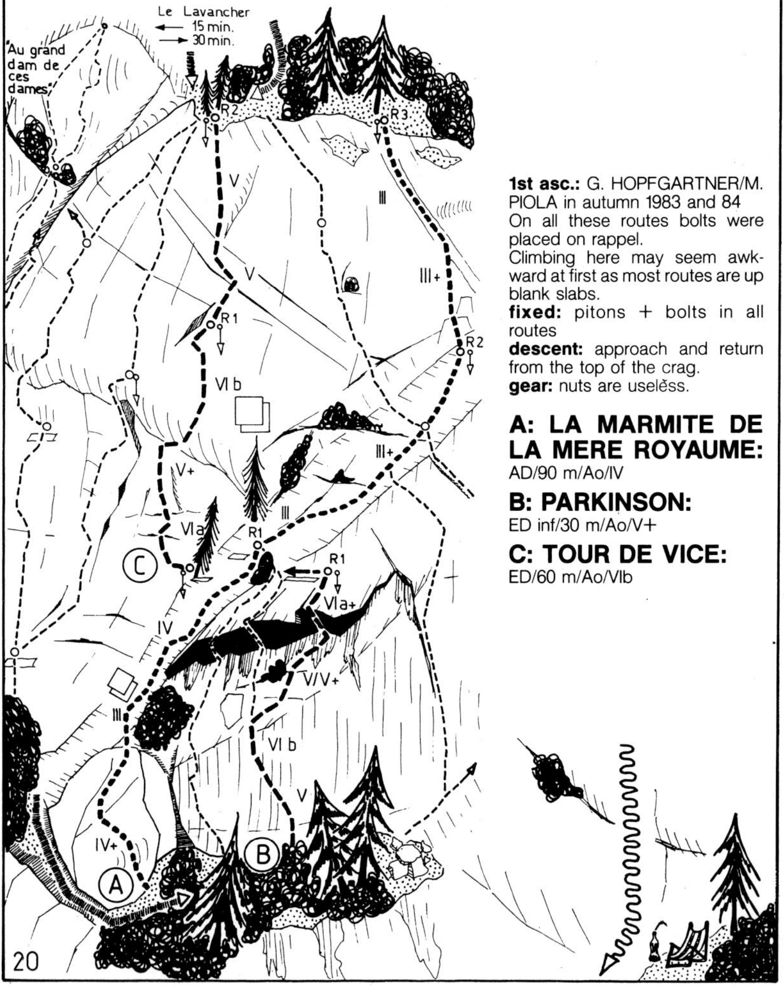

Le Lavancher
→ 15 min.
→ 30 min.

"Au grand dam de ces dames"

R2

R3

V

III

V

III+

R1

R2

VI b

V+

III+

VI a

III

R1

C

R1

VI a+

IV

V/V+

III

VI b

V

IV+

A

B

20

1st asc.: G. HOPFGARTNER/M. PIOLA in autumn 1983 and 84
On all these routes bolts were placed on rappel.
Climbing here may seem awkward at first as most routes are up blank slabs.
fixed: pitons + bolts in all routes
descent: approach and return from the top of the crag.
gear: nuts are useless.

A: LA MARMITE DE LA MERE ROYAUME:
AD/90 m/Ao/IV

B: PARKINSON:
ED inf/30 m/Ao/V+

C: TOUR DE VICE:
ED/60 m/Ao/VIb

SLABS OF LA JOUX A.K.A. "PLAQUE BELLIN"

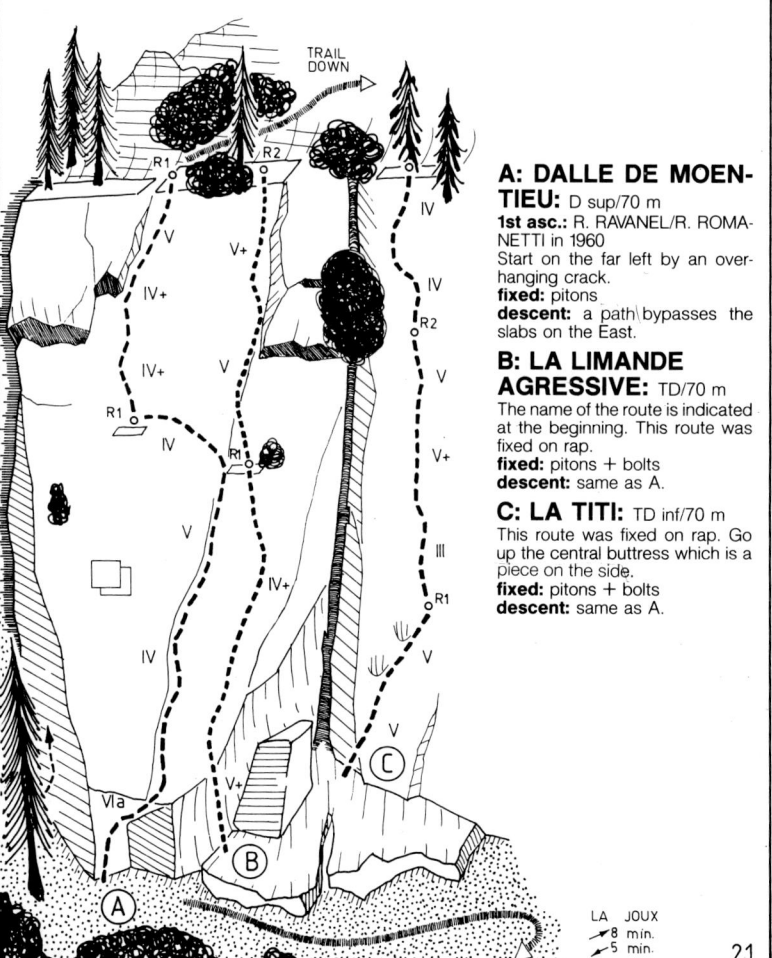

A: DALLE DE MOENTIEU: D sup/70 m
1st asc.: R. RAVANEL/R. ROMANETTI in 1960
Start on the far left by an overhanging crack.
fixed: pitons
descent: a path\bypasses the slabs on the East.

B: LA LIMANDE AGRESSIVE: TD/70 m
The name of the route is indicated at the beginning. This route was fixed on rap.
fixed: pitons + bolts
descent: same as A.

C: LA TITI: TD inf/70 m
This route was fixed on rap. Go up the central buttress which is a piece on the side.
fixed: pitons + bolts
descent: same as A.

SLABS OF LA JOUX A.K.A. "PLAQUE BELLIN"

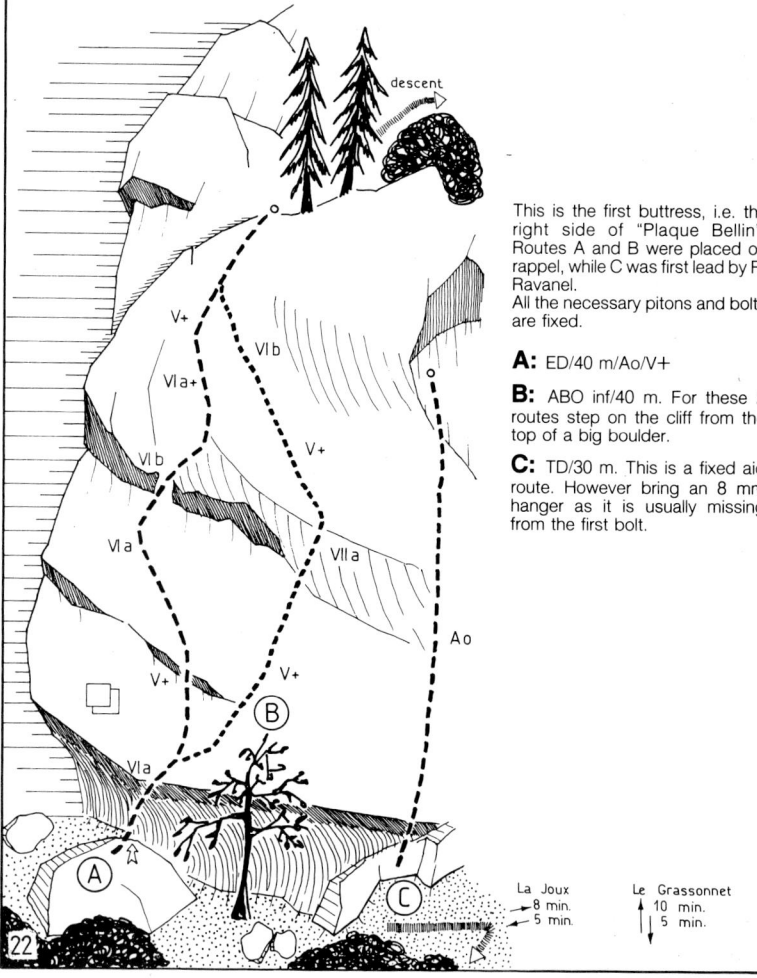

This is the first buttress, i.e. the right side of "Plaque Bellin". Routes A and B were placed on rappel, while C was first lead by R. Ravanel.
All the necessary pitons and bolts are fixed.

A: ED/40 m/Ao/V+

B: ABO inf/40 m. For these 2 routes step on the cliff from the top of a big boulder.

C: TD/30 m. This is a fixed aid route. However bring an 8 mm hanger as it is usually missing from the first bolt.

descent

V+
VIb
VIa+
VIb
V+
VIa
VIIa
V+
V+
Ao
VIa

A   B   C

La Joux
8 min.
5 min.

Le Grassonnet
10 min.
5 min.

22

SLAB OF VALLORCINE

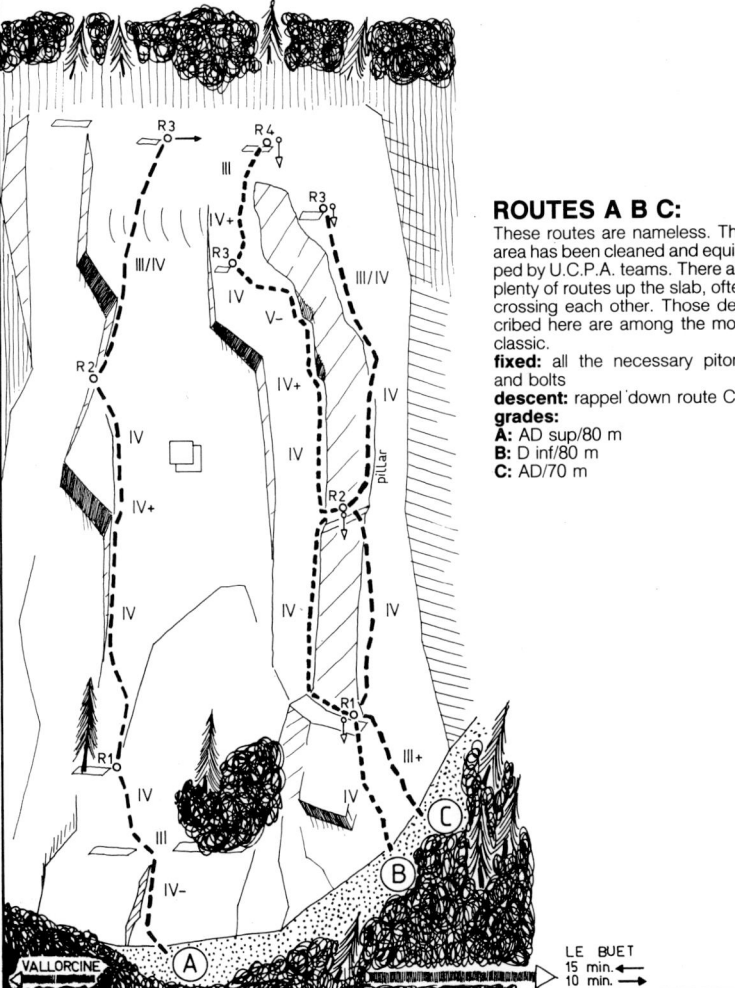

ROUTES A B C:

These routes are nameless. This area has been cleaned and equipped by U.C.P.A. teams. There are plenty of routes up the slab, often crossing each other. Those described here are among the most classic.

fixed: all the necessary pitons and bolts

descent: rappel down route C.

grades:
A: AD sup/80 m
B: D inf/80 m
C: AD/70 m

LE BUET
15 min. ←
10 min. →

23

AREA n° 2

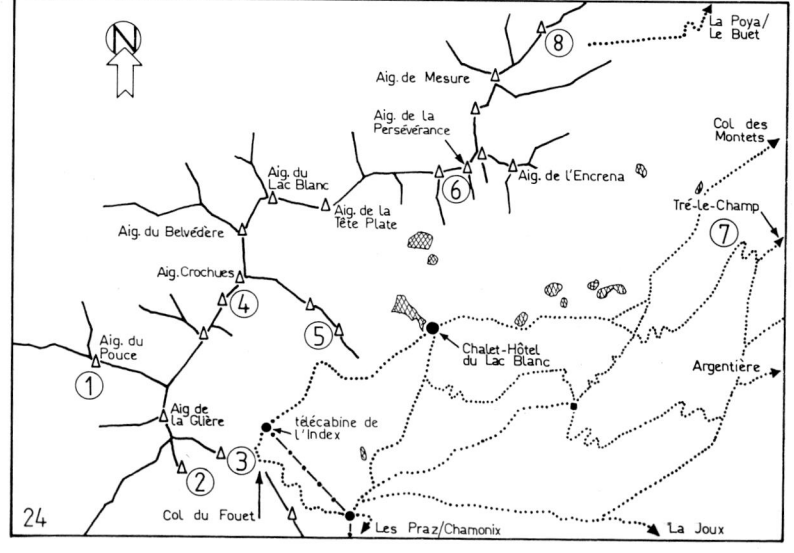

Aig. de Mesure

Aig. de la Persévérance

Aig. du Lac Blanc

Aig. du Belvédère

Aig. de la Tête Plate

Aig. de l'Encrena

La Poya/Le Buet

Col des Montets

Tré-le-Champ

⑦

Argentière

⑧

⑥

Aig. Crochues ④

⑤

Aig. du Pouce

①

Aig. de la Glière

② ③

Col du Fouet

télécabine de l'Index

Chalet-Hôtel du Lac Blanc

La Joux

Les Praz/Chamonix

AREA N. 2   LES AIGUILLES ROUGES

With beautiful Mont Blanc in the background, this area offers a wide range of climbs accessible to most climbers. Even though there are no real glaciers, one should be extremely careful with lingering snowfields in the early season.

Télécabine de l'Index, upper station (2385 m)
This building, which is the starting point for numerous climbs, does not provide any accomodation for the night.

Chalet-hôtel du Lac Blanc (2352 m) No phone.
From the upper station of Télécabine de l'Index follow a marked trail North, going round the South-east ridge of the Aiguilles Crochues and reach Lac Blanc in 50 minutes. This shelter can also be reached from Argentière, Tré-le-champ or Col des Montets.

Approaches to the cliffs:
1. South face of Aiguille du Pouce
From the Télécabine de l'Index walk up the valley to a pass which is just North of Aig. de la Glière. On the other side, walk down steep slopes to the west and make a detour on the left which leads to the base of the cliff.

2. Chapelle de la Glière
From the Télécabine de l'Index, cross to the South-west side of the Fuet pass and go down the Evettes valley for about a hundred meters, thus crossing beneath Aig. de l'Index. Keep crossing at the same level, by-pass the first spur and step in the gully which separates that spur from the South ridge of Chapelle de la Glière.

3. Aiguille de l'Index
From the Télécabine reach the gully coming from the Index pass.

4. East face and crossing of Aiguilles Crochues
From the Télécabine de l'Index follow the Lac Blanc path to the Crochues valley which you walk up towards the gully coming from the Aig. des Crochues pass.

5. West face of Tour des Crochues
Same as 4 but cross the valley diagonally to reach the base of the cliff.

6. Aiguille de la Persévérance et Aiguille des Chamois
From the Chalet-Hôtel du Lac Blanc move North up some grassy hills towards the talus coming down from the pass between the two summits.

7. South-east side of Dalles de la Remuaz
From Tré-le-Champ follow the "Tour du Mont Blanc" (Grand Balcon) path towards the Chésery lakes. You have reached the slabs when the path gets closer to the cliffs after a series of switchbacks.

8. East face of Aiguille nord-est de Praz-Torrent
From "Le Buet" follow the path leading South from the top of a skilift thus reaching "La Tête de Praz-Torrent" and then the base of the cliff.

SOUTH FACE OF AIGUILLE DU POUCE 2874 m

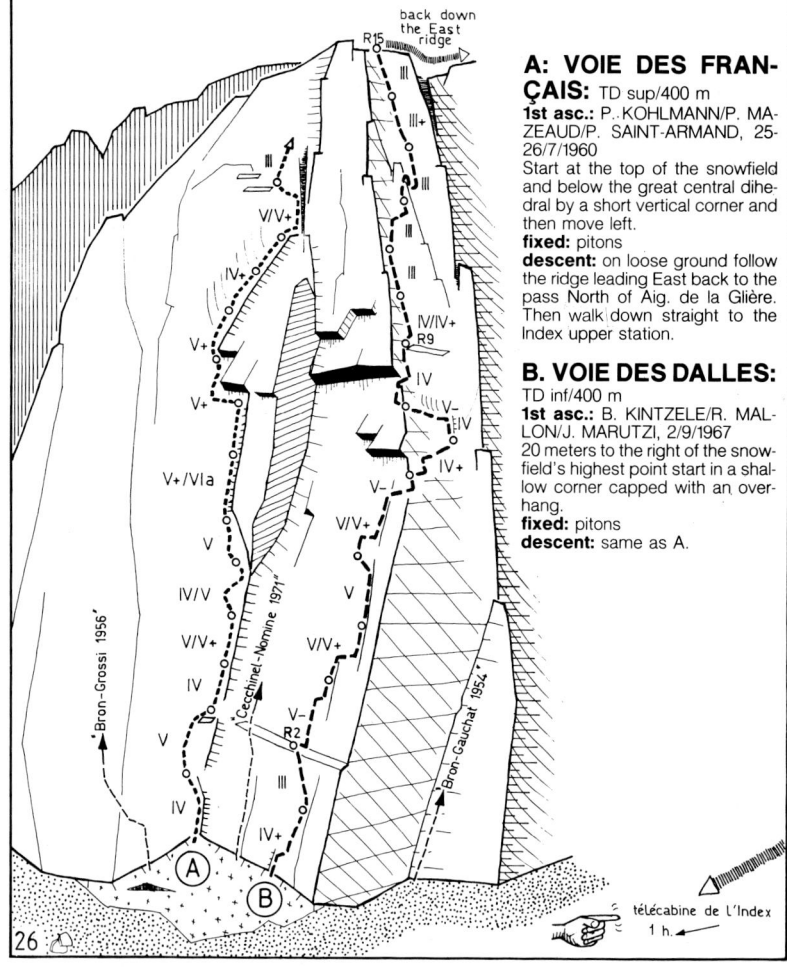

A: VOIE DES FRANÇAIS: TD sup/400 m

1st asc.: P. KOHLMANN/P. MAZEAUD/P. SAINT-ARMAND, 25-26/7/1960

Start at the top of the snowfield and below the great central dihedral by a short vertical corner and then move left.

fixed: pitons

descent: on loose ground follow the ridge leading East back to the pass North of Aig. de la Glière. Then walk down straight to the Index upper station.

B. VOIE DES DALLES: TD inf/400 m

1st asc.: B. KINTZELE/R. MALLON/J. MARUTZI, 2/9/1967

20 meters to the right of the snowfield's highest point start in a shallow corner capped with an overhang.

fixed: pitons

descent: same as A.

télécabine de L'Index
1 h. ◄─

CHAPELLE DE LA GLIERE 2663 m

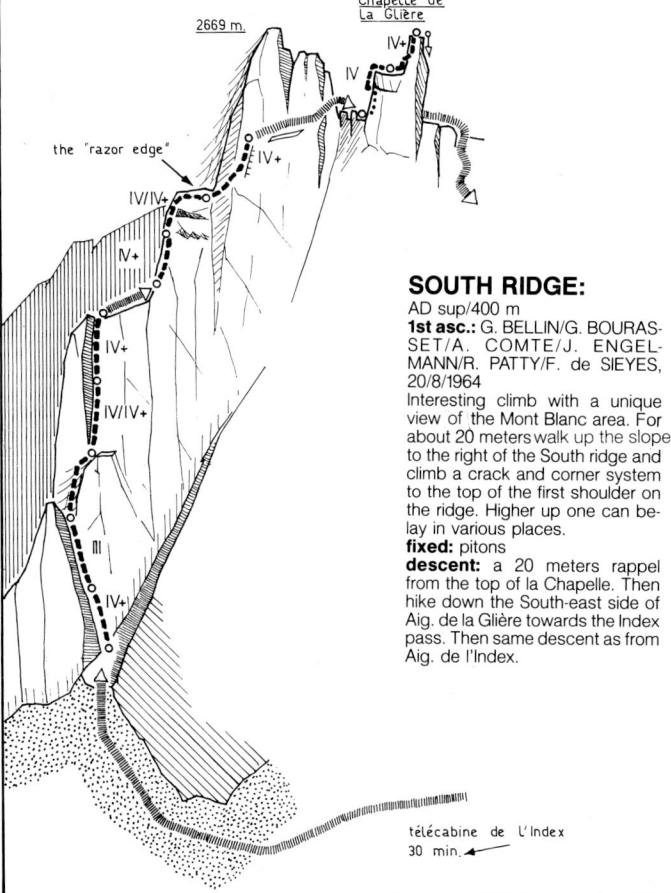

Chapelle de La Glière

the "razor edge"

2669 m.

IV+

IV

IV+

IV/IV+

IV+

IV+

IV/IV+

III

IV+

SOUTH RIDGE:

AD sup/400 m
1st asc.: G. BELLIN/G. BOURAS-SET/A. COMTE/J. ENGEL-MANN/R. PATTY/F. de SIEYES, 20/8/1964
Interesting climb with a unique view of the Mont Blanc area. For about 20 meters walk up the slope to the right of the South ridge and climb a crack and corner system to the top of the first shoulder on the ridge. Higher up one can belay in various places.
fixed: pitons
descent: a 20 meters rappel from the top of la Chapelle. Then hike down the South-east side of Aig. de la Glière towards the Index pass. Then same descent as from Aig. de l'Index.

télécabine de L'Index
30 min.

AIGUILLE DE L'INDEX 2595 m

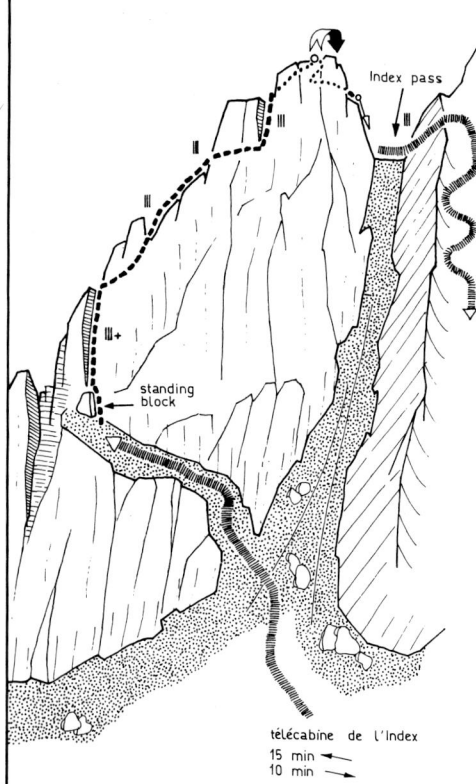

SOUTH EAST RIDGE:

PD sup/AD inf/100 m

1st asc.: Mlle AGUSSOL/H. BE-NIN/M. DAMESNE/J. de LEPI-NEY/T. de LEPINEY, 16/8/1913

This short climb, easily done in a couple of hours, can make a pleasant extension to another climb in the same area. Reach the wide grassy ledge across the East face and follow it almost to its end. Start near a big standing flake and climb a corner to the ridge. Then generally stay on the right-hand side of the ridge. There are lots of stances suitable for belays.

fixed: a big ring for the 40 meters rappel

descent: from the top, follow a short diagonal ledge in the West left face and reach an easy ledge leading right to the top of the rappel.

From the Index pass one can hike straight down the gully but it is advisable to climb up to the ridge (25 m/III) which forms the left bank of that gully. On a discontinuous track walk down the ridge. Near the bottom cross left and via easy slabs reach the snowfield or the slope.

EAST FACE AND CROSSING OF AIGUILLES CROCHUES 2837 m

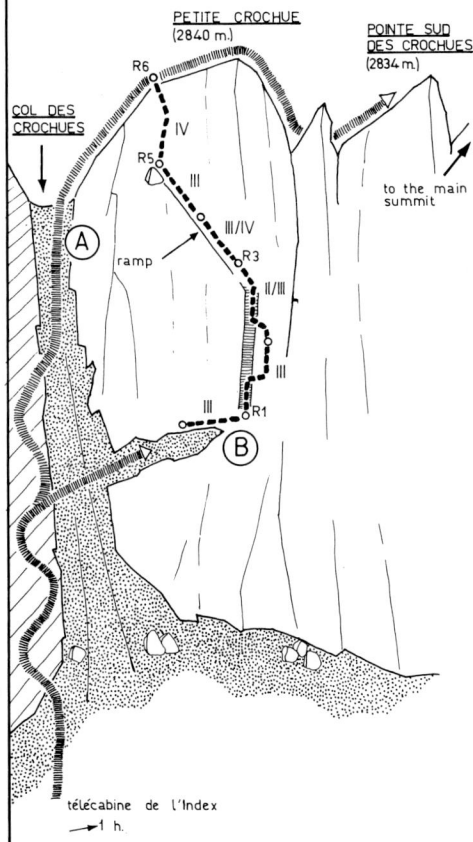

PETITE CROCHUE
(2840 m.)

POINTE SUD
DES CROCHUES
(2834 m.)

R6

IV

R5

III

COL DES
CROCHUES

Ⓐ

III/IV

ramp

R3

II/III

III

III

Ⓑ

R1

to the main
summit

télécabine de l'Index
→ 1 h.

A: TRAVERSEE DES AIGUILLES CRO-CHUES: PD

1st asc.: P. le BEC/T. de LEPI-NEY, 16/8/1920

Even though one can start the traverse from the Crochues pass it is more elegant to first climb the East face of Petite Crochue. Walk up to the pass left of the gully on steep grass and easy rock and then follow the easy ridge.

fixed: /

descent: continue the ridge easi-ly North up to the Dards pass. Then snowfields and taluses lead back to Lac Blanc.

B: FACE EST DE LA PETITE CROCHUE:

AD/130 m

1st asc.: R. SIMOND/X, 1960

Hike up part of the gully coming from the Crochues pass on its left side and then cross over to the big ledge at the base of the East face.

From the end of the ledge cross diagonally right to reach a gully-chimney (R1). Climb the chimney and the right-hand spur (R2) thus reaching the start of an obvious ramp.

fixed: /

descent: from the top either come back to the Crochues pass or continue the traverse.

SOUTH WEST FACE OF TOUR DES CROCHUES

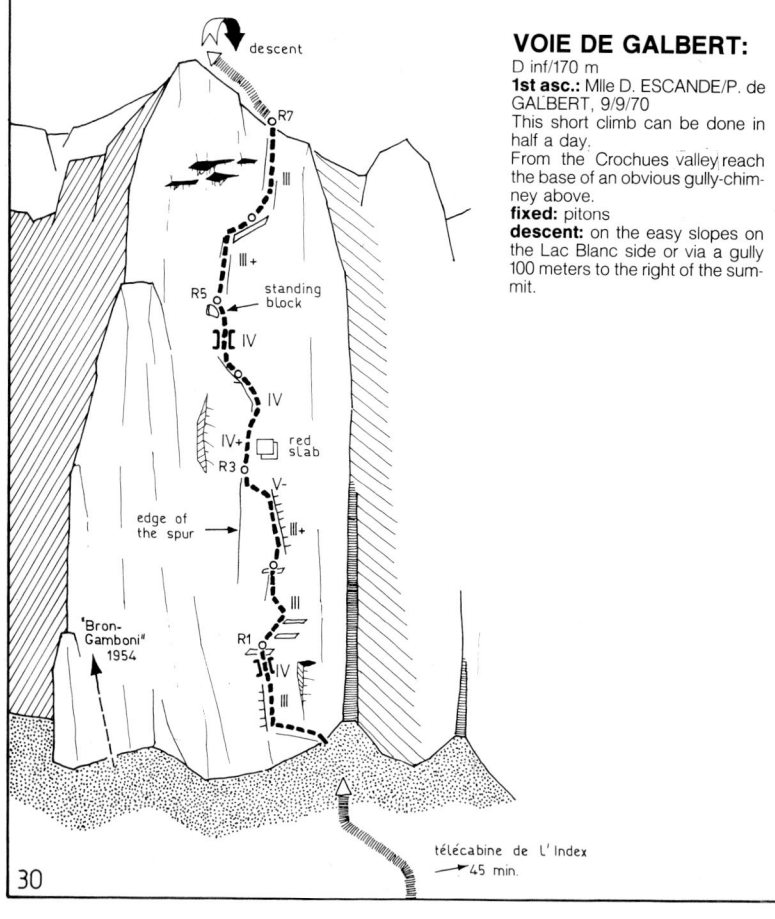

descent

R7

III

III+

R5

standing block

IV

IV

IV+

red slab

R3

V-

III+

edge of the spur

III

R1

IV

III

"Bron-Gamboni" 1954

télécabine de L'Index
← 45 min.

VOIE DE GALBERT:
D inf/170 m
1st asc.: Mlle D. ESCANDE/P. de GALBERT, 9/9/70
This short climb can be done in half a day.
From the Crochues valley reach the base of an obvious gully-chimney above.
fixed: pitons
descent: on the easy slopes on the Lac Blanc side or via a gully 100 meters to the right of the summit.

AIGUILLE DE LA PERSEVERANCE 2901 m
and AIGUILLE DES CHAMOIS 2902 m

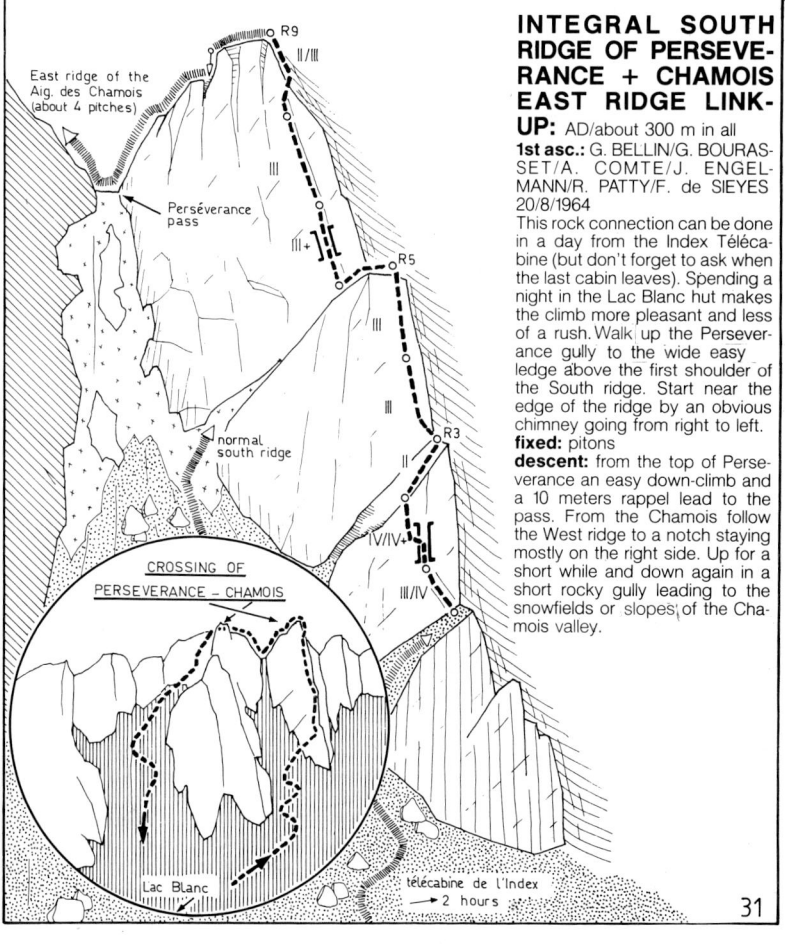

East ridge of the Aig. des Chamois (about 4 pitches)

R9

II/III

Persévérance pass

III

III+

R5

III

III

normal south ridge

R3

II

IV/IV

III/IV

CROSSING OF PERSEVERANCE – CHAMOIS

Lac Blanc

télécabine de l'Index
→ 2 hours

INTEGRAL SOUTH RIDGE OF PERSEVERANCE + CHAMOIS EAST RIDGE LINK-UP: AD/about 300 m in all

1st asc.: G. BELLIN/G. BOURASSET/A. COMTE/J. ENGELMANN/R. PATTY/F. de SIEYES 20/8/1964

This rock connection can be done in a day from the Index Télécabine (but don't forget to ask when the last cabin leaves). Spending a night in the Lac Blanc hut makes the climb more pleasant and less of a rush. Walk up the Perseverance gully to the wide easy ledge above the first shoulder of the South ridge. Start near the edge of the ridge by an obvious chimney going from right to left.
fixed: pitons

descent: from the top of Perseverance an easy down-climb and a 10 meters rappel lead to the pass. From the Chamois follow the West ridge to a notch staying mostly on the right side. Up for a short while and down again in a short rocky gully leading to the snowfields or slopes of the Chamois valley.

31

SOUTH EAST SIDE OF REMUAZ SLABS

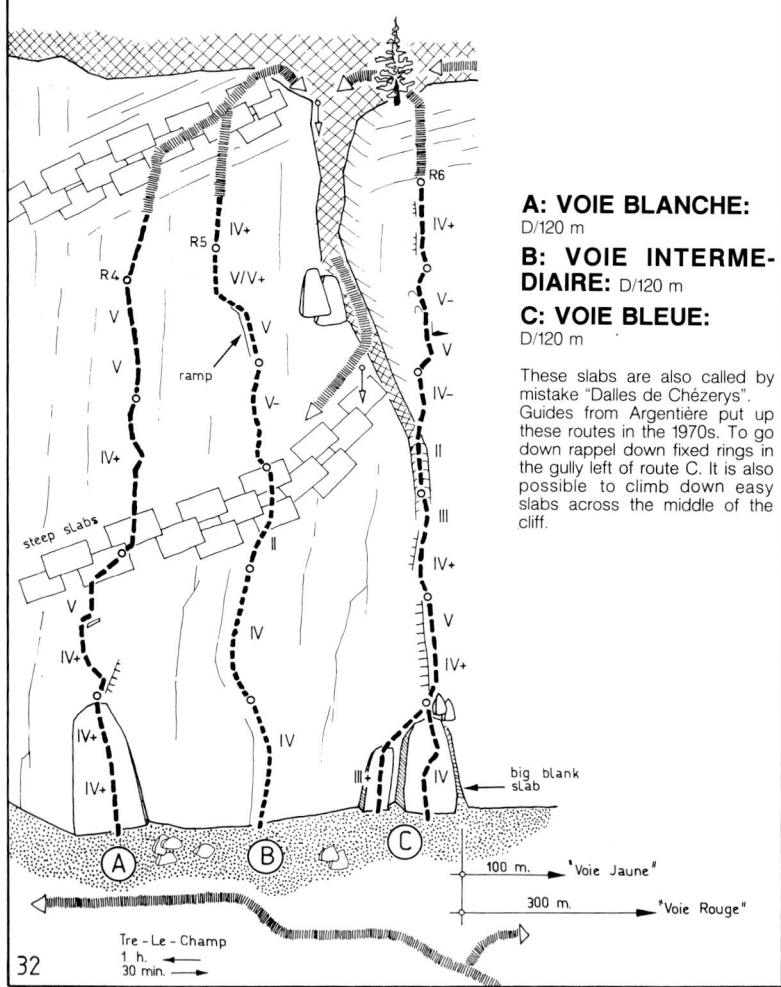

A: VOIE BLANCHE: D/120 m

B: VOIE INTERMEDIAIRE: D/120 m

C: VOIE BLEUE: D/120 m

These slabs are also called by mistake "Dalles de Chézerys". Guides from Argentière put up these routes in the 1970s. To go down rappel down fixed rings in the gully left of route C. It is also possible to climb down easy slabs across the middle of the cliff.

R6

IV+

V–

V

IV–

II

III

IV+

V

IV+

IV

III

IV

big blank slab

R5

IV+

V/V+

V

ramp

V–

IV

R4

V

V

IV+

steep slabs

V

IV+

IV+

IV+

A   B   C

100 m.   "Voie Jaune"

300 m.   "Voie Rouge"

Tre – Le – Champ
1 h. ←
30 min. →

SOUTH EAST SIDE OF REMUAZ SLABS

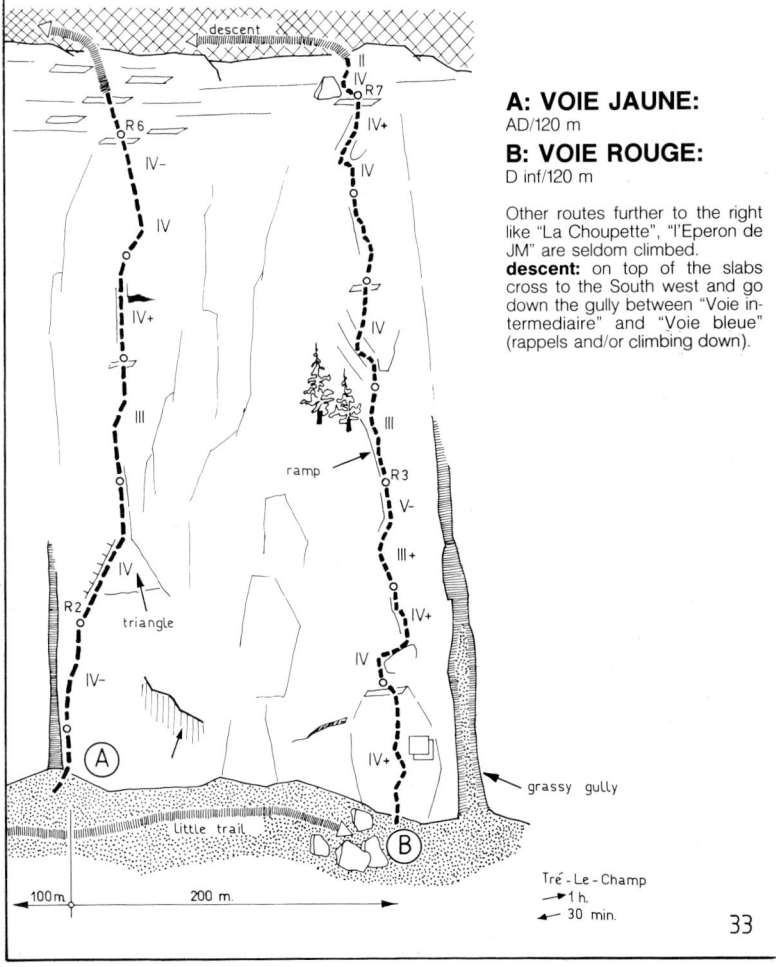

A: VOIE JAUNE:
AD/120 m

B: VOIE ROUGE:
D inf/120 m

Other routes further to the right like "La Choupette", "l'Eperon de JM" are seldom climbed.
descent: on top of the slabs cross to the South west and go down the gully between "Voie intermediaire" and "Voie bleue" (rappels and/or climbing down).

descent

II
IV
R7
IV+
IV

R6
IV-
IV

IV+

III

ramp
III
R3
V-
III+
IV+
IV

IV

IV+

grassy gully

R2
IV
triangle
IV-

Ⓐ

little trail

Ⓑ

100 m.   200 m.

Tré - Le - Champ
→ 1 h.
← 30 min.

33

AIGUILLE NORD EST DE PRAZ-TORRENT 2473 m
EAST FACE

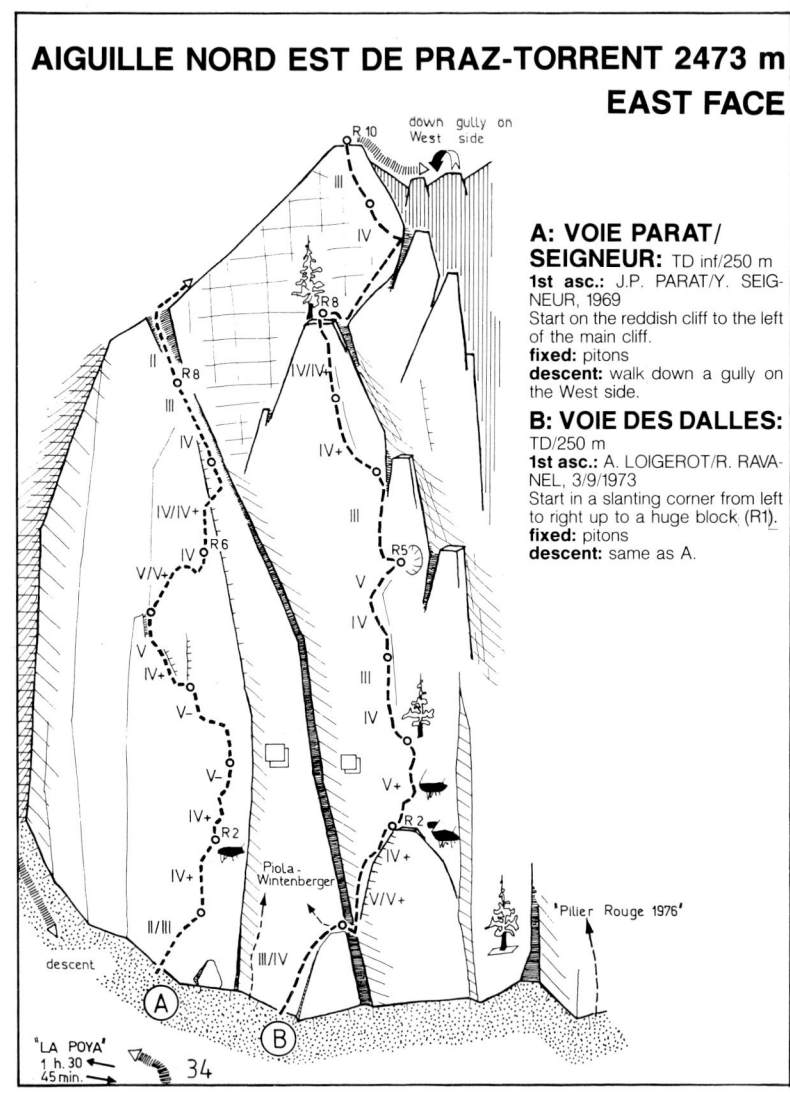

A: VOIE PARAT/SEIGNEUR: TD inf/250 m
1st asc.: J.P. PARAT/Y. SEIGNEUR, 1969
Start on the reddish cliff to the left of the main cliff.
fixed: pitons
descent: walk down a gully on the West side.

B: VOIE DES DALLES: TD/250 m
1st asc.: A. LOIGEROT/R. RAVANEL, 3/9/1973
Start in a slanting corner from left to right up to a huge block (R1).
fixed: pitons
descent: same as A.

down gully on West side

R 10

III

IV

R8

II R 8

IV/IV+

III

IV

IV+

IV/IV+

IV R 6

V/V+

III

R 5

V

IV

V

IV+

III

V−

IV

V−

V+

IV+ R 2

R 2

IV+

Piola-Wintenberger

IV+

V/V+

II/III

III/IV

'Pilier Rouge 1976'

descent

(A)

(B)

"LA POYA"
1 h. 30
45 min.

34

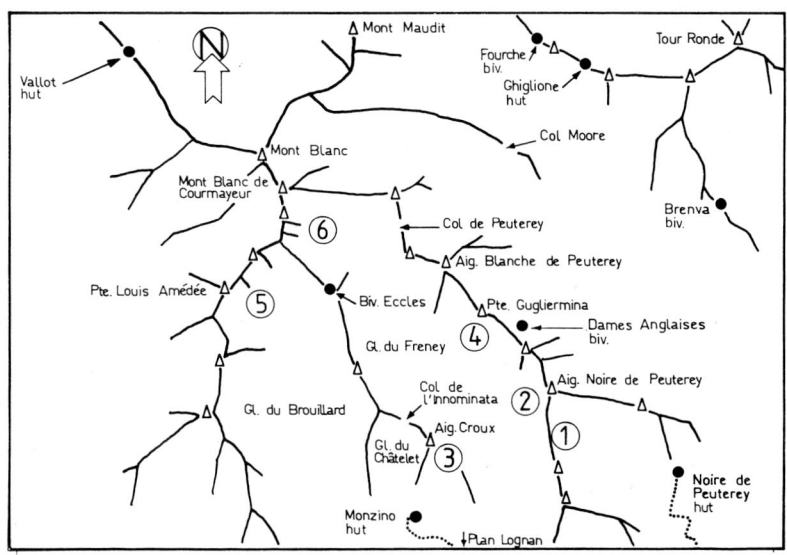

AREA N. 3   THE ITALIAN SIDE OF MONT BLANC

On this wild and spectacular side of the mountain the routes leading to the top of Mont Blanc, after endless ridges, are quite committing. These are ideal routes for whoever wants to add a very alpine dimension to the sport of rock climbing.

Noire de Peuterey hut (A.K.A. Borelli hut) (2310 m) No phone.
From the Chalets of Peuterey (1507 m) cross the stream running from the "Fauteuil des Allemands" and walk up faint tracks along its right bank. After a few rock bands cross the stream again, moving towards the "Fauteuil des Allemands" (another few rock moves, I/III) and then move right towards the hut (2h 30 min).

Monzino hut (2590 m) Phone: (0165) 80.95.53
From Plan Lognan (250 m after "La Visaille", Italian Val Veny, 1680 m) follow the well marked path to the hut climbing several rock bands on the way (cables) (2.30 to 3 hours). It is sometimes possible to have your rucksacks carried by the small téléphérique from Plan Lognan.

Eccles shelter (3850 m) No phone.
From Monzino hut reach the Châtelet glacier (between the South and South-east ridges of Innominata), step above on easy slopes and move left to cross over the lower shoulder of the Innominata South ridge. Walk up the Brouillard glacier and the slopes beneath the Pointe Eccles and the shelter (5 hours).

Ghiglione shelter (3690 m) No phone.
From Torino hut, cross the Flambeaux pass and diagonally walk down to the "Combe Maudite" (upper part of Geant glacier). Cross below the Tour Ronde North face and reach a steep snow slope beneath the Trident pass. Climb up the slope (occasional fixed ropes) and reach the shelter just to the left of the pass (2h 30 min).

Vallot hut (4362 m) No phone/Emergency phone.
Located by the "Rochers Foudroyés" on the Bosses ridge (normal descent route from top of Mont Blanc). This hut can be used in case of trouble.

Approaches to the cliffs:
1. South ridge of Aig. Noire de Peuterey
From the Noire de Peuterey hut cross the stream and walk up the moraine towards the base of Pointe Gamba.
2. West face of Aig. Noire de Peuterey
From Monzino hut grassy slopes lead to the Châtelet glacier and the Innominata pass. Go down its North side and cross the Frêney glacier (numerous crevasses) to the base of the cliff (3h 30 min).
3. South-east face of Aig. Croux
From Monzino hut a track leads to the snowfields at the base of the South-east side of Aig. Croux.
4. South-west face of P.te Gugliermina
Same as 2 but walk up Frêney glacier while crossing it.
5. South-east side of P.te Louis Amédée
a) From Eccles shelter cross horizontally beneath Pointe Eccles for about 40 meters towards the North-west. An easy descent leads to the upper part of the Brouillard glacier and the base of the pillars.
b) From Monzino hut, follow the way to the Eccles shelter but cross directly towards the pillars.
6. Frêney side of Mont Blanc
From Ghiglione shelter, reach the Brenva glacier and cross it towards the Moore pass. After the pass walk beneath the Pilier d'Angle East face (chance of ice fall), and climb up the North-east side of the Peuterey pass. Reach the base of the pillars on the other side. Timing varies a lot with the snow conditions.

SOUTH RIDGE OF AIGUILLE NOIRE OF PEUTEREY
3773 m

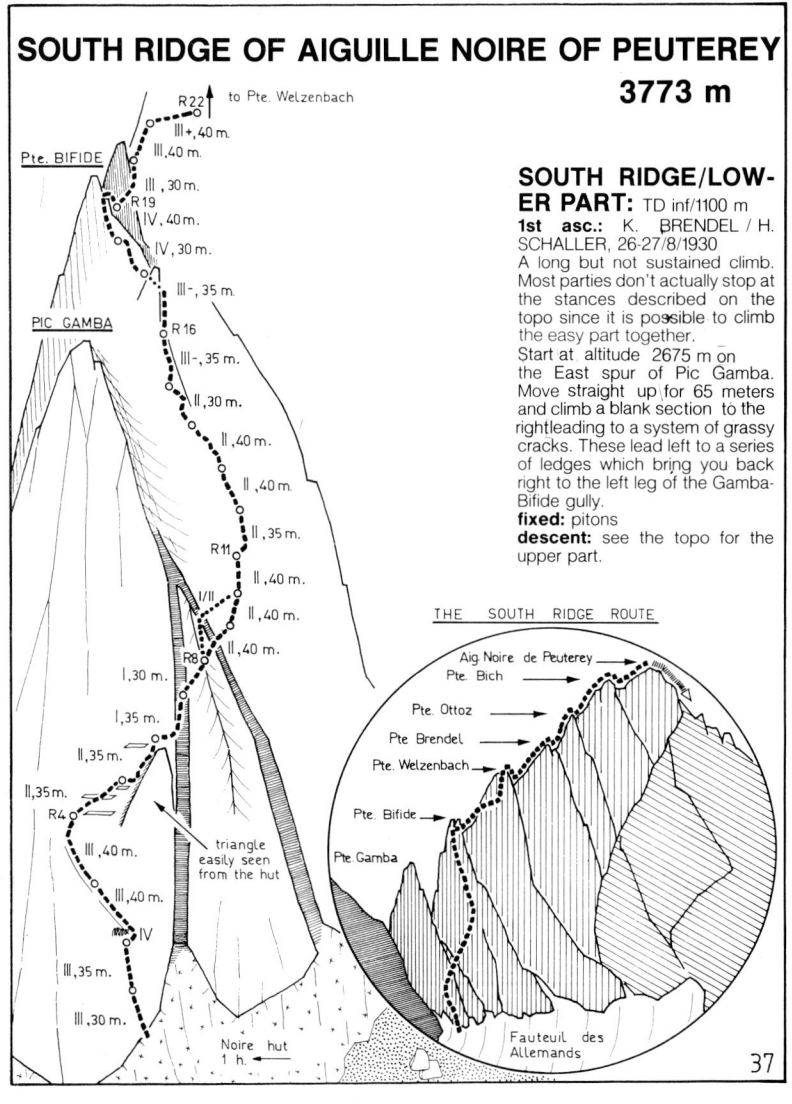

to Pte. Welzenbach

R22

III+, 40 m.

III, 40 m.

Pte. BIFIDE

III, 30 m.

R19

IV, 40 m.

IV, 30 m.

III-, 35 m.

R16

PIC GAMBA

III-, 35 m.

II, 30 m.

II, 40 m.

II, 40 m.

II, 35 m.

R11

II, 40 m.

I/II

II, 40 m.

II, 40 m.

R8

I, 30 m.

I, 35 m.

II, 35 m.

II, 35 m.

R4

III, 40 m.

III, 40 m.

IV

III, 35 m.

III, 30 m.

triangle
easily seen
from the hut

Noire hut
1 h. ←

SOUTH RIDGE/LOWER PART: TD inf/1100 m
1st asc.: K. BRENDEL / H. SCHALLER, 26-27/8/1930
A long but not sustained climb. Most parties don't actually stop at the stances described on the topo since it is possible to climb the easy part together.
Start at altitude 2675 m on the East spur of Pic Gamba. Move straight up for 65 meters and climb a blank section to the rightleading to a system of grassy cracks. These lead left to a series of ledges which bring you back right to the left leg of the Gamba-Bifide gully.
fixed: pitons
descent: see the topo for the upper part.

THE   SOUTH   RIDGE   ROUTE

Aig. Noire de Peuterey →
Pte. Bich →
Pte. Ottoz →
Pte. Brendel →
Pte. Welzenbach →
Pte. Bifide →
Pte. Gamba

Fauteuil des Allemands

37

SOUTH RIDGE OF AIGUILLE NOIRE OF PEUTEREY
3773 m

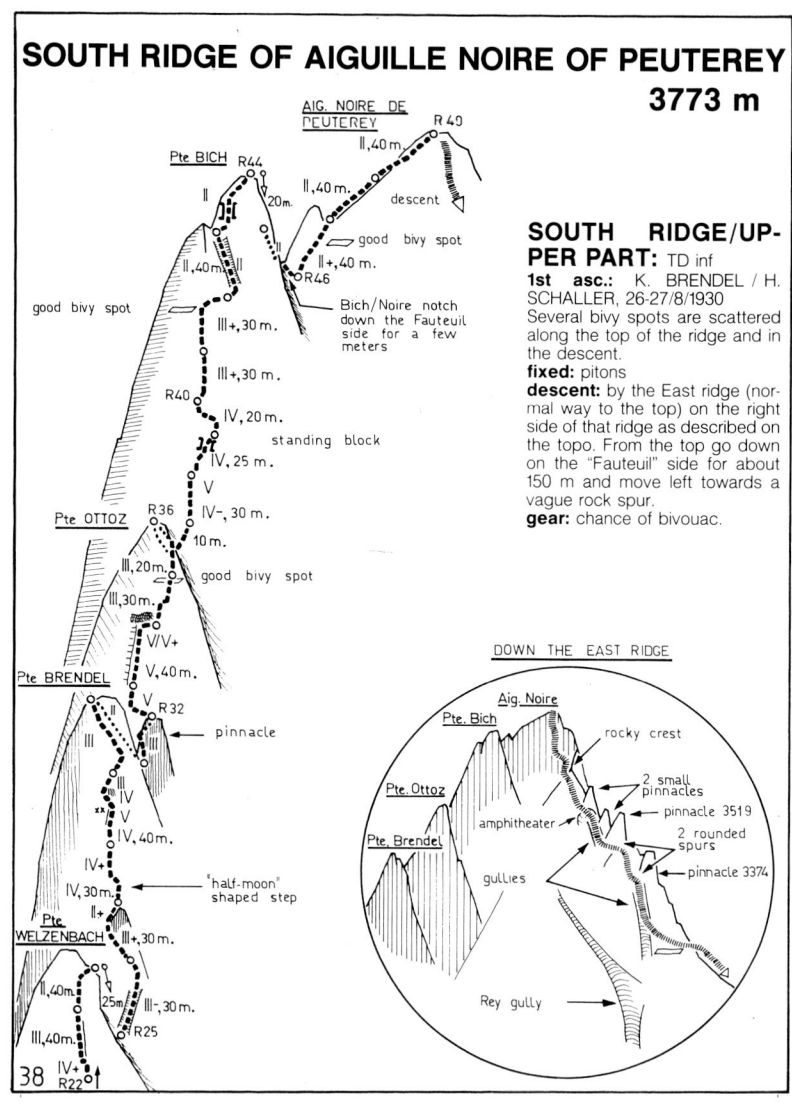

SOUTH RIDGE/UPPER PART: TD inf

1st asc.: K. BRENDEL / H. SCHALLER, 26-27/8/1930
Several bivy spots are scattered along the top of the ridge and in the descent.
fixed: pitons
descent: by the East ridge (normal way to the top) on the right side of that ridge as described on the topo. From the top go down on the "Fauteuil" side for about 150 m and move left towards a vague rock spur.
gear: chance of bivouac.

(Topo labels:)

AIG. NOIRE DE PEUTEREY — R 40
Pte BICH — R 44
good bivy spot
descent
good bivy spot
II, 40 m.
20 m.
II, 40 m.
II+, 40 m. — R 46
Bich/Noire notch down the Fauteuil side for a few meters
II, 40 m.
III
III+, 30 m.
III+, 30 m.
R 40
IV, 20 m. — standing block
IV, 25 m.
V
IV-, 30 m.
Pte OTTOZ — R 36
10 m.
III, 20 m. — good bivy spot
III, 30 m.
V/V+
V, 40 m.
Pte BRENDEL — R 32 — pinnacle
III
IV
xx — IV
IV, 40 m.
IV+
IV, 30 m. — "half-moon" shaped step
II+
Pte WELZENBACH — II+, 30 m.
II, 40 m. — 25 m — III-, 30 m. — R 25
III, 40 m.
38 — IV+ — R 22

DOWN THE EAST RIDGE

Aig. Noire
Pte Bich — rocky crest
Pte. Ottoz — 2 small pinnacles — pinnacle 3519
amphitheater — 2 rounded spurs
Pte. Brendel — pinnacle 3374
gullies
Rey gully

WEST FACE OF AIGUILLE NOIRE OF PEUTEREY

3773 m

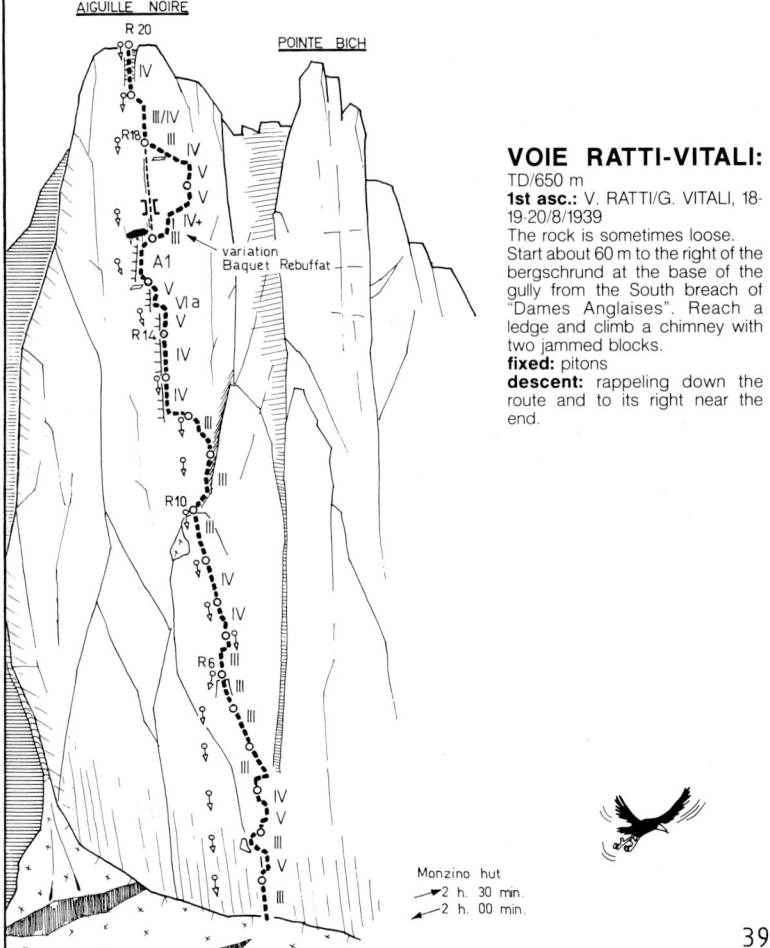

AIGUILLE NOIRE

R 20

IV

III/IV

R19 III

IV

V V

V

IV+

A1

variation
Baquet Rebuffat

V

VI a

R14 V

IV

IV

III

III

R10

III

IV

IV

R6 III

III

III

IV

V

III

V

III

POINTE BICH

VOIE RATTI-VITALI:

TD/650 m

1st asc.: V. RATTI/G. VITALI, 18-19-20/8/1939

The rock is sometimes loose.
Start about 60 m to the right of the bergschrund at the base of the gully from the South breach of "Dames Anglaises". Reach a ledge and climb a chimney with two jammed blocks.

fixed: pitons

descent: rappeling down the route and to its right near the end.

Monzino hut
2 h. 30 min.
2 h. 00 min.

39

SOUTH EAST FACE OF AIGUILLE CROUX 3251 m

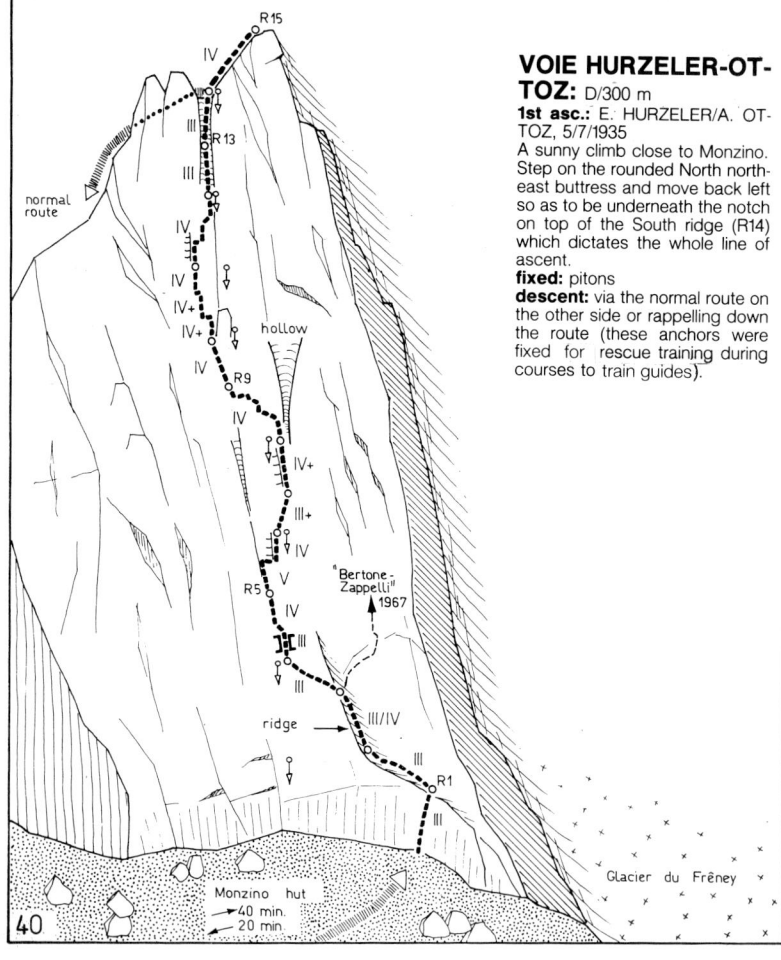

VOIE HURZELER-OT-TOZ: D/300 m

1st asc.: E. HURZELER/A. OT-TOZ, 5/7/1935

A sunny climb close to Monzino. Step on the rounded North north-east buttress and move back left so as to be underneath the notch on top of the South ridge (R14) which dictates the whole line of ascent.

fixed: pitons

descent: via the normal route on the other side or rappelling down the route (these anchors were fixed for rescue training during courses to train guides).

R15
IV
III
R13
III
IV
IV
IV+
IV+
IV
hollow
R9
IV
IV+
III+
IV
R5
V
IV
III
"Bertone-Zappelli" 1967
III
ridge
III/IV
III
R1
III
normal route

Monzino hut
40 min.
20 min.

Glacier du Frêney

40

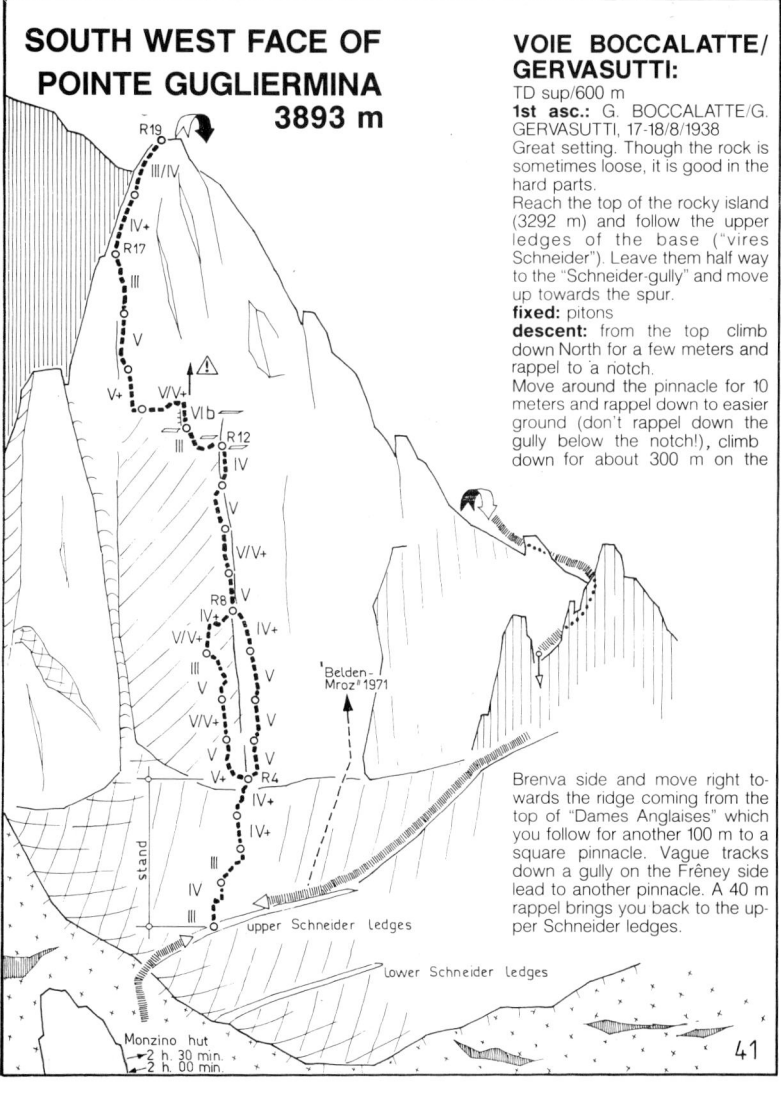

SOUTH WEST FACE OF POINTE GUGLIERMINA
3893 m

VOIE BOCCALATTE/GERVASUTTI:

TD sup/600 m

1st asc.: G. BOCCALATTE/G. GERVASUTTI, 17-18/8/1938

Great setting. Though the rock is sometimes loose, it is good in the hard parts.

Reach the top of the rocky island (3292 m) and follow the upper ledges of the base ("vires Schneider"). Leave them half way to the "Schneider-gully" and move up towards the spur.

fixed: pitons

descent: from the top climb down North for a few meters and rappel to a notch.

Move around the pinnacle for 10 meters and rappel down to easier ground (don't rappel down the gully below the notch!), climb down for about 300 m on the Brenva side and move right towards the ridge coming from the top of "Dames Anglaises" which you follow for another 100 m to a square pinnacle. Vague tracks down a gully on the Frêney side lead to another pinnacle. A 40 m rappel brings you back to the upper Schneider ledges.

Labels on topo:

R19
III/IV
IV+
R17
III
V
V+   V/V+
VIb
III   R12
IV
V
V/V+
V
R8
IV+   IV+
V/V+
III   V
V
V/V+
V
V+   R4
IV+
IV+
III
IV
III

stand

"Belden-Mroz" 1971

upper Schneider ledges

lower Schneider ledges

Monzino hut
2 h. 30 min.
2 h. 00 min.

41

PILIER ROUGE DU BROUILLARD - SOUTH EAST SIDE OF POINTE AMEDEE 4460 m

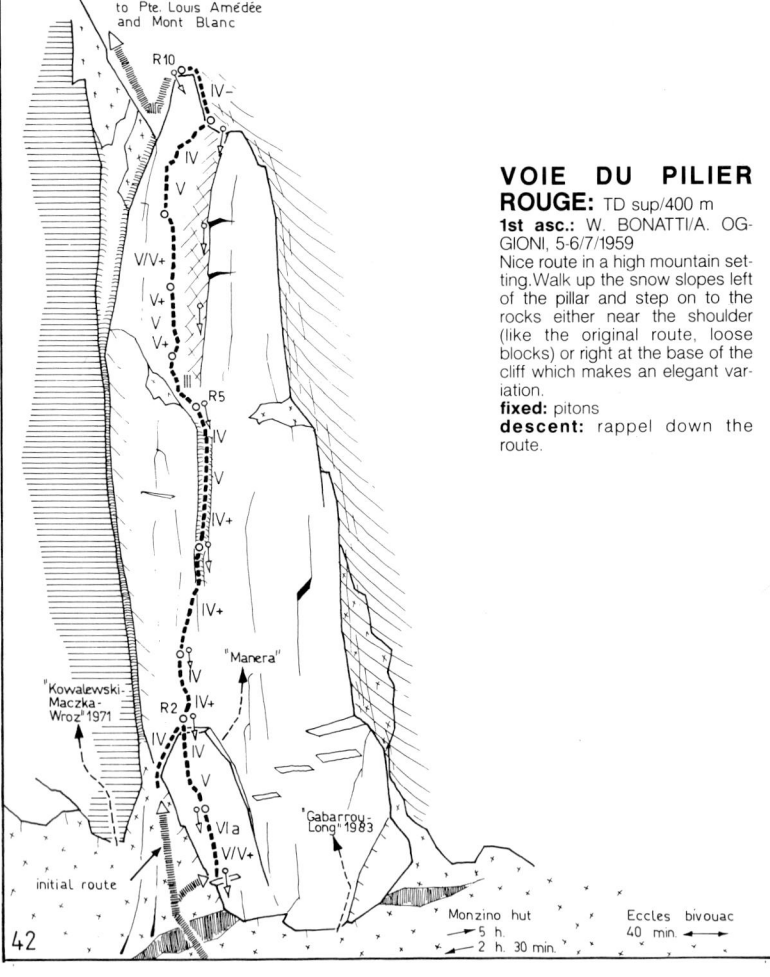

VOIE DU PILIER ROUGE: TD sup/400 m

1st asc.: W. BONATTI/A. OGGIONI, 5-6/7/1959

Nice route in a high mountain setting. Walk up the snow slopes left of the pillar and step on to the rocks either near the shoulder (like the original route, loose blocks) or right at the base of the cliff which makes an elegant variation.

fixed: pitons

descent: rappel down the route.

PILIER ROUGE DU BROUILLARD - SOUTH EAST SIDE OF POINTE AMEDEE 4460 m

Labels on topo:

R13 · IV+ · V+ · V · V+/VI a · VI b/c · VI a · VI b · R9 · V+ · IV+ · III · VI a · R6 · IV+ · VI b · VI b · A3 · VI b · A2 · VI c/VII a · V+ · R4 · V+ · VI b · V · V · VI a · R1 · IV+/V

rappel down

"Bonatti-Oggioni 1959"

Kowalewski-Maczka-Wroz 1971

"Dworak-Grochowski-Jedlinski 1971"

HELP...

Glacier du Brouillard

Monzino hut
5 h.
2 h. 30 min.

Eccles bivouac
40 min.

DIRECTISSIME DU PILIER ROUGE:

ED sup/400 m

1st asc.: P. GABARROU/A. LONG, 28-29/7/1983

An aesthetic line. This long approach takes you to one of the wildest areas of Mont Blanc. Starting from the Eccles shelter the whole route might be done in a day. Start in the middle by a right slanting corner.

fixed: pitons and bolts

descent: from the top of the pillar more or less rappelling down the same line as the Bonatti-Oggioni route.

gear: pitons, 165 feet ropes, chance of bivouac.

43

PILIERS DU FRENEY – A: PILIER DEROBE, 1963 · B: DIRECTISSIME JÖRI BARDILL, 1982
C: VOIE CLASSIQUE, 1961 – Photo: M. Piola.

DIRECTISSIME JÖRI BARDILL: STARTING THE "CHANDELLE". – Photo: M. Piola.

FRENEY SIDE OF MONT BLANC 4807 m

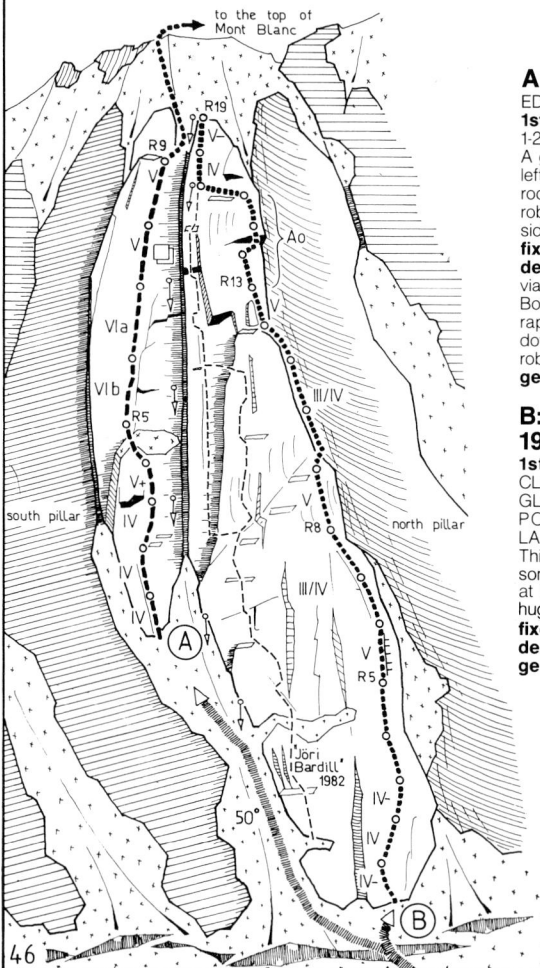

A: PILIER DEROBE

ED inf/300 m
1st asc.: T. FROST/J. HARLIN, 1-2/8/1963
A great route. Climb up the gully left of the Central Pillar (watch for rockfalls) and start the "Pilier Dérobé" by a crack system on its left side before moving back right.
fixed: pitons
descent: from top of Mont Blanc via the normal route ("Arête des Bosses"). However, one can also rappel (50 m/165 feet ropes) down the gorge between the Dérobé and Central Pillars.
gear: chance of bivouac.

B: VOIE CLASSIQUE

1961: TD sup/500 m
1st asc.: C. BONINGTON/J. CLOUGH/R. DESMAISON/J. DU- GLOSZ/P. JULIEN/I. PIUSSI/Y. POLLET-VILLARD/D. WHIL- LANS, 27-28-29/8/1961
This high altitude climb includes some mixed climbing too. Start at the spur to the right of a huge corner.
fixed: pitons
descent: same as A.
gear: chance of bivouac.

Ghiglione hut
3 to 6 h.
(up to 50° slopes)

FREENEY SIDE OF MONT BLANC 4807 m

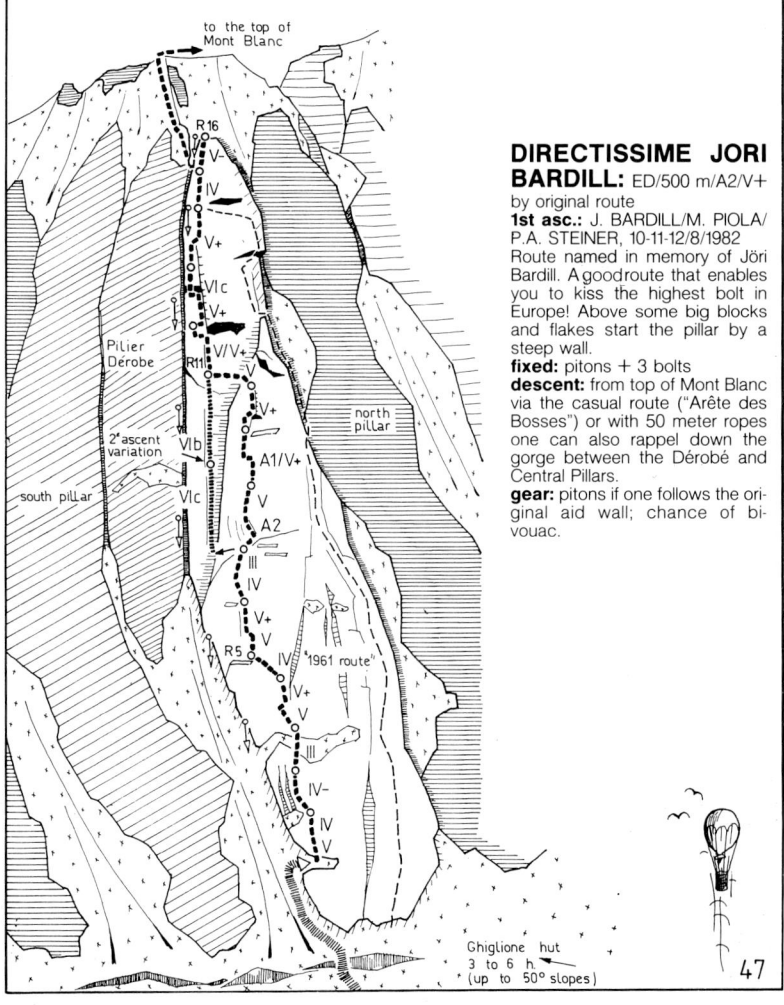

to the top of
Mont Blanc

R 16

V-

IV

V+

VIc

V+

V/V+

Pilier
Dérobe

R11

VIb

2ª ascent
variation

VIc

V+

A1/V+

north
pillar

south pillar

V

A2

III

IV

V+

V

R5

IV '1961 route'

V+

V

III

IV-

IV

V

Ghiglione hut
3 to 6 h
(up to 50° slopes)

DIRECTISSIME JORI BARDILL: ED/500 m/A2/V+

by original route

1st asc.: J. BARDILL/M. PIOLA/ P.A. STEINER, 10-11-12/8/1982

Route named in memory of Jöri Bardill. A good route that enables you to kiss the highest bolt in Europe! Above some big blocks and flakes start the pillar by a steep wall.

fixed: pitons + 3 bolts

descent: from top of Mont Blanc via the casual route ("Arête des Bosses") or with 50 meter ropes one can also rappel down the gorge between the Dérobé and Central Pillars.

gear: pitons if one follows the original aid wall; chance of bivouac.

47

AREA n° 4

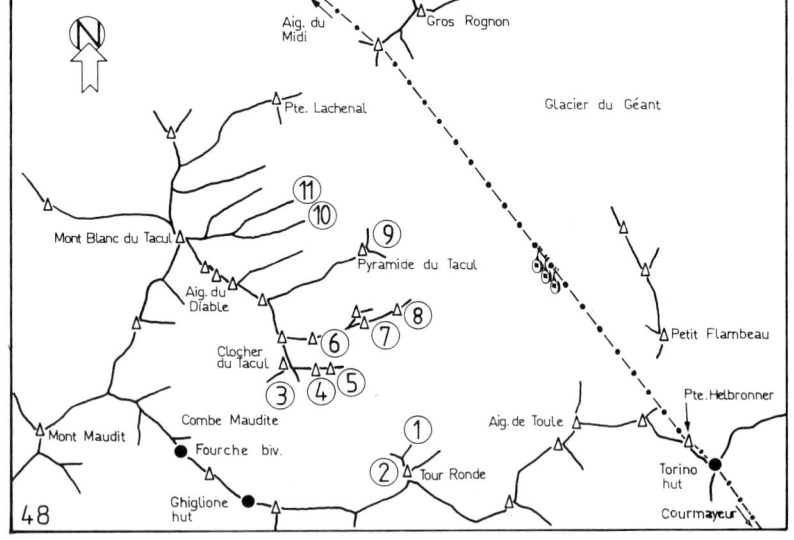

AREA N. 4   MONT BLANC DU TACUL/TOUR RONDE

They are scattered in a wild setting, they are surrounded by eternal snow, they are one of the best areas and above all their granite is the hardest and finest. Who are they? The outcrops of Mont Blanc du Tacul.

Torino hut, Col du Géant (3371 m) Phone: (0165) 84.22.47
This hut located at the upper téléphérique station can be reached from Courmayeur or from Chamonix via the Aig. du Midi téléphérique and Helbronner gondola.

Approaches to the cliffs (possible with skis all year round):
1. North-east ridge of Tour Ronde
a) From the Géant pass, cross the Flambeaux pass and walk down diagonally North-west towards the upper Géant glacier at an altitude of about 3300 m. Go up West towards "Combe Maudite" staying left of a crevassed area and walk beneath Tour Ronde's North face.
b) From Aig. du Midi, reach the Midi pass and then cross the pass between the "Gros Rognon" and "Pointe Lachenal". Walk down towards Pointe Adolphe Rey and cross South through a crevassed area.
2. West side of Tour Ronde
Same approach as 1.
3. South face of Clocher du Tacul
a) From the Géant pass, same approach as 1 but move right, to the North-west, after the crevassed area.
b) From Aig. du Midi same as 1, but stay right of the crevassed area around Pointe Adolphe Rey, moving to the South-west and usually sticking close to the cliffs.
4. Chandelle du Tacul
Same approach as 3.
5. South-west and East faces of Trident du Tacul
Same approach as 3.
6. South, South-east, and East faces of Grand Capucin
Same approach as 3.
7. Petit Capucin
Same approach as 3.
8. South-east face of Pointe Adolphe Rey
a) From the Col du Géant same as 1 to about 3300 m, then cross the Géant glacier to the North-west and towards Pointe Adolphe Rey dealing as best as possible with the crevassed area.
b) From Aig. du Midi, same approach as 3 to the base of the cliff.
9. Pyramide du Tacul
Same approach as 8.
10. Pilier des Trois Pointes
Same as 8 but walk up the glacier North of Pyramide du Tacul.
11. Gervasutti pillar
Same approach as 10.

NORTH EAST SIDE OF TOUR RONDE 3792 m

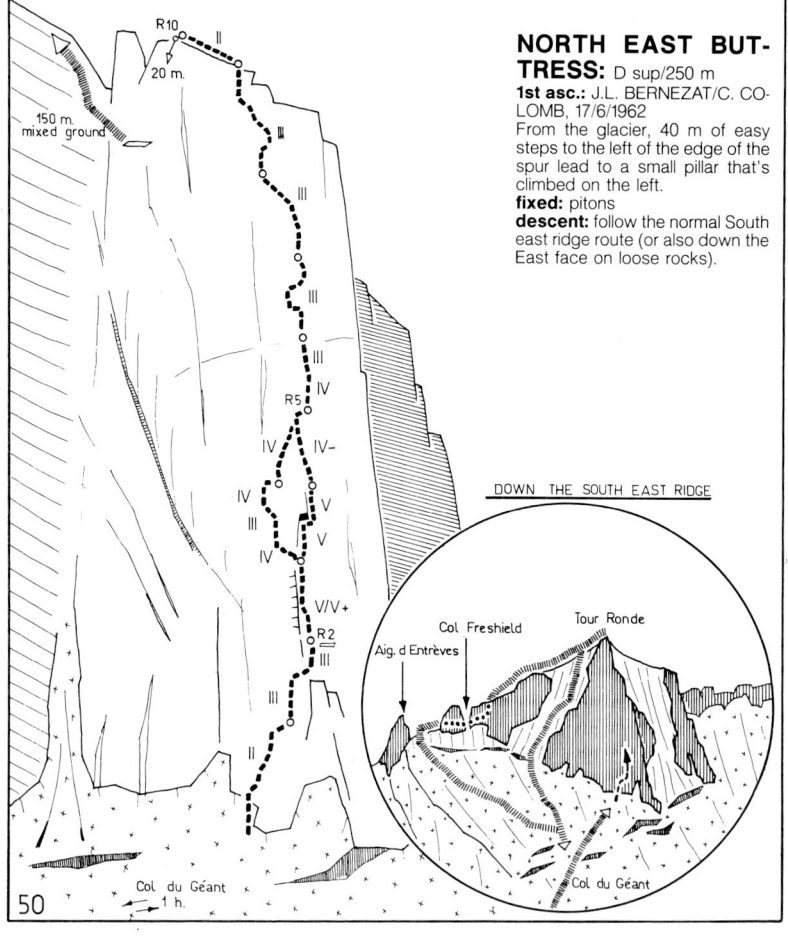

NORTH EAST BUT-TRESS: D sup/250 m

1st asc.: J.L. BERNEZAT/C. CO-LOMB, 17/6/1962

From the glacier, 40 m of easy steps to the left of the edge of the spur lead to a small pillar that's climbed on the left.

fixed: pitons

descent: follow the normal South east ridge route (or also down the East face on loose rocks).

R10

II

20 m.

150 m. mixed ground

II

III

III

III

III

III

R5 IV

IV IV−

IV V

III V

IV V/V+

R2

III

II

II

DOWN THE SOUTH EAST RIDGE

Aig. d Entrèves

Col Freshield

Tour Ronde

Col du Géant

Col du Géant
1 h.

50

WEST SIDE OF TOUR RONDE 3792 m

WEST BUTTRESS
TD/300 m

1st asc.: C. MOLLIER/G. PAYOT, 23/7/1961

A sunny side in the afternoon. The bergschrund is sometimes hard to cross. From the right reach the small pillar, which is about 100 meters high and below a big quarz crack.

fixed: pitons

descent: rappel down the route.

R9
III +
III
V/V+
V/V+
IV+
IV
IV
V
R6
V+
VIa
V+
V/V+
R3
IV
IV
V
V+
V
R1
V
VIa
V/V+ Ro
40°

"Chabod-Gervasutti" 1934

Col du Géant
1 h. 15 min

SOUTH FACE OF CLOCHER DU TACUL 3853 m

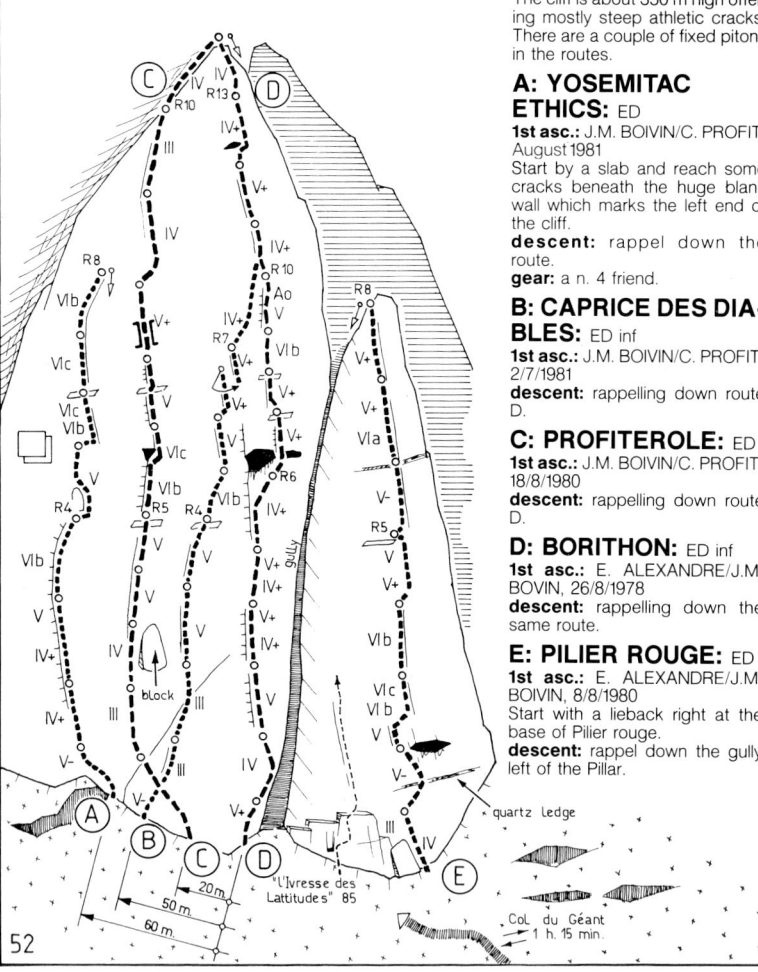

The cliff is about 350 m high offering mostly steep athletic cracks. There are a couple of fixed pitons in the routes.

A: YOSEMITAC ETHICS: ED
1st asc.: J.M. BOIVIN/C. PROFIT, August 1981
Start by a slab and reach some cracks beneath the huge blank wall which marks the left end of the cliff.
descent: rappel down the route.
gear: a n. 4 friend.

B: CAPRICE DES DIABLES: ED inf
1st asc.: J.M. BOIVIN/C. PROFIT, 2/7/1981
descent: rappelling down route D.

C: PROFITEROLE: ED
1st asc.: J.M. BOIVIN/C. PROFIT, 18/8/1980
descent: rappelling down route D.

D: BORITHON: ED inf
1st asc.: E. ALEXANDRE/J.M. BOVIN, 26/8/1978
descent: rappelling down the same route.

E: PILIER ROUGE: ED
1st asc.: E. ALEXANDRE/J.M. BOIVIN, 8/8/1980
Start with a lieback right at the base of Pilier rouge.
descent: rappel down the gully left of the Pillar.

CHANDELLE DU TACUL 3561 m

R9
IV+
VIa
V
V/V+
R7
V/V+
VIb
VIc var.
Ao
V+ IV R5
IV+ IV+
V
IV+
V
V+
V
"Lanfranconi-Cosson" 1972
V+ R3
VIa
V
VIb
V+
V
V+ R1

Trident gully

Col du Géant
1 h. 15 min.

53

SOUTH FACE: ED/150 m
1st asc.: W. BONATTI/R. GAL-LIENI, 3-4/8/1960
A very nice and sunny free climb. Climb up the Trident gully for about 20 m, reach the cliff and cross left for 5 m to climb a crack that splits the steep slabs.
fixed: pitons
descent: rappel down the route.

SOUTH WEST AND EAST FACES OF TRIDENT DU TACUL 3639 m

VOIE LEPINEY:

D/200 m

1st asc.: Mme A. DAMESNE/M. DAMESNE / J. de LEPINEY, 13/9/1919

The view on Grand Capucin is breathtaking.

The route moves from the South-west to the East face. For about 60 m up the gully coming from the Trident notch and then the easy rocks on its right. Move right to reach a wide terrace and a corner that leads right, to the East face.

fixed: pitons

descent: rappel down the East face and the Aiguillettes gully (bergschrund).

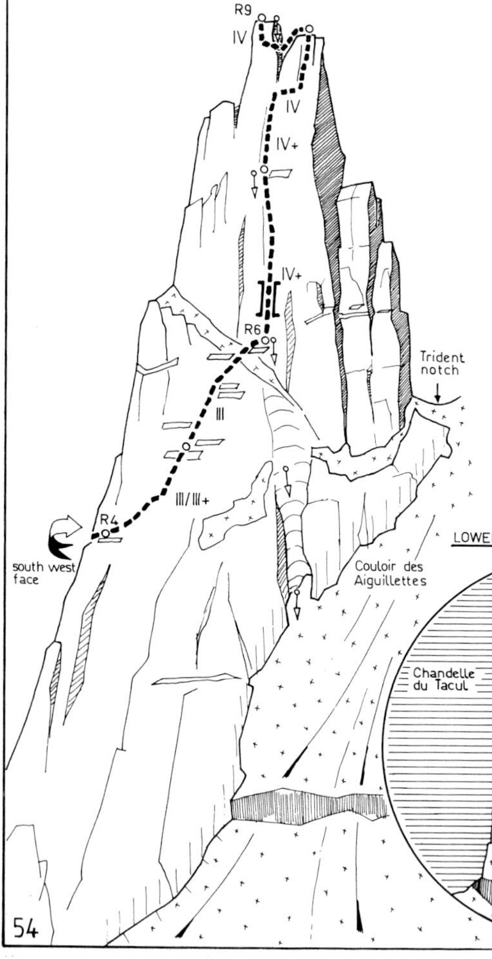

R9

IV

IV

IV+

IV+

R6

III

III/III+

R4

south west face

Trident notch

Couloir des Aiguillettes

LOWERT PART OF SOUTH WEST FACE

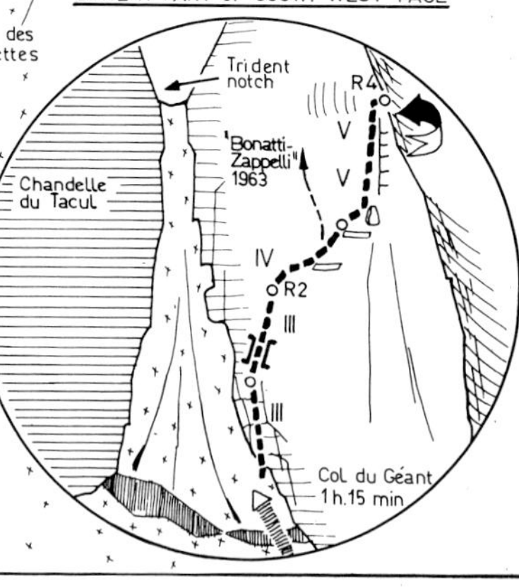

Trident notch

R4

"Bonatti-Zappelli" 1963

V

V

Chandelle du Tacul

IV

R2

III

III

Col du Géant 1 h.15 min

SOUTH BUTTRESS OF GRAND CAPUCIN 3838 m

O SOLE MIO...

ED/300 m/Ao/VIa

1st asc.: M. PIOLA/P.A. STEINER, 21-22/4/1984

A really great climb, varied and sunny.

The route goes up the South buttress of Grand Capucin. Look for an obvious crack in its lower part and start beneath it, near a carved arrow (R1).

fixed: pitons + 15 bolts

descent: rappel down the route to the big terrace on the "Swiss route" (R5) and then down the big corner of that route.

SOUTH BUTTRESS OF GRAND CAPUCIN 3838 m

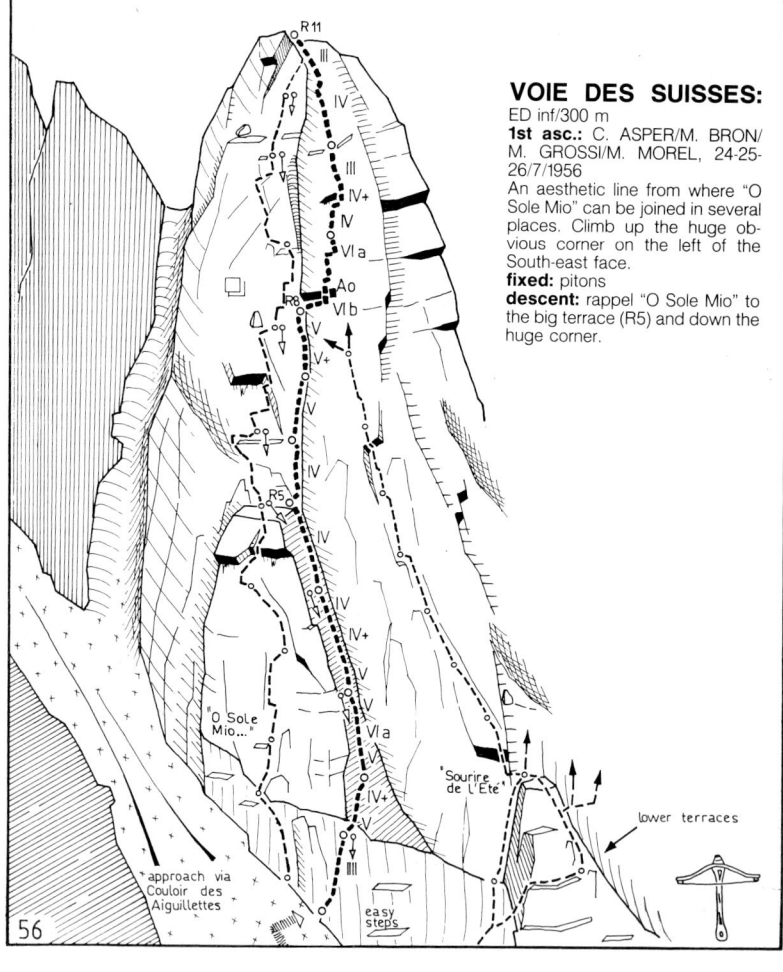

VOIE DES SUISSES:

ED inf/300 m
1st asc.: C. ASPER/M. BRON/ M. GROSSI/M. MOREL, 24-25-26/7/1956
An aesthetic line from where "O Sole Mio" can be joined in several places. Climb up the huge obvious corner on the left of the South-east face.
fixed: pitons
descent: rappel "O Sole Mio" to the big terrace (R5) and down the huge corner.

R 11
III
IV
III
IV+
IV
VI a
Ao
VI b
V
V+
V
IV
IV
IV
IV+
V
V
VI a
V
IV+
III

"O Sole Mio..."

"Sourire de L'Ete"

lower terraces

approach via Couloir des Aiguillettes

easy steps

SOUTH FACE OF GRAND CAPUCIN – A: O SOLE MIO..., 1984 – B: VOIE DES SUISSES, 1956 – C: LE SOURIRE DE L'ETE, 1981 – D: VOYAGE SELON GULLIVER, 1982 – E: FLA– GRANT DELIRE, 1983 – Photo: F. Labande.

SOUTH EAST FACE OF GRAND CAPUCIN 3838 m

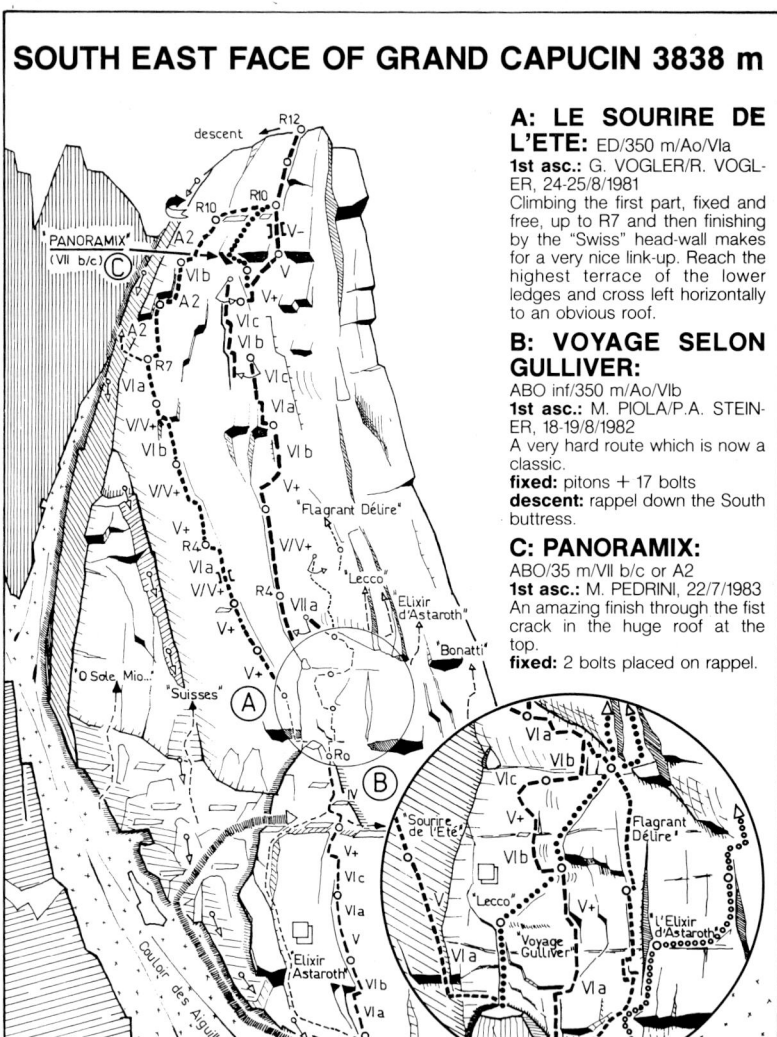

A: LE SOURIRE DE L'ETE:
ED/350 m/Ao/VIa

1st asc.: G. VOGLER/R. VOGLER, 24-25/8/1981

Climbing the first part, fixed and free, up to R7 and then finishing by the "Swiss" head-wall makes for a very nice link-up. Reach the highest terrace of the lower ledges and cross left horizontally to an obvious roof.

B: VOYAGE SELON GULLIVER:
ABO inf/350 m/Ao/VIb

1st asc.: M. PIOLA/P.A. STEINER, 18-19/8/1982

A very hard route which is now a classic.

fixed: pitons + 17 bolts
descent: rappel down the South buttress.

C: PANORAMIX:
ABO/35 m/VII b/c or A2

1st asc.: M. PEDRINI, 22/7/1983

An amazing finish through the fist crack in the huge roof at the top.

fixed: 2 bolts placed on rappel.

EAST FACE OF GRAND CAPUCIN – A: FACE EST CLASSIQUE (BONATTI-GHIGO), 1951 – B: L'ELIXIR D'ASTAROTH, 1981 – C: DIRECTE DES CAPUCINES, 1983 – Photo: J. Winkler.

(A)   (B)   (C)

EAST FACE OF GRAND CAPUCIN 3838 m

The "triple direct", combining "Elixir", "Gulliver" and "Panoramix" (ABO/450 m) is an extremely hard and sustained link-up, with only one point of aid (the 3rd pendulum on Gulliver).

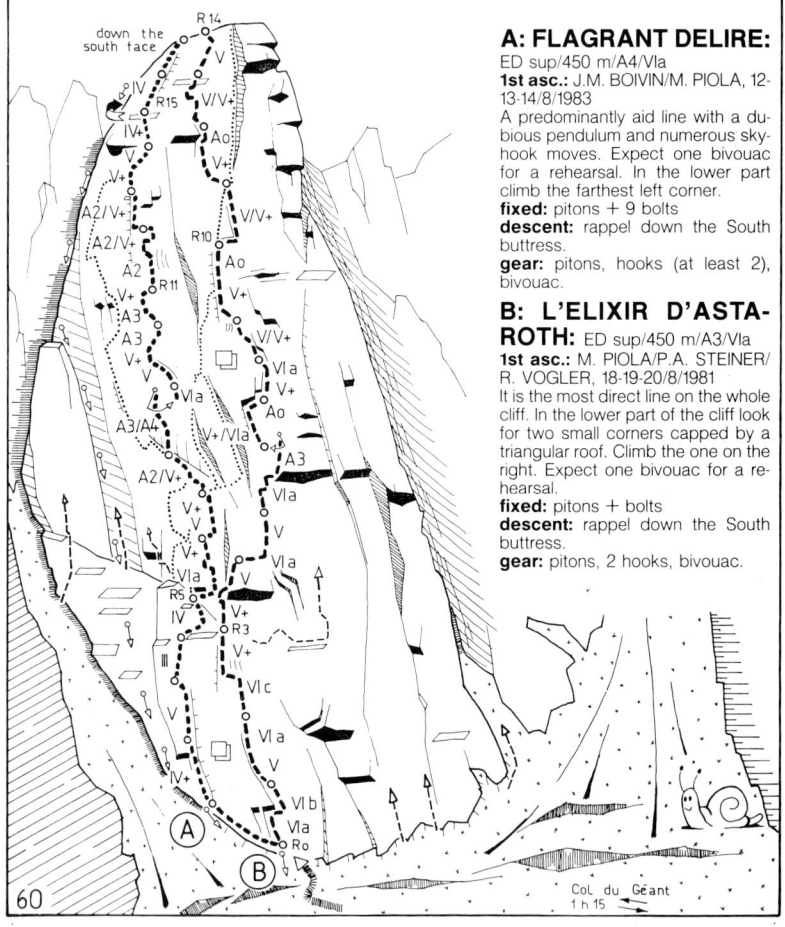

A: FLAGRANT DELIRE:

ED sup/450 m/A4/VIa
1st asc.: J.M. BOIVIN/M. PIOLA, 12-13-14/8/1983
A predominantly aid line with a dubious pendulum and numerous sky-hook moves. Expect one bivouac for a rehearsal. In the lower part climb the farthest left corner.
fixed: pitons + 9 bolts
descent: rappel down the South buttress.
gear: pitons, hooks (at least 2), bivouac.

B: L'ELIXIR D'ASTA-ROTH: ED sup/450 m/A3/VIa

1st asc.: M. PIOLA/P.A. STEINER/ R. VOGLER, 18-19-20/8/1981
It is the most direct line on the whole cliff. In the lower part of the cliff look for two small corners capped by a triangular roof. Climb the one on the right. Expect one bivouac for a rehearsal.
fixed: pitons + bolts
descent: rappel down the South buttress.
gear: pitons, 2 hooks, bivouac.

EAST FACE OF GRAND CAPUCIN 3838 m

VOIE BONATTI-GHIGO:

ED sup/350 m
1st asc.: W. BONATTI/L. GHIGO,
20-21-22/7/1951
The first ascent was done on aid
and the route is still equipped in
such a way.
From the Aiguillettes gully traverse
right on the ledges that split the first
third of the cliff, or start by the first
three pitches of "Elixir" which makes
for a very long and sustained
route.
fixed: numerous pitons
descent: rappel down the South
buttress.

EAST FACE OF GRAND CAPUCIN 3838 m

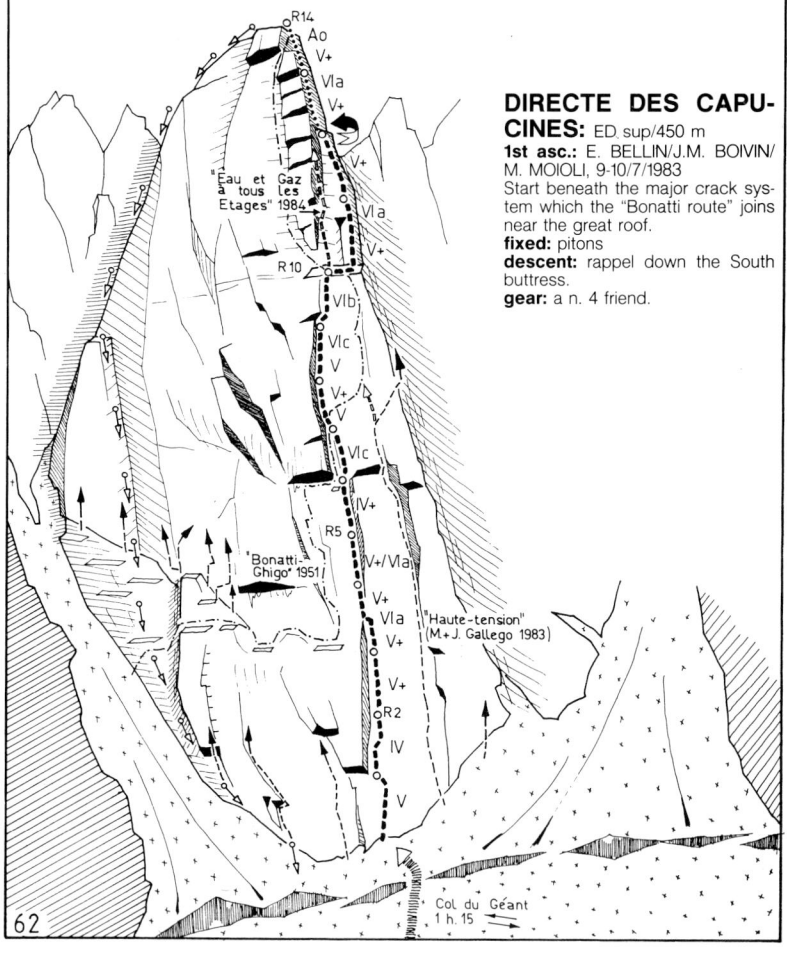

DIRECTE DES CAPU-CINES: ED. sup/450 m
1st asc.: E. BELLIN/J.M. BOIVIN/ M. MOIOLI, 9-10/7/1983
Start beneath the major crack system which the "Bonatti route" joins near the great roof.
fixed: pitons
descent: rappel down the South buttress.
gear: a n. 4 friend.

R14
Ao
V+
VIa
V+
V+
"Eau et Gaz à tous les Etages" 1984
VIa
V+
R 10
VIb
VIc
V
V+
V
VIc
IV+
R5
V+/VIa
"Bonatti-Ghigo" 1951
V+
VIa   "Haute-tension" (M+J. Gallego 1983)
V+
V+
R 2
IV
V
Col du Géant
1 h. 15

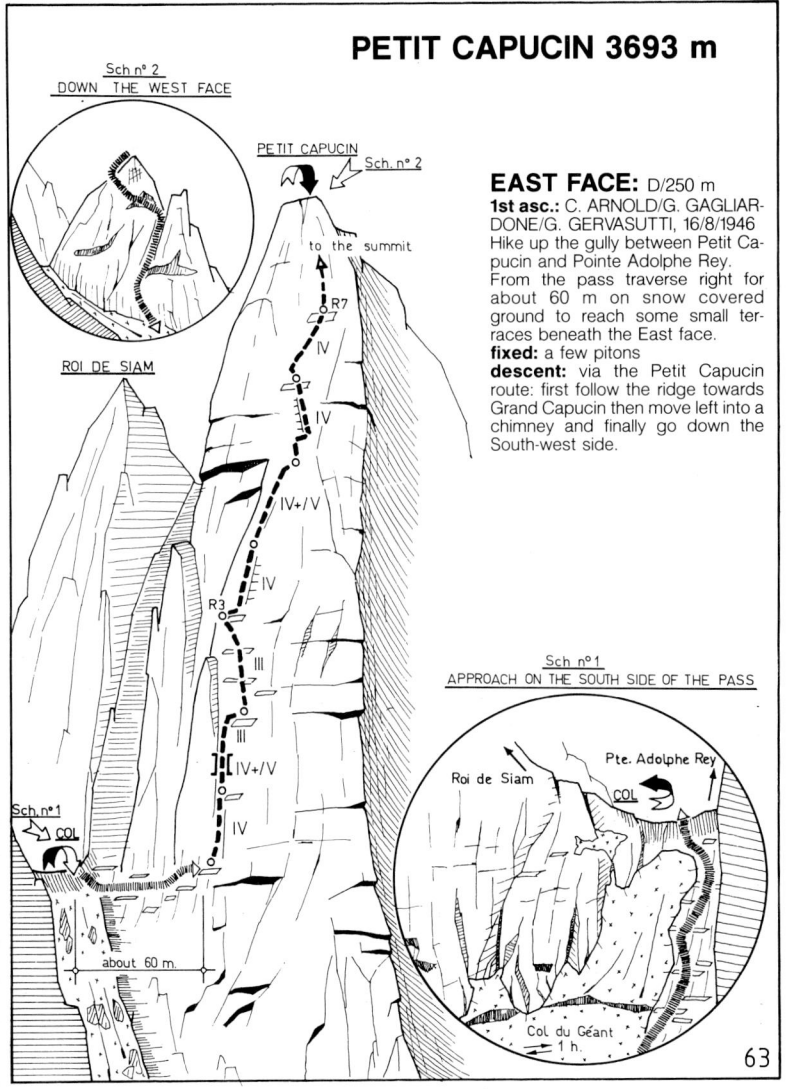

PETIT CAPUCIN 3693 m

Sch n° 2
DOWN THE WEST FACE

PETIT CAPUCIN

Sch. n° 2

to the summit

ROI DE SIAM

R7

IV

IV

IV+/V

IV

R3

III

III

IV+/V

IV

Sch. n°1

COL

about 60 m.

EAST FACE: D/250 m
1st asc.: C. ARNOLD/G. GAGLIAR-
DONE/G. GERVASUTTI, 16/8/1946
Hike up the gully between Petit Capucin and Pointe Adolphe Rey.
From the pass traverse right for
about 60 m on snow covered
ground to reach some small terraces beneath the East face.
fixed: a few pitons
descent: via the Petit Capucin
route: first follow the ridge towards
Grand Capucin then move left into a
chimney and finally go down the
South-west side.

Sch n° 1
APPROACH ON THE SOUTH SIDE OF THE PASS

Pte. Adolphe Rey

Roi de Siam

COL

Col du Géant
1 h.

63

SOUTH EAST FACE OF POINTE ADOLPHE REY
3535 m

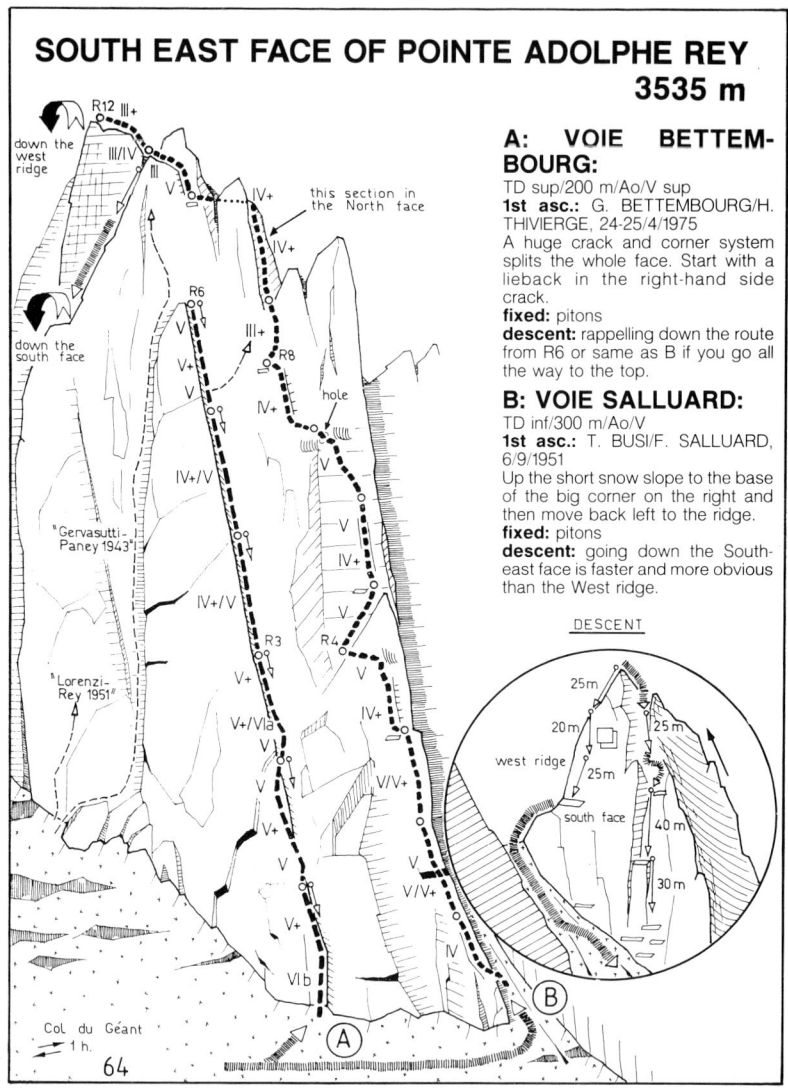

A: VOIE BETTEMBOURG:

TD sup/200 m/Ao/V sup

1st asc.: G. BETTEMBOURG/H. THIVIERGE, 24-25/4/1975

A huge crack and corner system splits the whole face. Start with a lieback in the right-hand side crack.

fixed: pitons

descent: rappelling down the route from R6 or same as B if you go all the way to the top.

B: VOIE SALLUARD:

TD inf/300 m/Ao/V

1st asc.: T. BUSI/F. SALLUARD, 6/9/1951

Up the short snow slope to the base of the big corner on the right and then move back left to the ridge.

fixed: pitons

descent: going down the Southeast face is faster and more obvious than the West ridge.

DESCENT

POINTE ADOLPHE REY, VOIE BETTEMBOURG – Photo: A. Gogna.

SOUTH EAST FACE OF POINTE ADOLPHE REY
3535 m

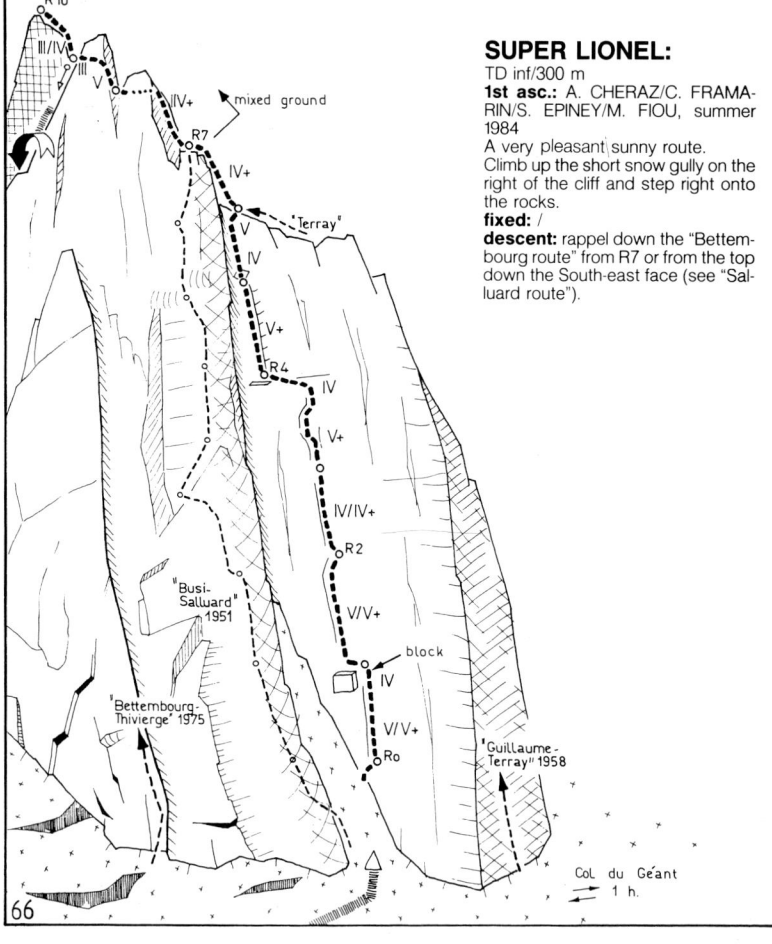

R 10

III/IV

III

V

IV+

mixed ground

R7

IV+

"Terray"

V

IV

V+

R4

IV

V+

IV/IV+

R2

V/V+

block

IV

V/V+

Ro

"Busi-
Salluard"
1951

"Bettembourg-
Thivierge" 1975

"Guillaume-
Terray" 1958

Col du Géant
1 h.

SUPER LIONEL:
TD inf/300 m
1st asc.: A. CHERAZ/C. FRAMA-
RIN/S. EPINEY/M. FIOU, summer
1984
A very pleasant sunny route.
Climb up the short snow gully on the
right of the cliff and step right onto
the rocks.
fixed: /
descent: rappel down the "Bettembourg route" from R7 or from the top
down the South-east face (see "Salluard route").

PYRAMIDE DU TACUL 3468 m

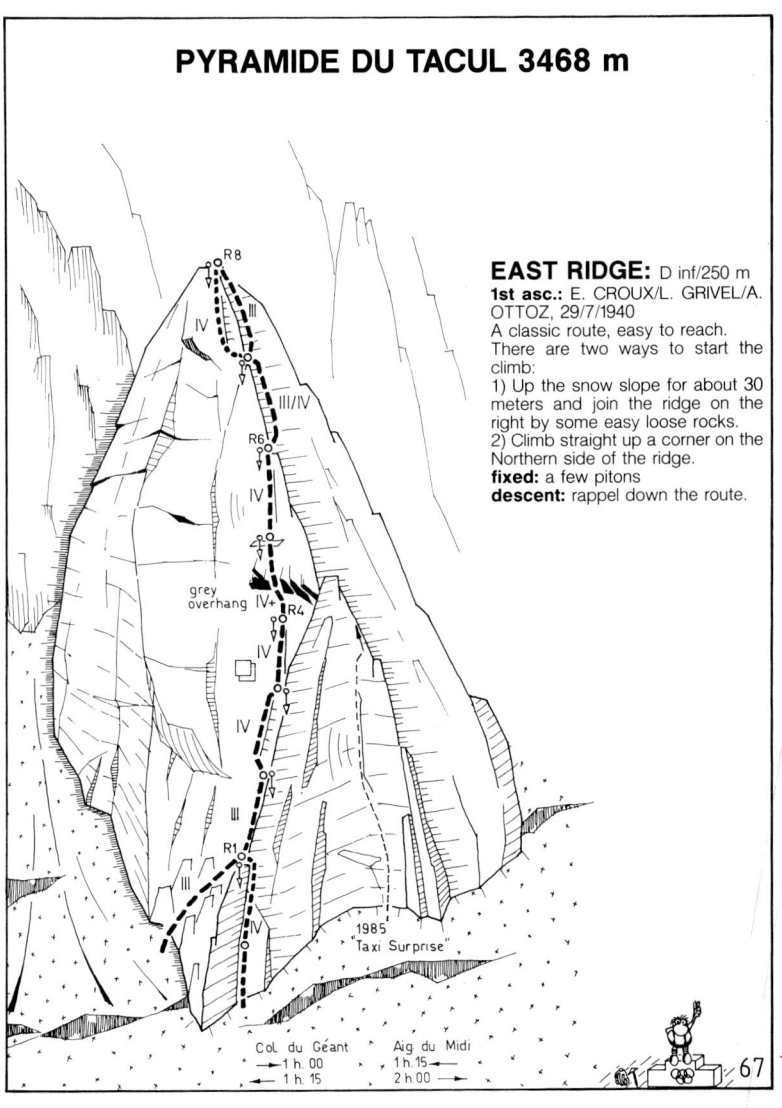

EAST RIDGE: D inf/250 m
1st asc.: E. CROUX/L. GRIVEL/A. OTTOZ, 29/7/1940
A classic route, easy to reach.
There are two ways to start the climb:
1) Up the snow slope for about 30 meters and join the ridge on the right by some easy loose rocks.
2) Climb straight up a corner on the Northern side of the ridge.
fixed: a few pitons
descent: rappel down the route.

R8
IV
III
III/IV
R6
IV
grey overhang IV+ R4
IV
IV
IV
III
R1
III
IV
1985 "Taxi Surprise"

Col du Géant
→ 1 h. 00
← 1 h. 15

Aig du Midi
1 h. 15 ←
2 h. 00 →

EAST SIDE OF MONT BLANC DU TACUL - PILIER DES TROIS POINTES

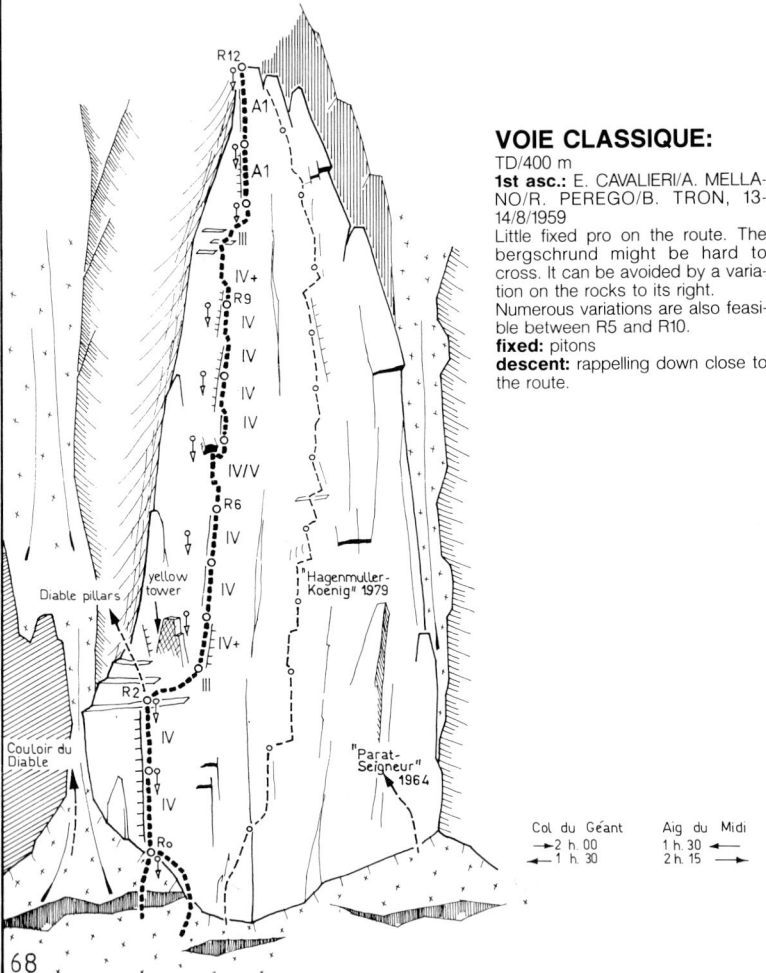

VOIE CLASSIQUE:

TD/400 m

1st asc.: E. CAVALIERI/A. MELLANO/R. PEREGO/B. TRON, 13-14/8/1959

Little fixed pro on the route. The bergschrund might be hard to cross. It can be avoided by a variation on the rocks to its right. Numerous variations are also feasible between R5 and R10.

fixed: pitons

descent: rappelling down close to the route.

R12

A1

A1

III

IV+

R9

IV

IV

IV

IV

IV/V

R6

IV

IV

yellow
tower

IV

"Hagenmuller-
Koenig" 1979

IV+

III

R2

Diable pillars

IV

Couloir du
Diable

IV

"Parat-
Seigneur"
1964

Ro

Col du Géant	Aig du Midi
→ 2 h. 00	1 h. 30 ←
← 1 h. 30	2 h. 15 →

EAST SIDE OF MONT BLANC DU TACUL - PILIER DES TROIS POINTES

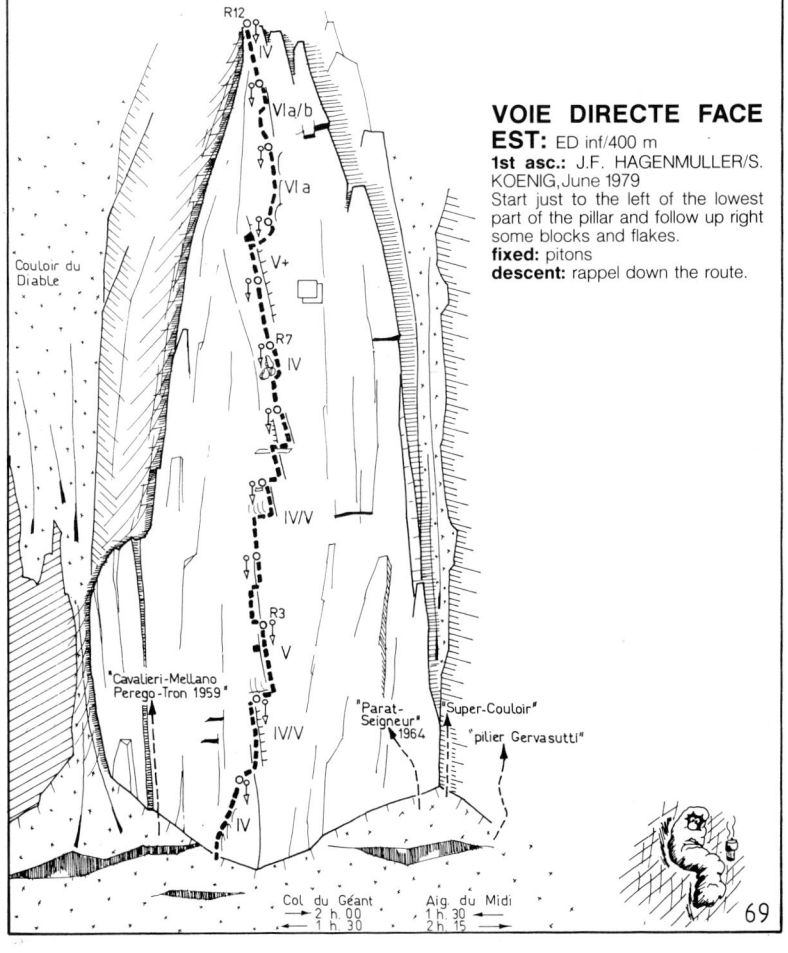

VOIE DIRECTE FACE EST: ED inf/400 m

1st asc.: J.F. HAGENMULLER/S. KOENIG, June 1979

Start just to the left of the lowest part of the pillar and follow up right some blocks and flakes.

fixed: pitons

descent: rappel down the route.

R12

IV

VIa/b

VI a

V+

R7

IV

IV/V

R3

V

"Cavalieri-Mellano
Perego-Tron 1959"

IV/V

IV

Couloir du
Diable

"Parat-
Seigneur"
1964

"Super-Couloir"

"pilier Gervasutti"

Col du Géant
→ 2 h. 00
← 1 h. 30

Aig. du Midi
1 h. 30 →
2 h. 15 ←

EAST SIDE OF MONT BLANC DU TACUL 4248 m

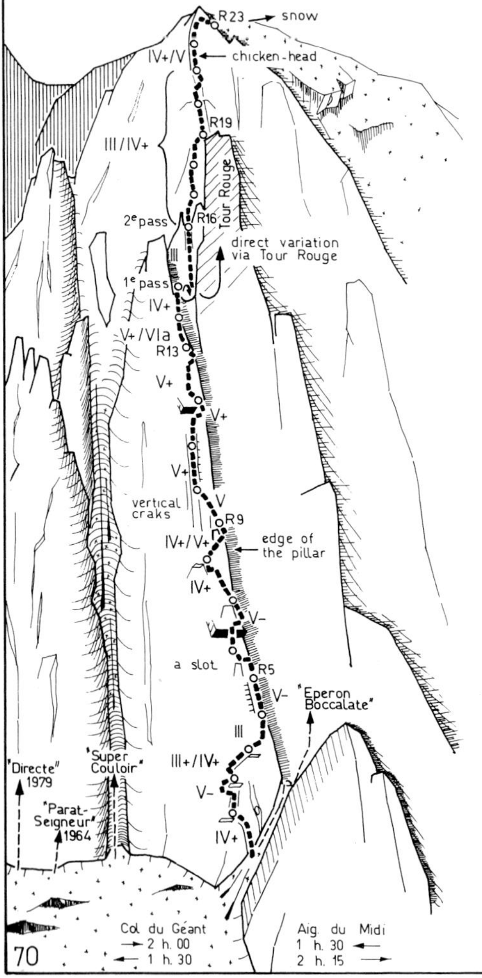

R23 → snow

IV+/V — chicken-head

III/IV+

R19

Tour Rouge

2ᵉ pass — R16

direct variation via Tour Rouge

III

1ᵉ pass

IV+

V+/VIa — R13

V+

V+

V+

vertical craks

V

R9

IV+/V+ — edge of the pillar

IV+

V−

a slot

R5

III — "Eperon Boccalate"

III+/IV+

V−

IV+

"Directe" 1979

"Super Couloir"

"Parat-Seigneur" 1964

Col du Géant
→ 2 h. 00
→ 1 h. 30

Aig. du Midi
1 h. 30 ←
2 h. 15 ←

PILIER GERVASUTTI:

TD/800 m

1st asc.: P. FORNELLI/G. MAURO, 29-30/7/1951

A very elegant line. The rock, which is fractured but solid, is very suitable for nuts.

Climb up a steep snow gully on the right of the pillar. A crack then leads to the pillar's edge.

fixed: pitons

descent: snow slopes lead to the top of Mont Blanc du Tacul from where one goes down the snow slopes of the North face (crevasses and bergschrunds).

gear: crampons and at least one ice-axe per party for the descent.

AREA n° 5

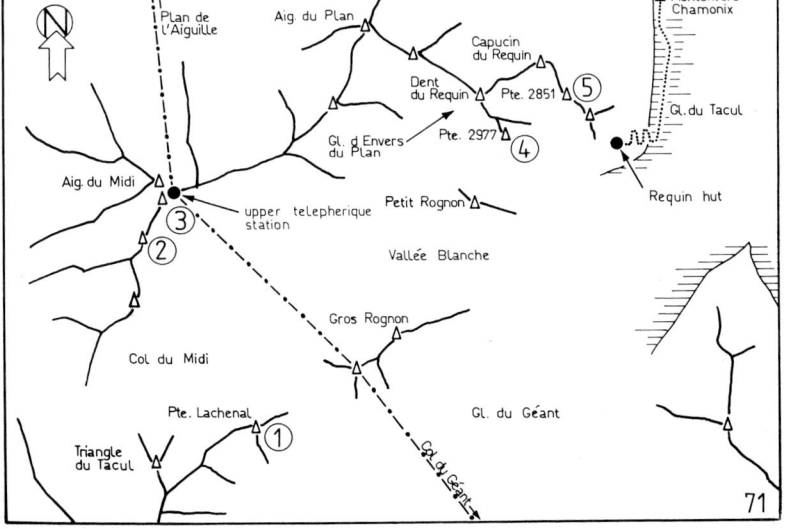

N

Plan de
l'Aiguille

Aig. du Plan

Capucin
du Requin

Montenvers
Chamonix

Dent
du Requin

Pte. 2851

⑤

Gl. d Envers
du Plan

Pte. 2977

④

Gl. du Tacul

Aig. du Midi

upper telepherique
station

③

②

Petit Rognon

Requin hut

Vallée Blanche

Col du Midi

Gros Rognon

Gl. du Géant

Pte. Lachenal

①

Triangle
du Tacul

Col du Géant

71

AREA N. 5   LE COL DU MIDI/DENT DU REQUIN

Despite its high altitude the Col du Midi area benefits from excellent climbing conditions very early in the season, sometimes even before the crags down in the valley. Climbing in spring is very appealing since one can then ski down the "Vallée Blanche".

Upper téléphérique station of Aig. du Midi (3800 m)
Bivouacking in the tunnels of the Piton Sud is barely tolerated by the téléphérique staff. However it is the only way of spending a night in that area. Bring all the necessary equipment, including water.

Requin hut (2516 m) Phone: (50) 53.16.96
a) From Montenvers (1909 m) reach "la Mer de Glace" and follow it up (sticking mostly to the right) until below the hut's shoulder. Go up to the hut by a system of ledges and an equipped trail (3 hours).
b) From Aig. du Midi follow the Southern side of the Midi-Plan ridge to the Envers du Plan glacier down which you go to the hut (20 min. with skis, 45 min. to 1 h 30 min on foot). Many, many crevasses in the summertime. In spring one can also follow the usual "Vallée Blanche" ski track.

Approaches to the cliffs:
1. South-east side of Pointe Lachenal
From Aig. du Midi reach the Midi pass and then cross the pass between the Gros Rognon and the Pointe Lachenal. Turn right to reach the base of the cliff.
2. South and East sides of Eperon des Cosmiques
From Aig. du Midi, after the tunnels, walk down the exposed snow ridge, cross the bergschrund and traverse below the South face of Aig. du Midi.
3. South face of Aig. du Midi
Same as 2.
4. South face of Pointe 2977 m
a) From Aig. du Midi same way as to the Requin hut.
b) From the Requin hut go up the snow slope which is left of the East face of Requin and avoid by the right some seracs from the Envers du Plan glacier.
5. East face of Pointe 2851 m
From the Requin hut traverse North below Pointe 2784 m and go up a short snow slope to the base of the cliff.

SOUTH FACE OF AIGUILLE DU MIDI – A: LA DAME DU LAC, 1982 – B: VOIE MAZEAUD, 1963 – C: MA DALTON, 1984 – D: SUPER DUPONT, 1984 – E: VOIE REBUFFAT, 1956 – Photo: M. Piola.

SOUTH FACE OF AIGUILLE DU MIDI, BENEATH MA DALTON'S ROOF (VIIb+) DURING THE FIRST ASCENT – Photo: G. Hopfgartner.

SOUTH EAST SIDE OF POINTE LACHENAL
3613 m

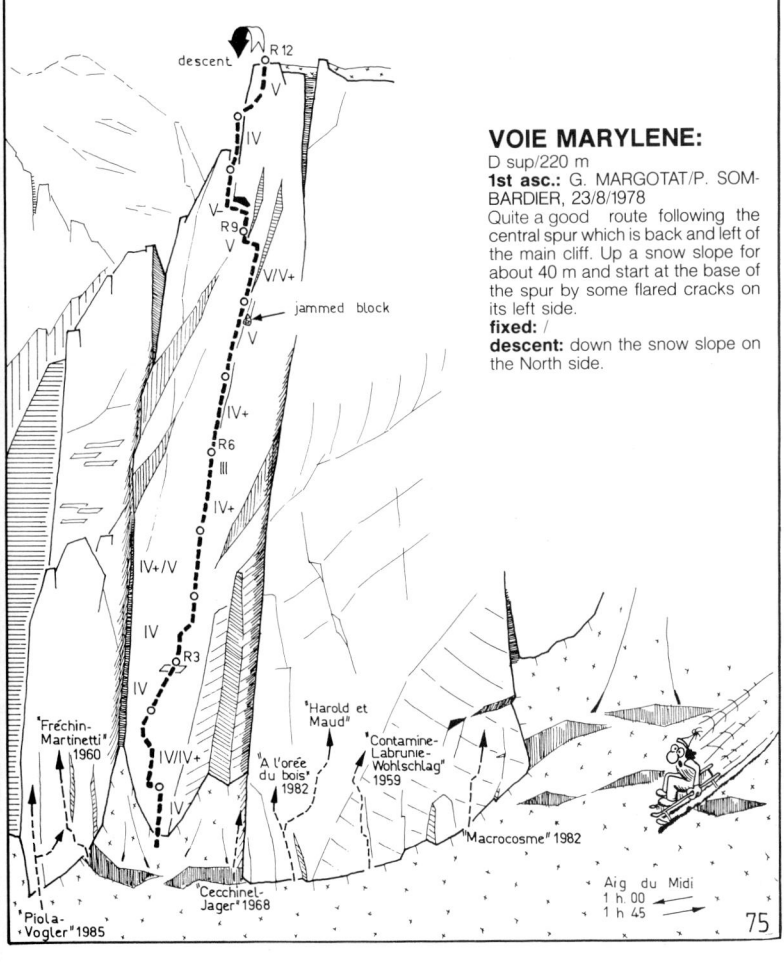

VOIE MARYLENE:
D sup/220 m
1st asc.: G. MARGOTAT/P. SOMBARDIER, 23/8/1978
Quite a good route following the central spur which is back and left of the main cliff. Up a snow slope for about 40 m and start at the base of the spur by some flared cracks on its left side.
fixed: /
descent: down the snow slope on the North side.

(diagram labels)

descent — R 12
V
IV
V—
R 9
V
V/V+
jammed block
V
IV+
R 6
III
IV+
IV+/V
IV
R 3
IV
IV/IV+
IV

"Fréchin-Martinetti" 1960

"Harold et Maud"

"Contamine-Labrunie-Wohlschlag" 1959

"A l'orée du bois" 1982

"Macrocosme" 1982

"Cecchinel-Jager" 1968

"Piola-Vogler" 1985

Aig du Midi
1 h. 00
1 h. 45

SOUTH EAST SIDE OF POINTE LACHENAL
3613 m

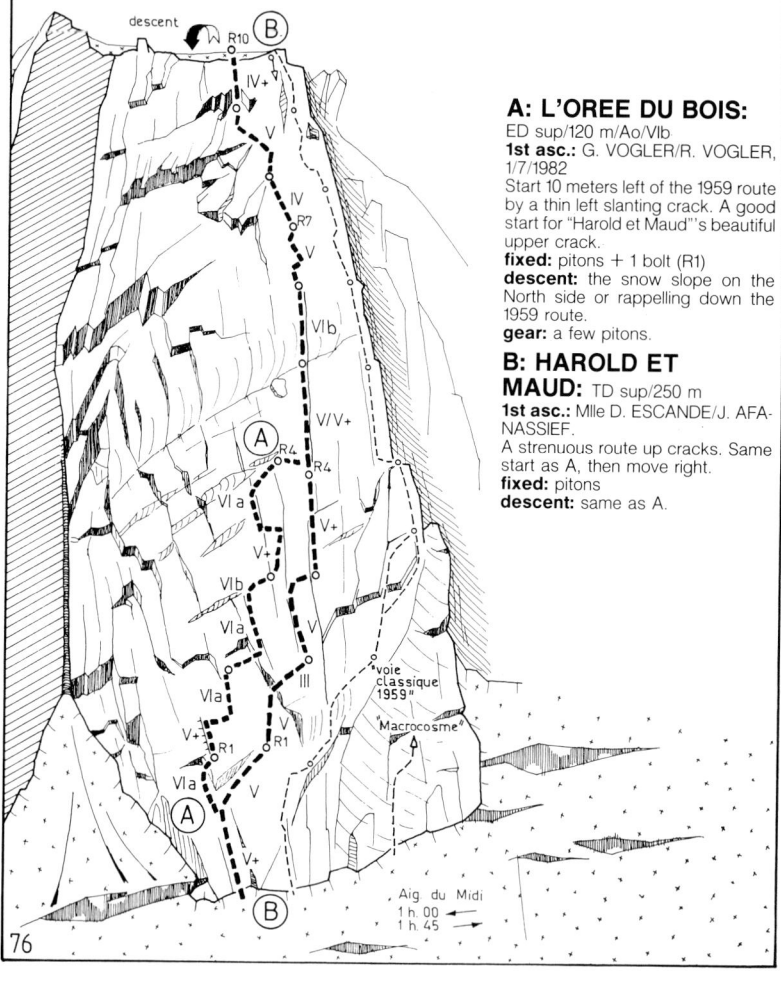

descent

R10 B

IV+

V

IV
R7

V

VIb

V/V+

A R4

R4

VIa

V+

V+

VIb

VIa

V

VIa

III

voie
classique
1959"

VIa

V+ R1

R1

V

"Macrocosme"

VIa

V

A

V+

B

Aig. du Midi
1 h. 00 ──►
1 h. 45 ──►

76

A: L'OREE DU BOIS:

ED sup/120 m/Ao/VIb
1st asc.: G. VOGLER/R. VOGLER,
1/7/1982
Start 10 meters left of the 1959 route
by a thin left slanting crack. A good
start for "Harold et Maud"'s beautiful
upper crack.
fixed: pitons + 1 bolt (R1)
descent: the snow slope on the
North side or rappelling down the
1959 route.
gear: a few pitons.

B: HAROLD ET
MAUD: TD sup/250 m

1st asc.: Mlle D. ESCANDE/J. AFA-
NASSIEF.
A strenuous route up cracks. Same
start as A, then move right.
fixed: pitons
descent: same as A.

STARTING A NEW ROUTE NEAR POINTE LACHENAL – Photo: M. Piola.

SOUTH EAST SIDE OF POINTE LACHENAL
3613 m

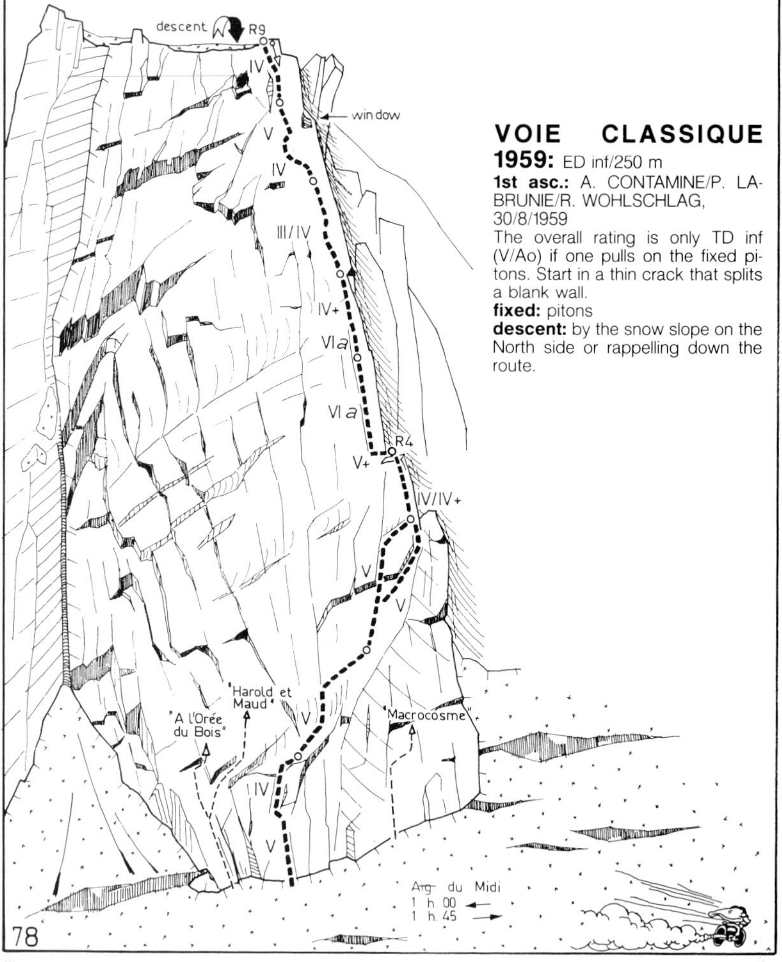

descent — R9

IV

window

V

IV

III/IV

IV+

VIa

VIa

R4

V+

IV/IV+

V

V

Harold et Maud

"A l'Orée du Bois"

V

Macrocosme

IV

V

Arg. du Midi
1 h. 00 ←
1 h. 45 →

VOIE CLASSIQUE

1959: ED inf/250 m
1st asc.: A. CONTAMINE/P. LA-BRUNIE/R. WOHLSCHLAG, 30/8/1959
The overall rating is only TD inf (V/Ao) if one pulls on the fixed pitons. Start in a thin crack that splits a blank wall.
fixed: pitons
descent: by the snow slope on the North side or rappelling down the route.

78

SOUTH AND EAST SIDES OF EPERON DES COSMIQUES

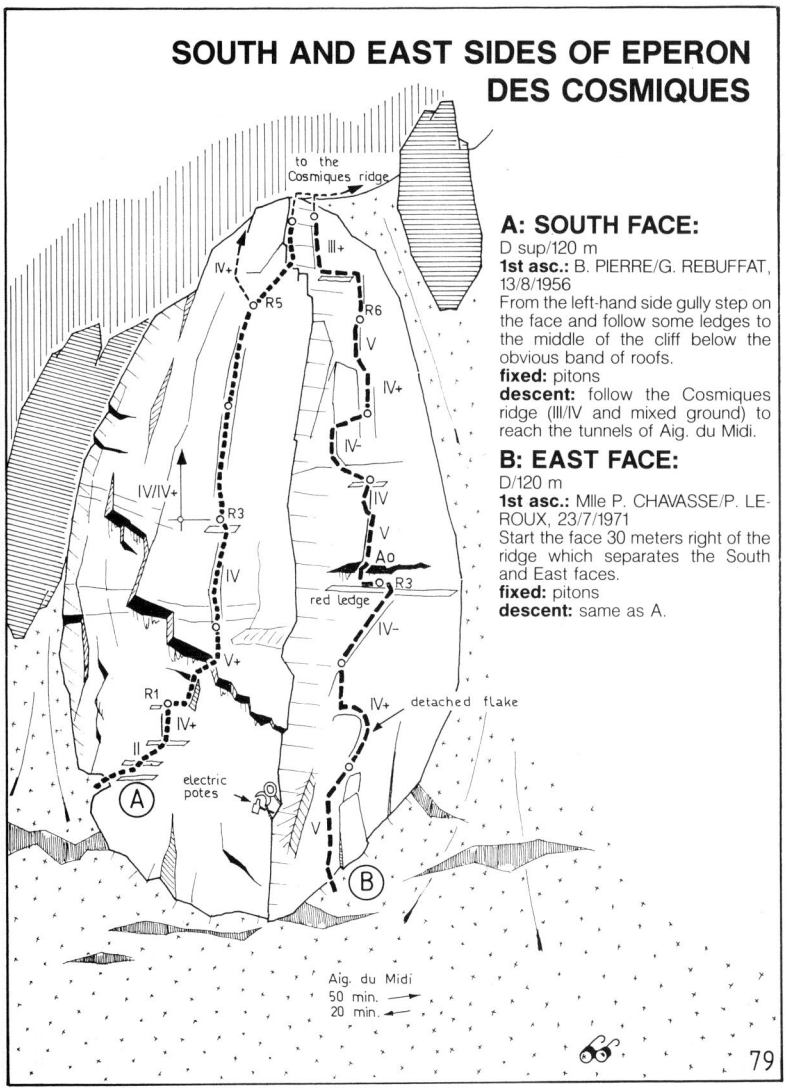

to the Cosmiques ridge

III+

IV+

V

R5

R6

V

IV+

IV-

IV

IV

V

Ao

IV/IV+

R3

R3

IV

red ledge

IV-

V+

R1

IV+

detached flake

II

IV+

electric potes

(A)

V

(B)

Aig. du Midi
50 min. ➡
20 min. ⬅

A: SOUTH FACE:

D sup/120 m
1st asc.: B. PIERRE/G. REBUFFAT,
13/8/1956
From the left-hand side gully step on the face and follow some ledges to the middle of the cliff below the obvious band of roofs.
fixed: pitons
descent: follow the Cosmiques ridge (III/IV and mixed ground) to reach the tunnels of Aig. du Midi.

B: EAST FACE:

D/120 m
1st asc.: Mlle P. CHAVASSE/P. LE-ROUX, 23/7/1971
Start the face 30 meters right of the ridge which separates the South and East faces.
fixed: pitons
descent: same as A.

SOUTH SOUTH WEST FACE OF AIGUILLE DU MIDI 3800 m

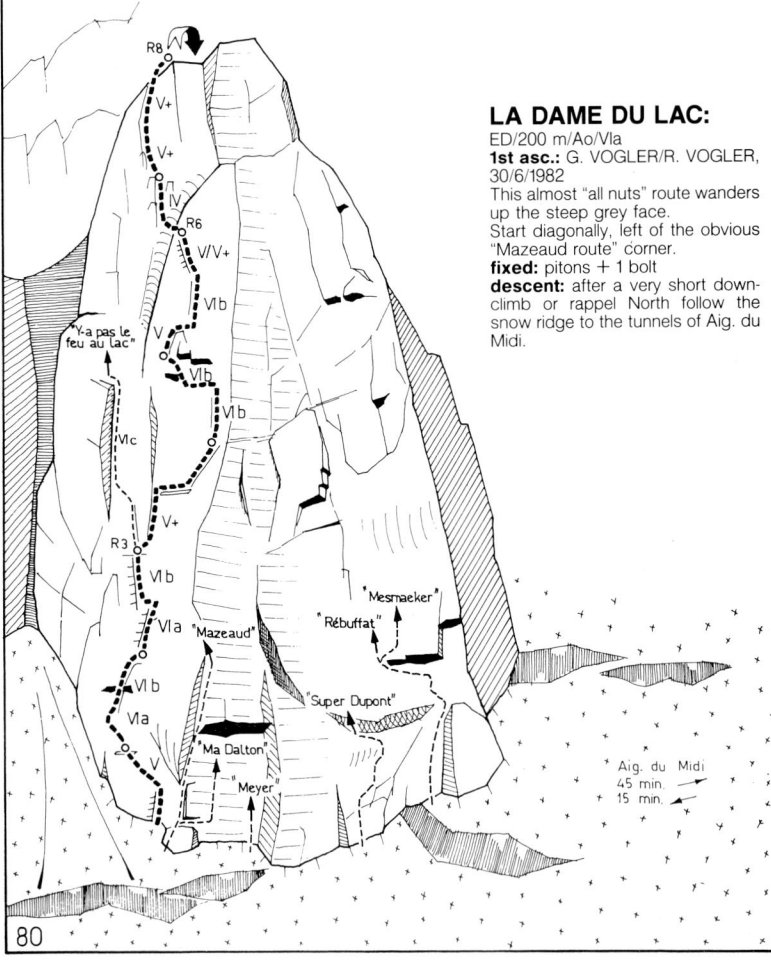

LA DAME DU LAC:
ED/200 m/Ao/VIa
1st asc.: G. VOGLER/R. VOGLER, 30/6/1982
This almost "all nuts" route wanders up the steep grey face.
Start diagonally, left of the obvious "Mazeaud route" corner.
fixed: pitons + 1 bolt
descent: after a very short down-climb or rappel North follow the snow ridge to the tunnels of Aig. du Midi.

R8
V+
V+
IV
R6
V/V+
VIb
"Y-a pas le feu au lac"
V
VIb
VIb
VIc
V+
R3
VIb
VIa
"Mazeaud"
VIb
VIa
V
Ma Dalton
"Meyer"
"Super Dupont"
"Rébuffat"
"Mesmaeker"

Aig. du Midi
45 min.
15 min.

80

SOUTH FACE OF AIGUILLE DU MIDI 3800 m

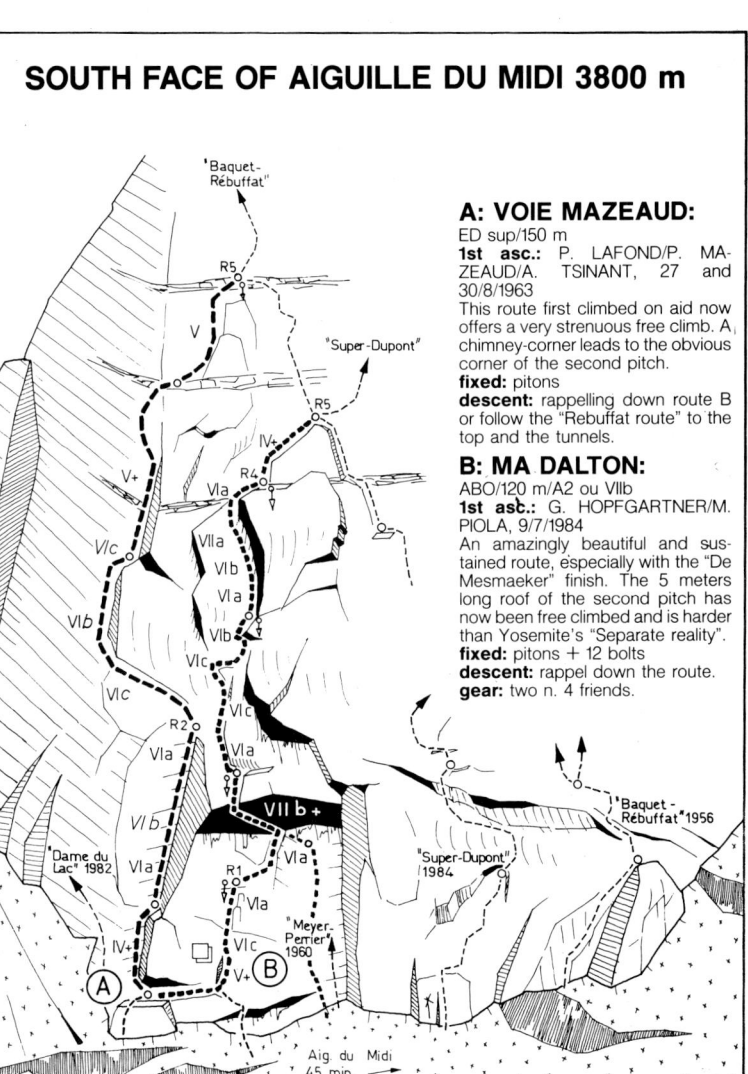

A: VOIE MAZEAUD:
ED sup/150 m
1st asc.: P. LAFOND/P. MAZEAUD/A. TSINANT, 27 and 30/8/1963
This route first climbed on aid now offers a very strenuous free climb. A chimney-corner leads to the obvious corner of the second pitch.
fixed: pitons
descent: rappelling down route B or follow the "Rebuffat route" to the top and the tunnels.

B: MA DALTON:
ABO/120 m/A2 ou VIIb
1st asc.: G. HOPFGARTNER/M. PIOLA, 9/7/1984
An amazingly beautiful and sustained route, especially with the "De Mesmaeker" finish. The 5 meters long roof of the second pitch has now been free climbed and is harder than Yosemite's "Separate reality".
fixed: pitons + 12 bolts
descent: rappel down the route.
gear: two n. 4 friends.

81

A: VOIE REBUFFAT:

TD sup/200 m
1st asc.: M. BAQUET/G. REBUF-FAT, 13/7/1956
A classic among classics. Start left of a big flake and go left of the big obvious roof.
fixed: pitons
descent: a short rappel North leads to the snow ridge and the tunnels.

B: VOIE CONTAMINE:

ED sup/200 m
1st asc.: M. BRON/C. BOZON/A. CONTAMINE, 1/9/1957
The 40 meters crack near the top is very sustained when freed, but can be easily aided too.
Start to the right of the great roof.
fixed: pitons
descent: from R6 rappel down "Super-Dupont".
Or from R8 rappel down 5 meters on the North-east side and then climb a steep crack which turns into a ramp.

C: JULES DE CHEZ SMITH D'EN FACE:

TD sup/70 m/Ao/Vla
1st asc.: G. HOPFGARTNER/M. PIOLA, 16/4/1983
A beautiful start for the "Contamine route".
The route goes up the blank slab on the edge of the South-east buttress.
fixed: pitons + 3 bolts
descent: rappel down the route.

SOUTH FACE OF AIGUILLE DU MIDI 3800 m

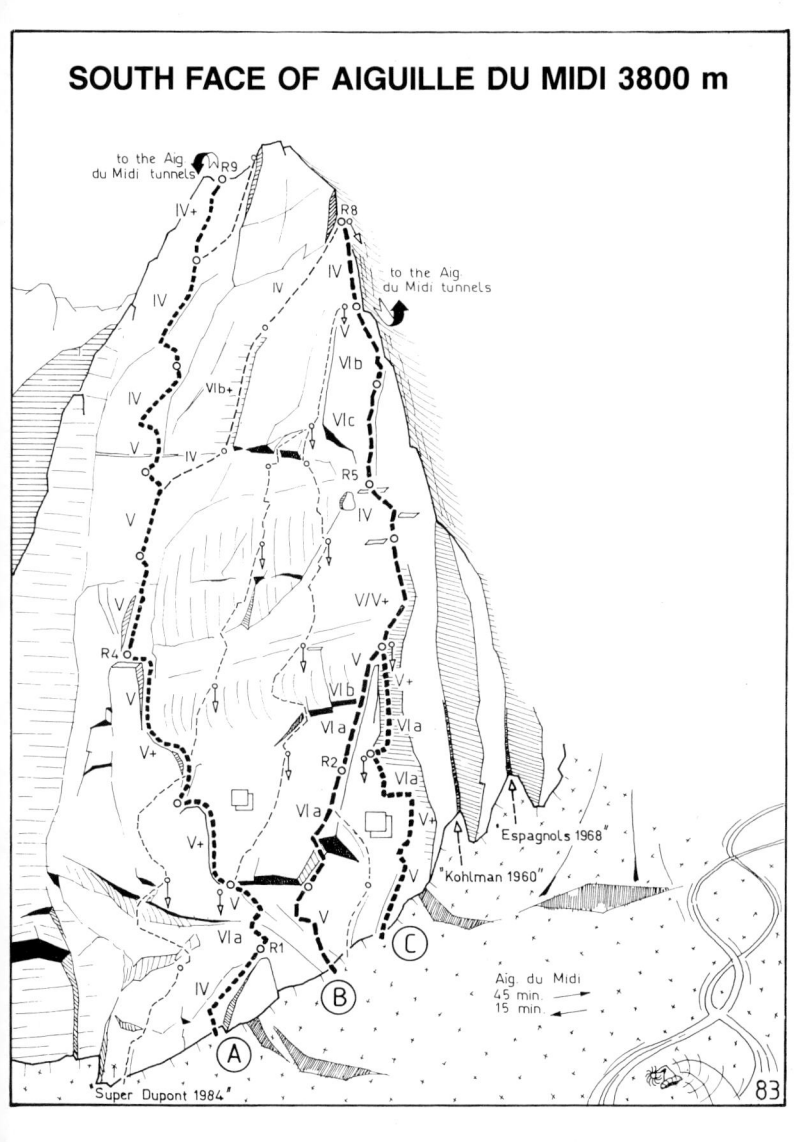

to the Aig du Midi tunnels

R9

IV+

IV   IV

IV   VIb+

V   IV

V

V

R4

V

V+

V+

V

VIa   R1

IV

Super Dupont 1984"

R8

IV

to the Aig du Midi tunnels

V

VIb

VIc

R5

IV

V/V+

V

VIb   V+

VIa   VIa

R2   VIa

VIa

VIa   V+

V

V

C

"Kohlman 1960"   "Espagnols 1968"

Aig. du Midi
45 min.
15 min.

B

A

83

SOUTH FACE OF AIGUILLE DU MIDI 3800 m

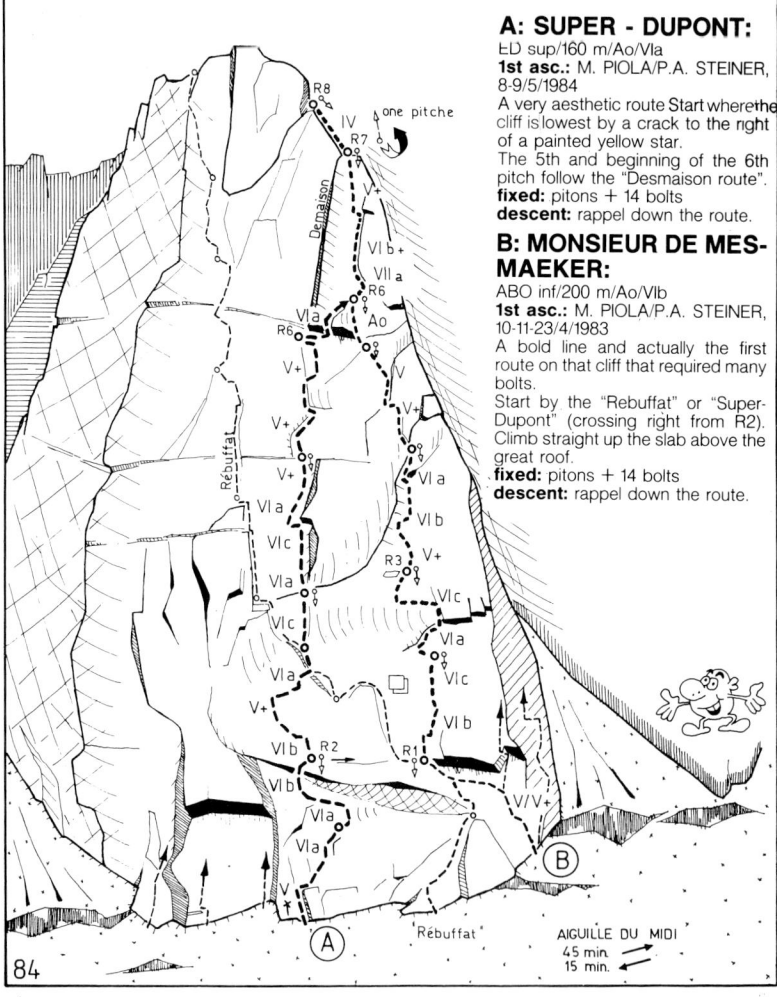

A: SUPER - DUPONT:
ED sup/160 m/Ao/VIa
1st asc.: M. PIOLA/P.A. STEINER,
8-9/5/1984
A very aesthetic route Start where the cliff is lowest by a crack to the right of a painted yellow star.
The 5th and beginning of the 6th pitch follow the "Desmaison route".
fixed: pitons + 14 bolts
descent: rappel down the route.

B: MONSIEUR DE MES-MAEKER:
ABO inf/200 m/Ao/VIb
1st asc.: M. PIOLA/P.A. STEINER,
10-11-23/4/1983
A bold line and actually the first route on that cliff that required many bolts.
Start by the "Rebuffat" or "Super-Dupont" (crossing right from R2).
Climb straight up the slab above the great roof.
fixed: pitons + 14 bolts
descent: rappel down the route.

AIGUILLE DU MIDI
45 min.
15 min.

SOUTH FACE OF AIGUILLE DU MIDI – A: MONSIEUR DE MESMAEKER, 1982 - B: VOIE CONTAMINE, 1957 - C: JULES DE CHEZ SMITH D'EN FACE, 1983 – Photo: M. Piola.

OUTCROPS OF DENT DU REQUIN – SOUTH FACE OF POINTE 2977 m

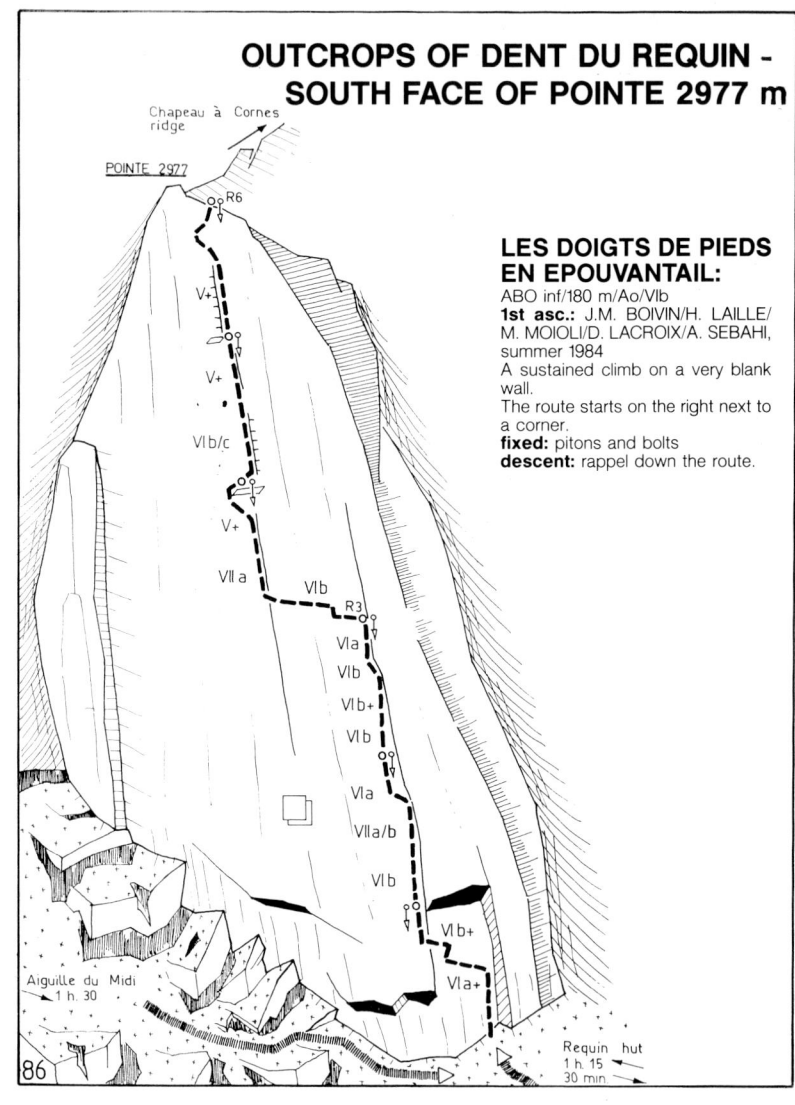

Chapeau à Cornes ridge

POINTE 2977

R6

V+

V+

VIb/c

V+

VII a

VIb

R3

VIa

VIb

VIb+

VIb

VIa

VIIa/b

VIb

VIb+

VIa+

Aiguille du Midi
→ 1 h. 30

86

Requin hut
1 h. 15 →
30 min. →

LES DOIGTS DE PIEDS EN EPOUVANTAIL:

ABO inf/180 m/Ao/VIb

1st asc.: J.M. BOIVIN/H. LAILLE/ M. MOIOLI/D. LACROIX/A. SEBAHI, summer 1984

A sustained climb on a very blank wall.

The route starts on the right next to a corner.

fixed: pitons and bolts
descent: rappel down the route.

OUTCROPS OF DENT DU REQUIN - EAST FACE OF POINTE 2851 m

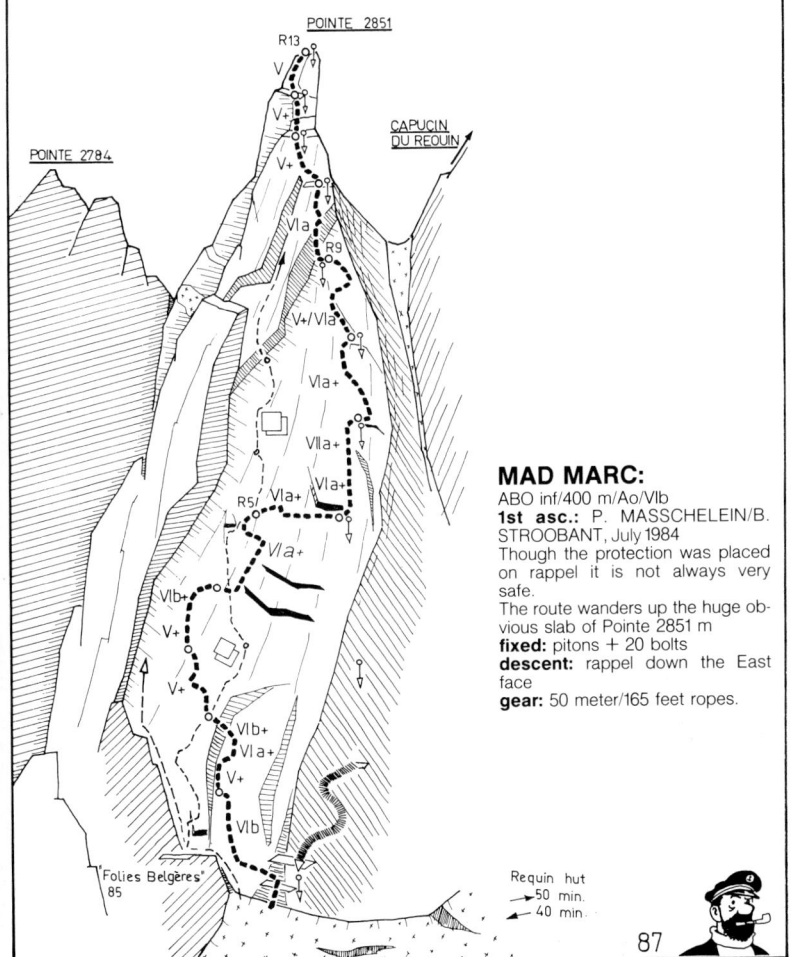

POINTE 2851

R13

V

V+

V+

VIa

R9

V+/VIa

VIa+

VIIa+

VIa+

R5/

VIa+

VIb+

V+

V+

VIb+

VIa+

V+

VIb

POINTE 2784

CAPUCIN DU REQUIN

'Folies Belgères' 85

MAD MARC:

ABO inf/400 m/Ao/VIb
1st asc.: P. MASSCHELEIN/B. STROOBANT, July 1984
Though the protection was placed on rappel it is not always very safe.
The route wanders up the huge obvious slab of Pointe 2851 m
fixed: pitons + 20 bolts
descent: rappel down the East face
gear: 50 meter/165 feet ropes.

Requin hut
→ 50 min.
← 40 min.

87

AREA n° 6

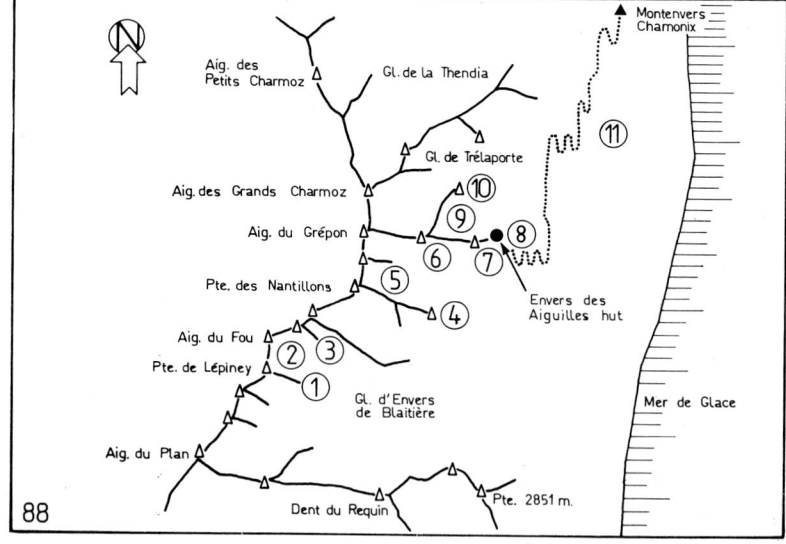

Aig. des Petits Charmoz

Gl. de la Thendia

Gl. de Trélaporte

Aig. des Grands Charmoz

Aig. du Grépon

Pte. des Nantillons

Aig. du Fou

Pte. de Lépiney

Gl. d'Envers de Blaitière

Aig. du Plan

Dent du Requin

Pte. 2851 m.

Envers des Aiguilles hut

Montenvers Chamonix

Mer de Glace

88

AREA N. 6   L'ENVERS DES AIGUILLES

This is the South-east side of the Aiguilles de Chamonix. Being very sunny and having so many good crags this area has undergone a spectacular development in the early 1980's and is now considered as the foremost place for climbing on granite.

L'Envers des Aiguilles hut (2523 m) No phone.
From Montenvers (1909 m) reach the "Mer de Glace" and follow it up until you see some big yellow arrows painted on the rocks on the right. Some ladders lead to a path that traverses beneath the small glacier of Trélaporte. The hut is beautifully perched on the lowest shoulder of the South-east ridge of Aig. de Roc (2h 30 min).

Approaches to the cliffs:
1. South-east buttress of Pointe Lépiney
From the hut cross horizontally and reach the Envers de Blaitière glacier. Keep very close to the base of the East buttress of "Première Pointe des Nantillons". Walk up the glacier moving South of Aig. de Blaitière's South-east ridge.
2. South face of Aig. du Fou
Same as 1.
3. East buttress of Aig. des Ciseaux
Same as 1.
4. East buttress of "Première Pointe des Nantillons"
From the hut cross horizontally to the South and go up a short snow slope to the base of the buttress.
5. East face of Pointe des Nantillons
From the hut go up the snow slopes sticking close to the South face of Aig. de Roc and cross towards the base of the cliff on the plateau of the glacier.
6. South side of Aig. de Roc (antécime)
From the hut go up the snow slopes and beneath the Tour Verte.
7. South-east side of Tour Verte
From the hut simply walk up the short moraine which leads to the base of the cliff.
8. Crags below the hut
Walk down the path. The routes start from the last switchback.
9. Lower East side of Aig. de Roc
From the hut cross the notch on the East ridge of Aig. de Roc and reach the Trélaporte glacier, follow this to the base of the cliffs.
10. South-east side of Tour Rouge
Same as 9 but cross the Trélaporte glacier diagonally.
11. Lower slabs of l'Envers des Aiguilles
a) From Montenvers: follow the Mer de Glace as if going to the Requin hut. At the junction of the glaciers of Leschaux and Tacul move right to avoid a crevassed area and reach the edge of the glacier. Big green triangles are painted on the nearby rocks: this is it!
b) From the Envers des Aiguilles hut: walk back down the trail until the end of the long traverse below Trélaporte glacier, just before a series of switchbacks on the moraine. Walk down the moraine towards a topographic sign, thus reaching the top of the slabs (a cairn shows the start of the rappels).

AT THE START OF PYRAMID (VIc) ON EAST FACE OF AIGUILLE DE ROC – Photo: M. Piola.

DURING THE FIRST ASCENT OF PEDRO-POLAR (VIb) ON THE EAST FACE OF AIGUIL-LE DE ROC – Photo: M. Piola.

SOUTH EAST BUTTRESS OF POINTE LEPINEY
3429 m

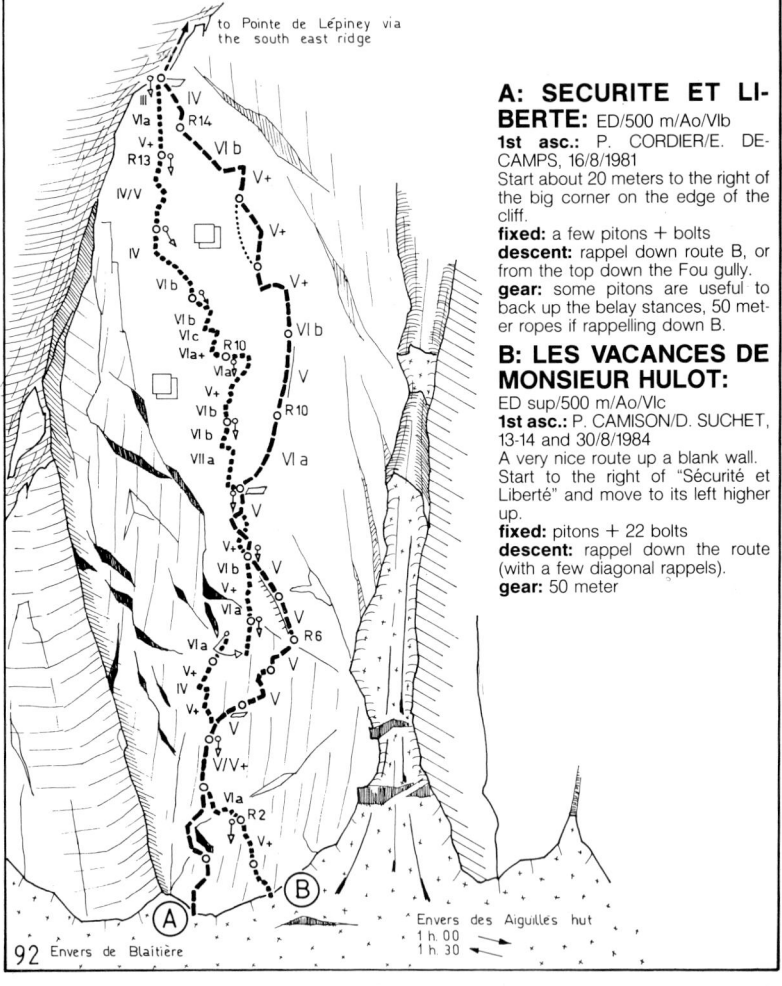

to Pointe de Lépiney via the south east ridge

A: SECURITE ET LI-BERTE: ED/500 m/Ao/VIb

1st asc.: P. CORDIER/E. DE-CAMPS, 16/8/1981

Start about 20 meters to the right of the big corner on the edge of the cliff.

fixed: a few pitons + bolts
descent: rappel down route B, or from the top down the Fou gully.
gear: some pitons are useful to back up the belay stances, 50 meter ropes if rappelling down B.

B: LES VACANCES DE MONSIEUR HULOT:

ED sup/500 m/Ao/VIc
1st asc.: P. CAMISON/D. SUCHET, 13-14 and 30/8/1984

A very nice route up a blank wall. Start to the right of "Sécurité et Liberté" and move to its left higher up.

fixed: pitons + 22 bolts
descent: rappel down the route (with a few diagonal rappels).
gear: 50 meter

Envers des Aiguilles hut
1 h. 00
1 h. 30

SOUTH FACE OF AIGUILLE DU FOU 3501 m

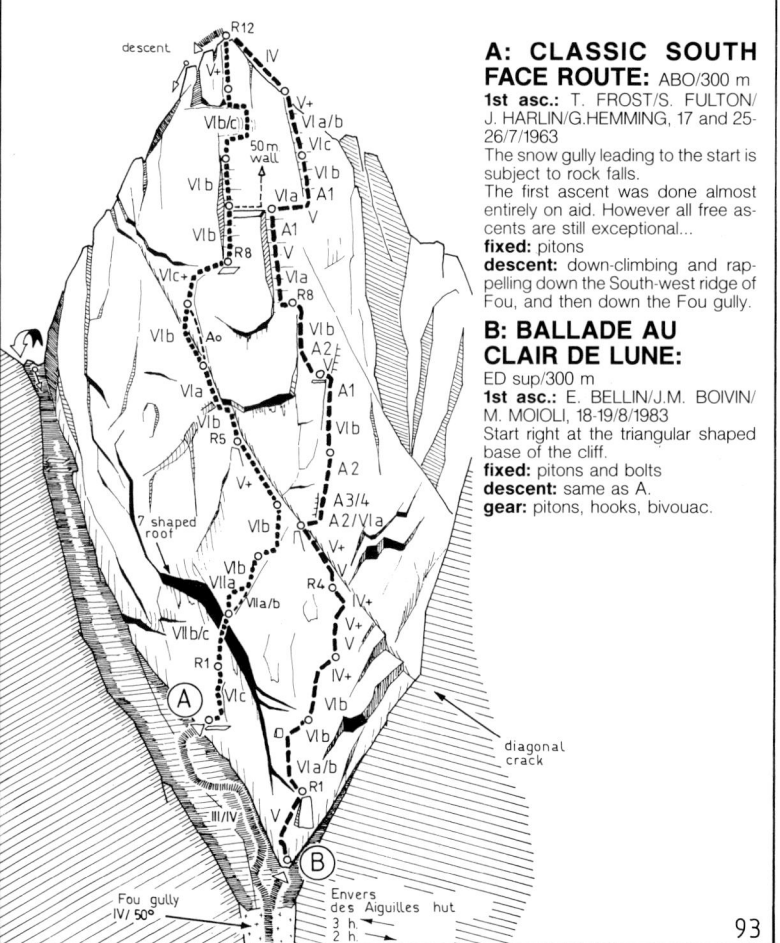

A: CLASSIC SOUTH FACE ROUTE:
ABO/300 m

1st asc.: T. FROST/S. FULTON/ J. HARLIN/G.HEMMING, 17 and 25-26/7/1963

The snow gully leading to the start is subject to rock falls.

The first ascent was done almost entirely on aid. However all free ascents are still exceptional...

fixed: pitons

descent: down-climbing and rappelling down the South-west ridge of Fou, and then down the Fou gully.

B: BALLADE AU CLAIR DE LUNE:
ED sup/300 m

1st asc.: E. BELLIN/J.M. BOIVIN/ M. MOIOLI, 18-19/8/1983

Start right at the triangular shaped base of the cliff.

fixed: pitons and bolts

descent: same as A.

gear: pitons, hooks, bivouac.

EAST BUTTRESS OF AIGUILLE DES CISEAUX - LOWER PART 3479 m

AIGUILLE DES
CISEAUX
(200 m.-II/III)

R12

II/III

R11   R11

IV

R10   R10

IV

V   R9
R9

III   IV

R8   R8

IV   V
R7   R7

IV   III+
R6   R6

R5   ]·[IV

V   R5
R4   III+

V   VIa R4
R3   IV+

VIa   R3

R2   R2   IV
V-   IV

R1   IV
V+   Ryan gully

Fou
south face

IV

A: LE FIL A COUDRE:
TD inf/400 m
1st asc.: E. BELLIN/P. CAMISON, 30/7/1984
Follow the Troussier route for one pitch, then traverse left.
fixed: pitons and bolts
descent: rappel down route B.

B: EPERON EST:
D/400 m
1st asc.: G. PRIORESCHI/J.M. TROUSSIER, 25/7/1978
A very nice climb with a spectacular view of the nearby South face.
Start by an obvious flake leading left from the base of the Ryan gully.
fixed: pitons
descent: rappel down the route.

(A)   (B)

Envers des
Aiguilles hut
1 h. 00 →
1 h. 30 →

EAST BUTTRESS OF PREMIERE POINTE DES NANTILLONS 2921 m

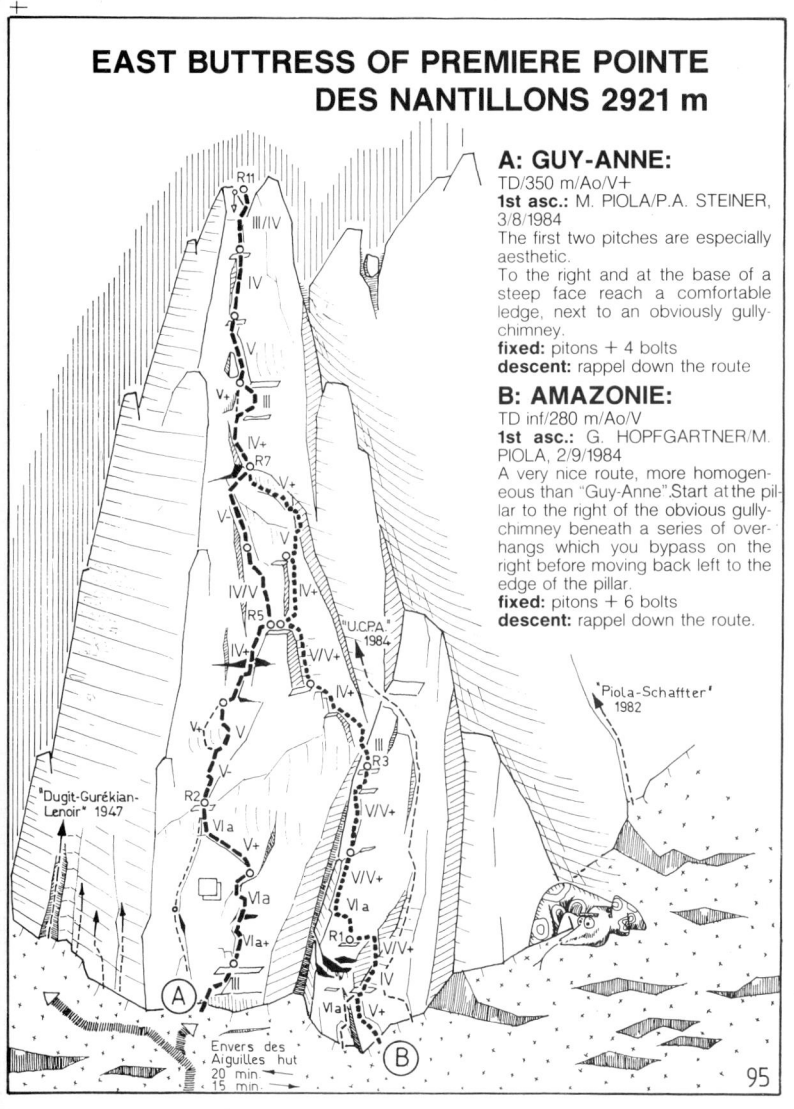

A: GUY-ANNE:

TD/350 m/Ao/V+

1st asc.: M. PIOLA/P.A. STEINER, 3/8/1984

The first two pitches are especially aesthetic.

To the right and at the base of a steep face reach a comfortable ledge, next to an obviously gully-chimney.

fixed: pitons + 4 bolts
descent: rappel down the route

B: AMAZONIE:

TD inf/280 m/Ao/V

1st asc.: G. HOPFGARTNER/M. PIOLA, 2/9/1984

A very nice route, more homogeneous than "Guy-Anne". Start at the pillar to the right of the obvious gully-chimney beneath a series of overhangs which you bypass on the right before moving back left to the edge of the pillar.

fixed: pitons + 6 bolts
descent: rappel down the route.

EAST FACE OF POINTE DES NANTILLONS
3359 m

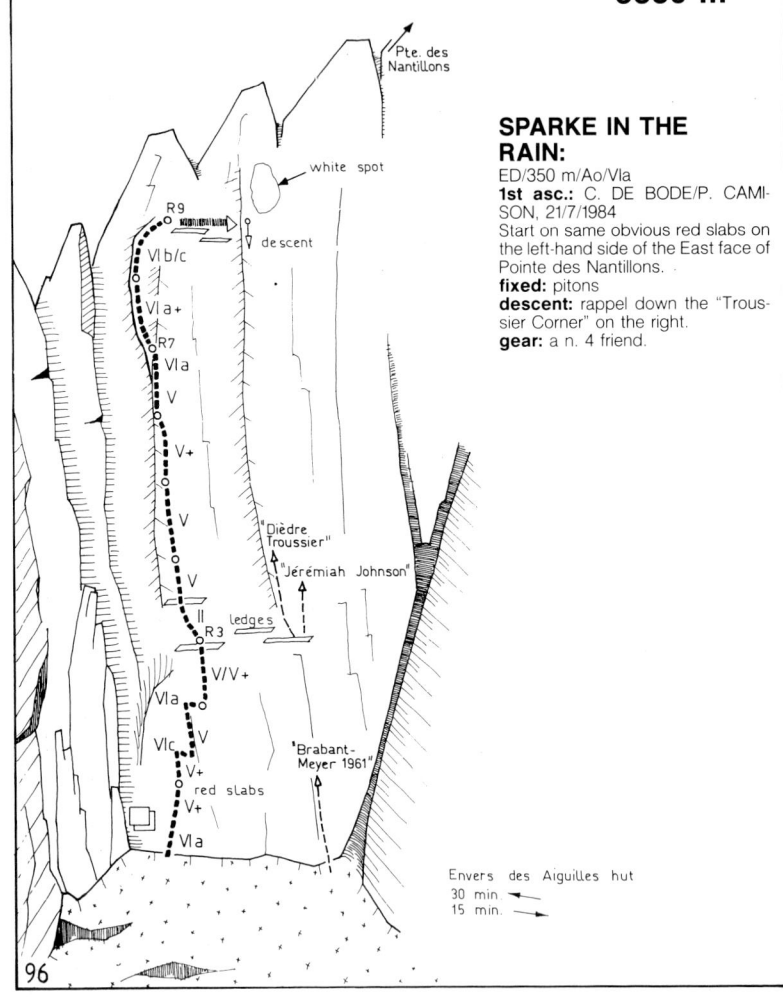

Pte. des Nantillons

white spot

R9

descent

VI b/c

VI a+

R7

VI a

V

V+

V

V

"Dièdre Troussier"

"Jérémiah Johnson"

II

R3

ledges

V/V+

VI a

VI c   V

V+

red slabs

V+

VI a

"Brabant-Meyer 1961"

Envers des Aiguilles hut
30 min. ◄
15 min. ►

SPARKE IN THE RAIN:
ED/350 m/Ao/VIa
1st asc.: C. DE BODE/P. CAMISON, 21/7/1984
Start on same obvious red slabs on the left-hand side of the East face of Pointe des Nantillons.
fixed: pitons
descent: rappel down the "Troussier Corner" on the right.
gear: a n. 4 friend.

SOUTH SIDE OF AIGUILLE DE ROC (ANTECIME)
3409 m

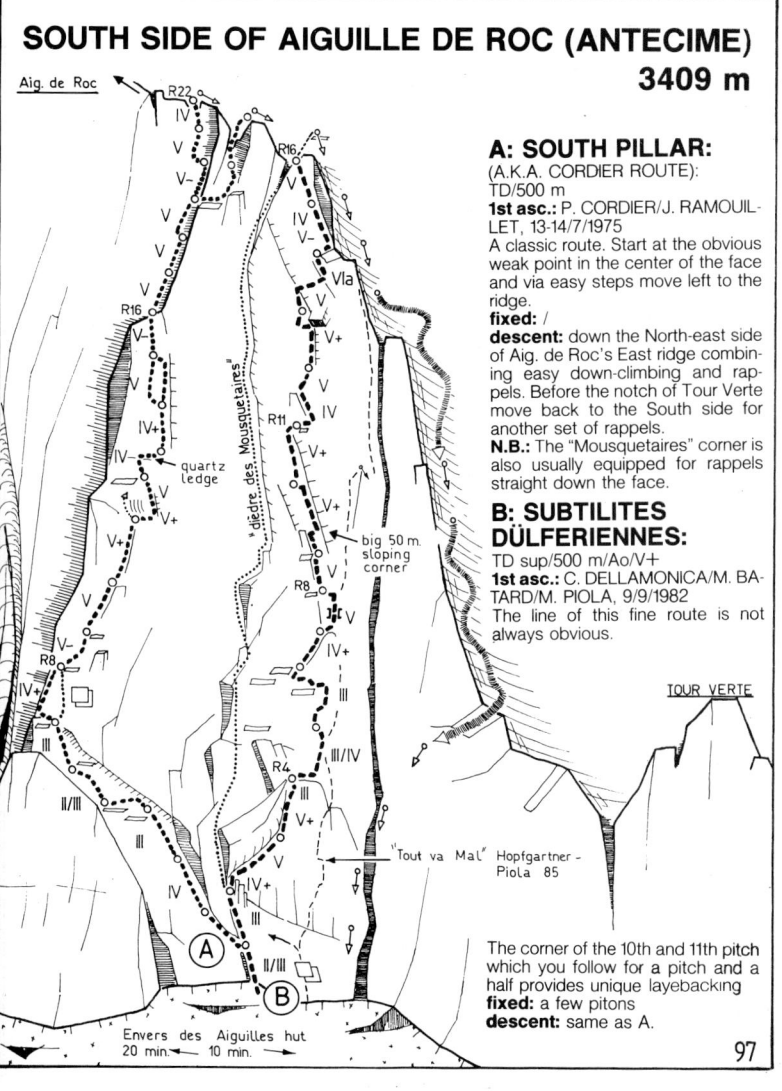

A: SOUTH PILLAR:

(A.K.A. CORDIER ROUTE):
TD/500 m
1st asc.: P. CORDIER/J. RAMOUIL-
LET, 13-14/7/1975
A classic route. Start at the obvious
weak point in the center of the face
and via easy steps move left to the
ridge.
fixed: /
descent: down the North-east side
of Aig. de Roc's East ridge combining easy down-climbing and rappels. Before the notch of Tour Verte
move back to the South side for
another set of rappels.
N.B.: The "Mousquetaires" corner is
also usually equipped for rappels
straight down the face.

B: SUBTILITES DÜLFERIENNES:

TD sup/500 m/Ao/V+
1st asc.: C. DELLAMONICA/M. BA-
TARD/M. PIOLA, 9/9/1982
The line of this fine route is not
always obvious.

The corner of the 10th and 11th pitch
which you follow for a pitch and a
half provides unique layebacking
fixed: a few pitons
descent: same as A.

DURING THE FIRST ASCENT OF SUBTILITES DÜLFERIENNES (V+) ON THE SOUTH
FACE OF AIGUILLE DE ROC - Photo: M. Piola.

SOUTH EAST SIDE OF TOUR VERTE 2760 m

LE PIEGE:

TD sup/200 m/Ao/V+

1st asc.: M. PIOLA/J.M. SCHEN-
KEL, 25/7/1984

A short but strenuous climb.

At the cliff's base look for three
short characteristic pillars, the first
one being right above the moraine.

Climb up the first pillar either straight
or moving right to a bolt.

fixed: pitons + 6 bolts

descent: rappel down the route.

R6
V
IV
V/V+
V+
VI a
V+
V
IV+
III/III
R2 VIa
V+
IV+
V
VIa V/V+

approach: Aig. de Roc east
face
Tour Rouge

Envers des
Aiguilles hut
7 min.
5 min.

1st asc.: M. PIOLA/J.M. SCHEN-
KEL/P. SPRUNGLI, summer 1984
Some of these routes like "Météo-
Bobo" are a good example of the
style of climbing encountered on the
cliffs above. The upper crag is less
interesting.
fixed: pitons+ 16 bolts
descent: rappel down or follow the
path to the hut

UNE HORRIBLE HIS- TOIRE DE PLUIE ET DE MAUVAIS TEMPS:
TD sup/45 m/Ao/V+

B: METEO-BOBO:
TD sup/45 m/Ao/V+

C: SCIENCE-FRIC- TION: D inf/25 m/Ao/V−

D: LE SPHYNX:
AD sup/60 m/Ao/V−

E: LE MATOU:
D inf/60 m/Ao/IV+

F: LE REFUGE EN T:
D/40 m/Ao/V

G: OMBRE ET SOLI- TUDE: TD/40 m/Ao/V+

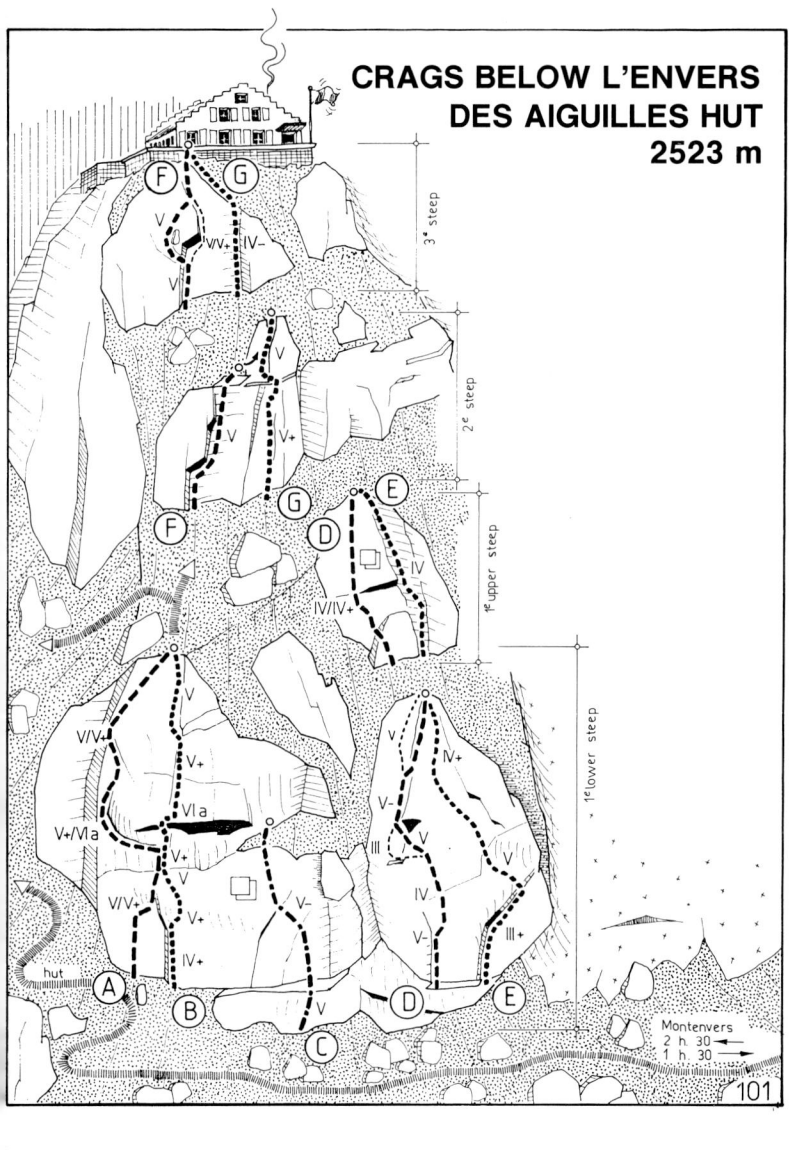

CRAGS BELOW L'ENVERS
DES AIGUILLES HUT
2523 m

LOWER EAST SIDE OF AIGUILLE DE ROC
3409 m

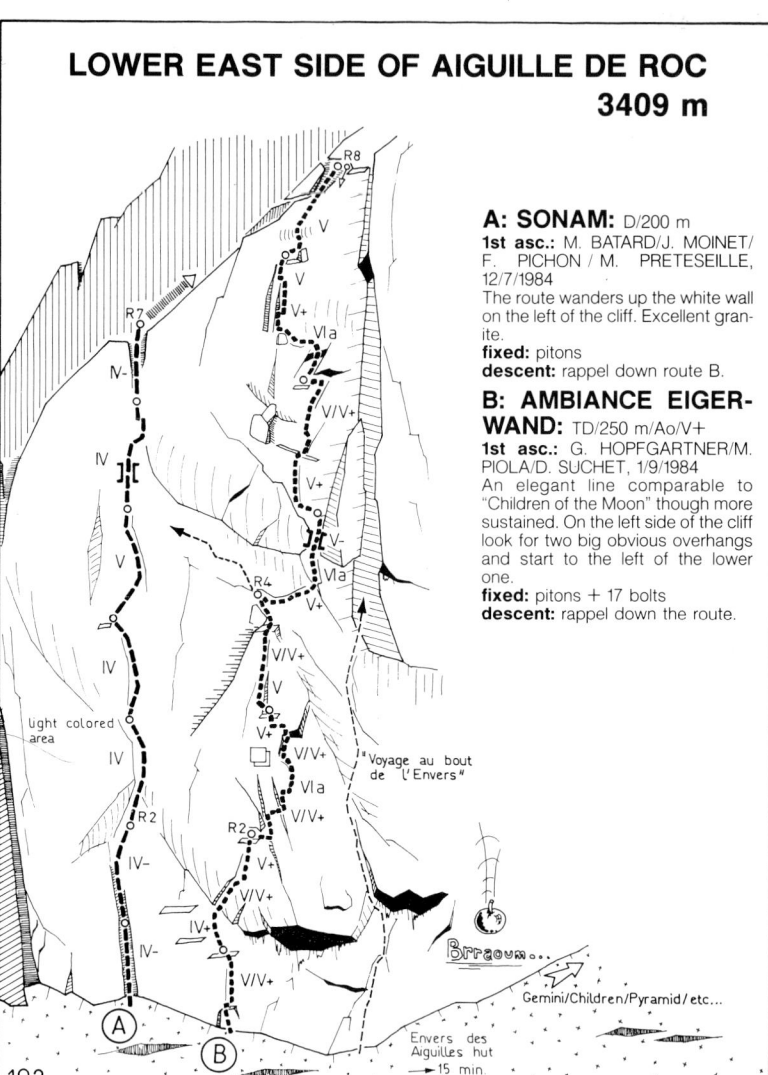

A: SONAM: D/200 m
1st asc.: M. BATARD/J. MOINET/ F. PICHON / M. PRETESEILLE, 12/7/1984
The route wanders up the white wall on the left of the cliff. Excellent granite.
fixed: pitons
descent: rappel down route B.

B: AMBIANCE EIGER-WAND: TD/250 m/Ao/V+
1st asc.: G. HOPFGARTNER/M. PIOLA/D. SUCHET, 1/9/1984
An elegant line comparable to "Children of the Moon" though more sustained. On the left side of the cliff look for two big obvious overhangs and start to the left of the lower one.
fixed: pitons + 17 bolts
descent: rappel down the route.

LOWER EAST SIDE OF AIGUILLE DE ROC
3409 m

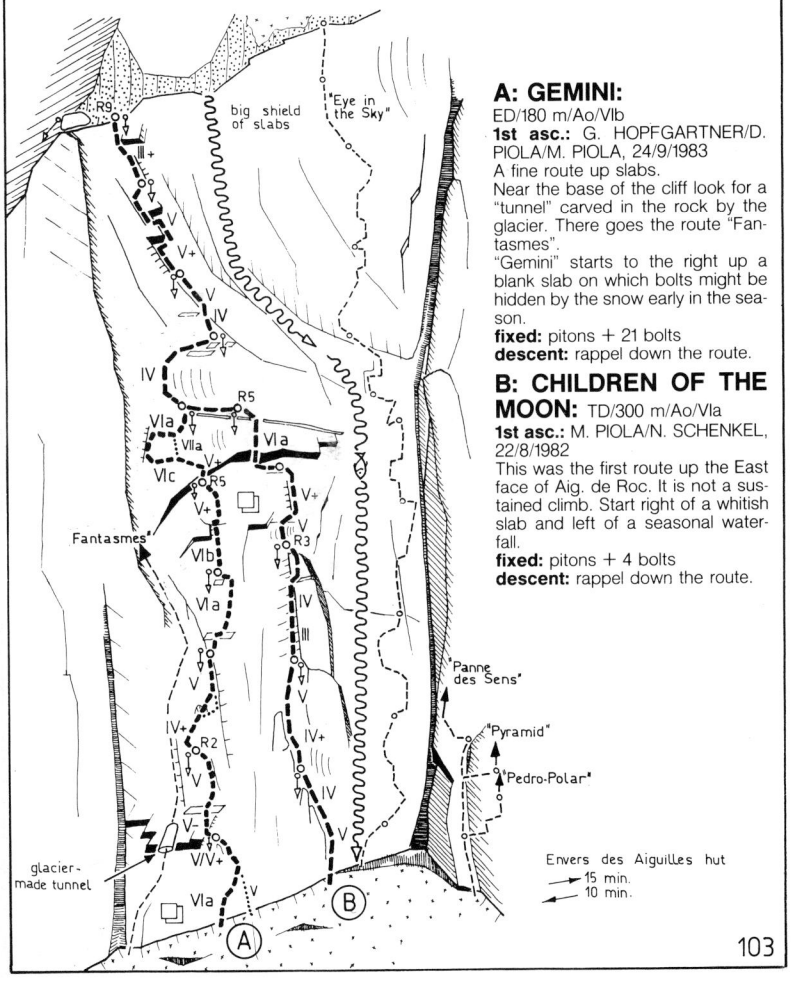

A: GEMINI:

ED/180 m/Ao/VIb

1st asc.: G. HOPFGARTNER/D. PIOLA/M. PIOLA, 24/9/1983

A fine route up slabs.

Near the base of the cliff look for a "tunnel" carved in the rock by the glacier. There goes the route "Fantasmes".

"Gemini" starts to the right up a blank slab on which bolts might be hidden by the snow early in the season.

fixed: pitons + 21 bolts
descent: rappel down the route.

B: CHILDREN OF THE MOON: TD/300 m/Ao/VIa

1st asc.: M. PIOLA/N. SCHENKEL, 22/8/1982

This was the first route up the East face of Aig. de Roc. It is not a sustained climb. Start right of a whitish slab and left of a seasonal waterfall.

fixed: pitons + 4 bolts
descent: rappel down the route.

A: EYE IN THE SKY:

ED inf/350 m/Ao/Vla

1st asc.: M. PEDRINI / M. PIOLA, 4-5/8/1983

The route goes right up the slaby shield which characterizes the East face of Aig. de Roc.

Start up a short ramp to the right of a seasonal waterfall and move back left on the slab.

fixed: pitons + 15 bolts

descent: fixed rappel anchors up to R5. From the top traverse down left on the ledges to reach the rappels of "Children".

B: PYRAMIDE:

ED inf/350 m/Ao/Vla

1st asc.: M. BATARD/M. PIOLA, 25/8/1982

Though the first ascent party had also climbed the rock triangle of the very top, parties now stop at R11.

Step on the steep pillar by a left-slanting corner.

fixed: pitons + 3 bolts

descent: from R10 rappel down "Pedro Polar" or "Panne des sens". From R12 same descent as route A. From the top of the triangle: rappel down the route to the ledges, then same as A.

LOWER EAST SIDE OF AIGUILLE DE ROC
3409 m

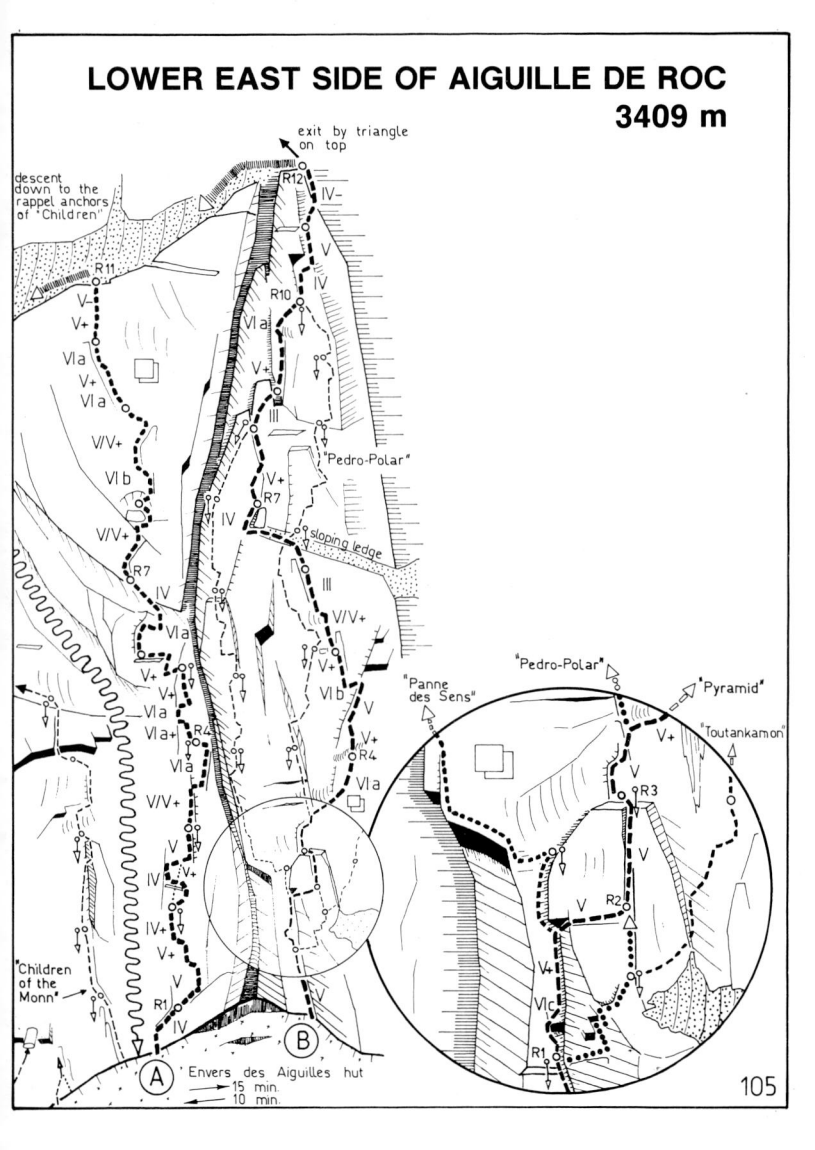

exit by triangle on top

R12

IV−

descent down to the rappel anchors of "Children"

V

IV

R10

R11

V

VIa

V+

VIa

V+

VIa

V/V+

VIb

V/V+

R7

IV

VIa

V+

V+

VIa

VIa+

R4

VIa

V/V+

V

IV

IV+

V+

V

R1

IV

"Pedro-Polar"

V+

R7

IV

sloping ledge

III

V/V+

V+

VIb

V+

VIa

"Children of the Monn"

"Panne des Sens"

A

B

Envers des Aiguilles hut
→ 15 min.
→ 10 min.

"Pedro-Polar"

"Pyramid"

"Toutankamon"

V+

V

R3

V

V

R2

V

V4

VIc

R1

105

LOWER EAST FACE OF AIGUILLE DE ROC – A: GEMINI, 1983 - B: CHILDREN OF THE MOON, 1982 - C: EYE IN THE SKY, 1983 - D: PANNE DES SENS, 1984 - E: PYRAMID, 1982 - F: PEDRO-POLAR, 1984 – Photo: P.A. Steiner.

STARTING VERTIGES DE L'AUTOMNE (VIa+) ON THE LOWER SLABS OF ENVERS DES AIGUILLES – Photo: M. Piola.

LOWER EAST SIDE OF AIGUILLE DE ROC
3409 m

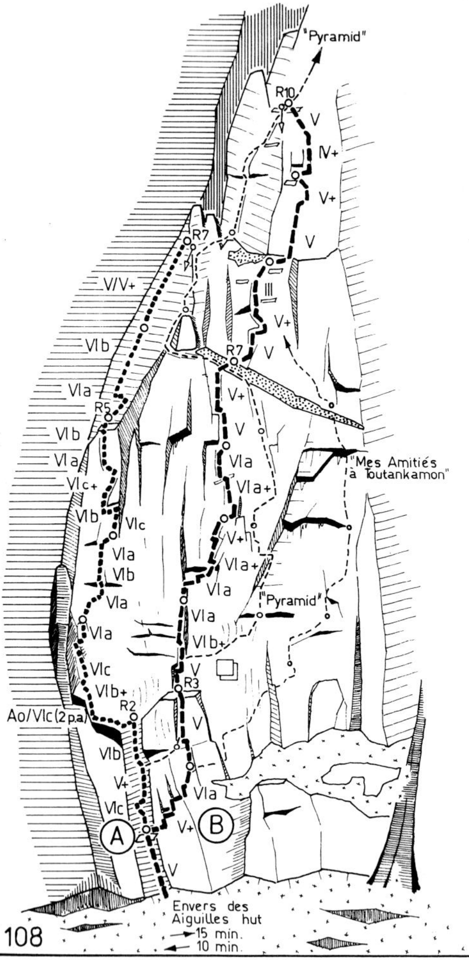

"Pyramid"

R10

V

IV+

V+

V

R7

V/V+

III

VIb

V+

VIa

R7

V

R5

V+

VIb

V

VIa

VIa

"Mes Amitiés
à Toutankamon"

VIc+

VIa+

VIb

VIc

V+

VIa

VIb

VIa+

VIa

VIa

"Pyramid"

VIa

VIa

VIb+

VIc

R3

VIb+

R2

Ao/VIc(2pa)

V

VIb

V+

VIa

VIc

(A)

V+ (B)

V

Envers des
Aiguilles hut
← 15 min.
← 10 min.

A: PANNE DES SENS: ABO/250 m/Ao/VIc
1st asc.: M. PIOLA/P.A. STEINER, 19-20/7/1984
A really hard but beautiful line up the edge of the spur.
It shares the first pitch with "Pyramide".
fixed: pitons + 25 bolts
descent: rappel down the route.

B: PEDRO-POLAR:
ED/300 m/Ao/VIa+
1st asc.: M. PIOLA/P.A. STEINER, 4/8/1984
A fine route, more sustained than "Pyramide".
Move right from the 1st stance of "Pyramide".
fixed: pitons + 13 bolts
descent: rappel down the route.

SOUTH EAST SIDE OF TOUR ROUGE 2899 m

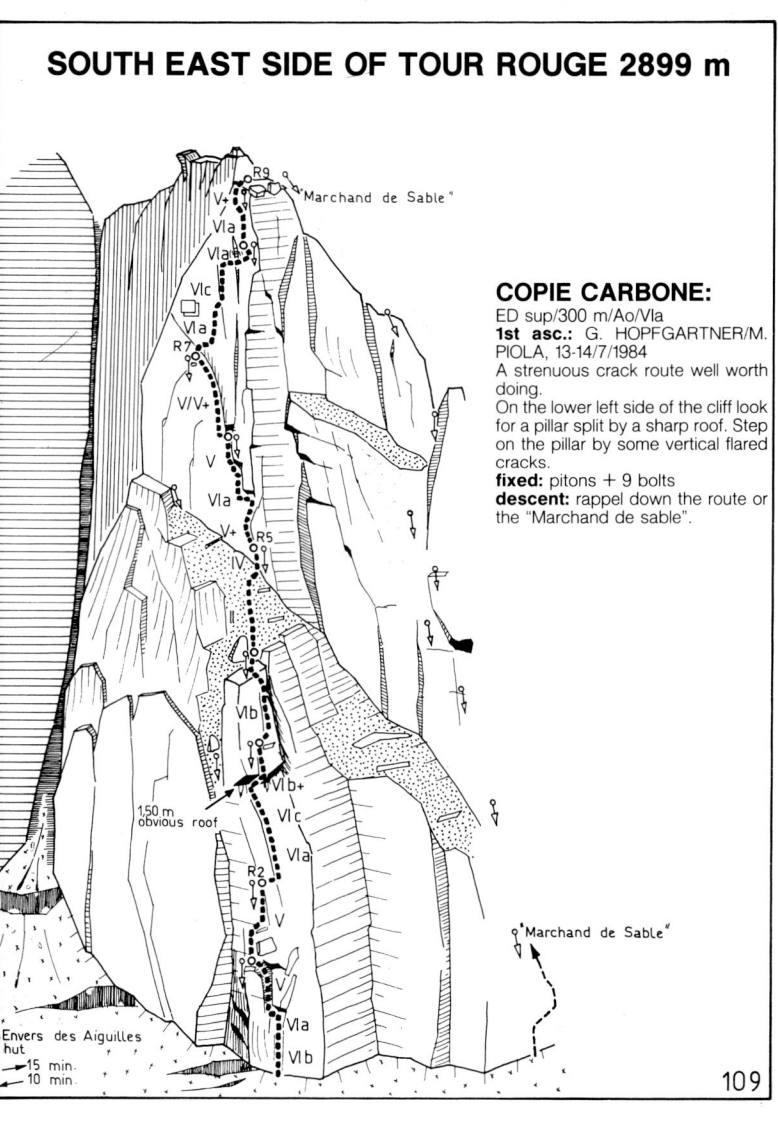

"Marchand de Sable"

R9

V+
VIa
VIa
VIc
VIa
R7
V/V+

V

VIa

V+   R5
IV

II

VIb

VIb+
VIc
VIa
R2
V

VIa
VIb

1,50 m
obvious roof

○ "Marchand de Sable"

Envers des Aiguilles
hut
15 min.
10 min.

COPIE CARBONE:

ED sup/300 m/Ao/VIa
1st asc.: G. HOPFGARTNER/M.
PIOLA, 13-14/7/1984
A strenuous crack route well worth
doing.
On the lower left side of the cliff look
for a pillar split by a sharp roof. Step
on the pillar by some vertical flared
cracks.
fixed: pitons + 9 bolts
descent: rappel down the route or
the "Marchand de sable".

SOUTH EAST SIDE OF TOUR ROUGE 2899 m

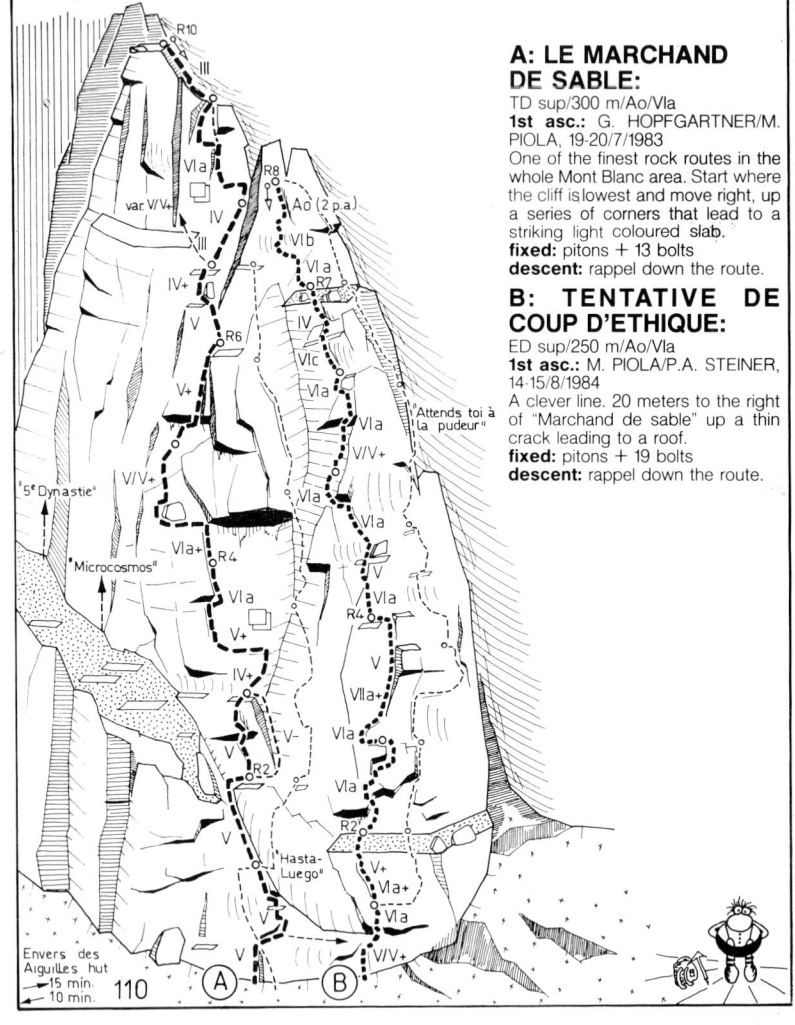

A: LE MARCHAND DE SABLE:

TD sup/300 m/Ao/VIa
1st asc.: G. HOPFGARTNER/M. PIOLA, 19-20/7/1983
One of the finest rock routes in the whole Mont Blanc area. Start where the cliff is lowest and move right, up a series of corners that lead to a striking light coloured slab.
fixed: pitons + 13 bolts
descent: rappel down the route.

B: TENTATIVE DE COUP D'ETHIQUE:

ED sup/250 m/Ao/VIa
1st asc.: M. PIOLA/P.A. STEINER, 14-15/8/1984
A clever line. 20 meters to the right of "Marchand de sable" up a thin crack leading to a roof.
fixed: pitons + 19 bolts
descent: rappel down the route.

110

Envers des Aiguilles hut
← 15 min.
← 10 min.

SOUTH EAST SIDE OF TOUR ROUGE 2899 m

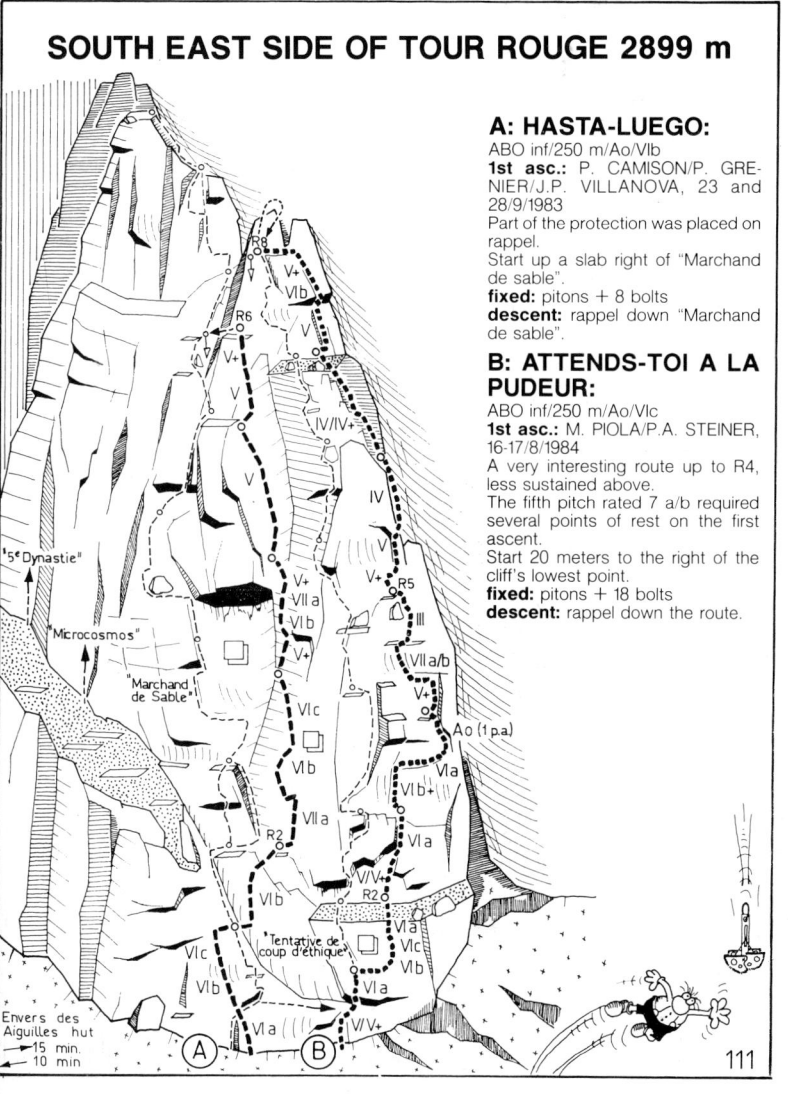

A: HASTA-LUEGO:

ABO inf/250 m/Ao/VIb
1st asc.: P. CAMISON/P. GRE-
NIER/J.P. VILLANOVA, 23 and
28/9/1983
Part of the protection was placed on
rappel.
Start up a slab right of "Marchand
de sable".
fixed: pitons + 8 bolts
descent: rappel down "Marchand
de sable".

B: ATTENDS-TOI A LA PUDEUR:

ABO inf/250 m/Ao/VIc
1st asc.: M. PIOLA/P.A. STEINER,
16-17/8/1984
A very interesting route up to R4,
less sustained above.
The fifth pitch rated 7 a/b required
several points of rest on the first
ascent.
Start 20 meters to the right of the
cliff's lowest point.
fixed: pitons + 18 bolts
descent: rappel down the route.

"5e Dynastie"

"Microcosmos"

"Marchand de Sable"

Envers des
Aiguilles hut
→ 15 min.
→ 10 min.

LOWER SLABS OF ENVERS DES AIGUILLES
2406 m

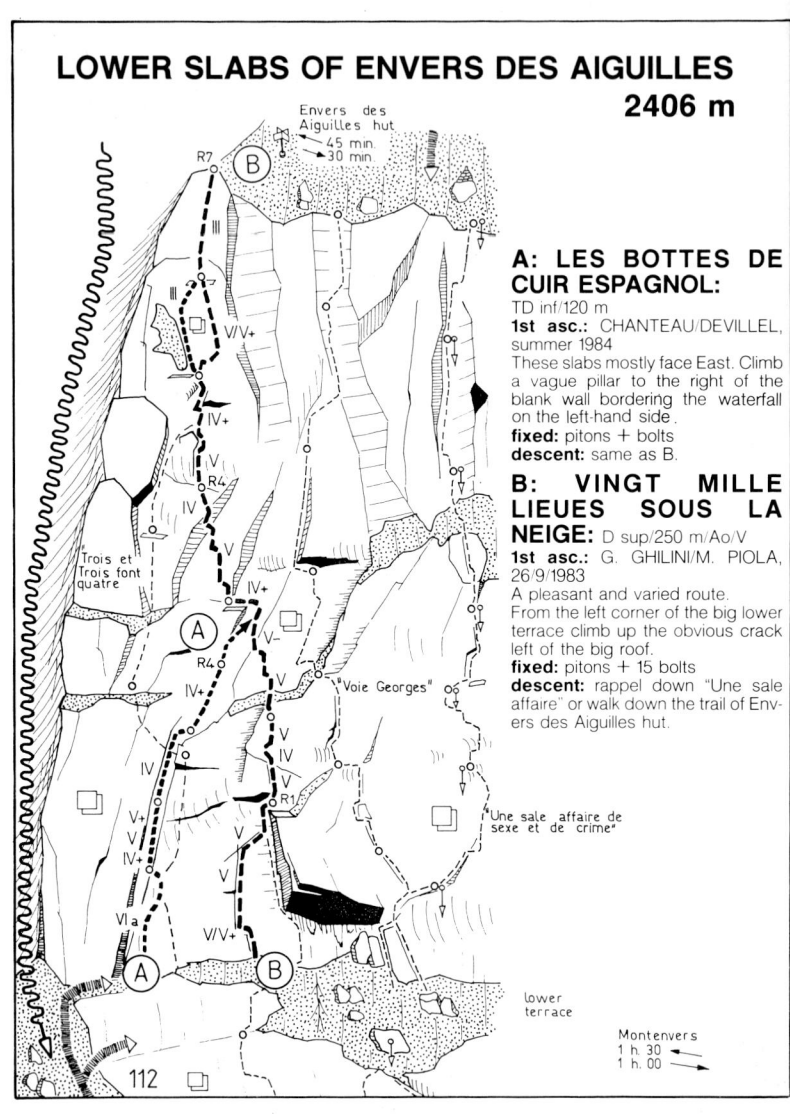

Envers des
Aiguilles hut
45 min.
30 min.

A: LES BOTTES DE CUIR ESPAGNOL:

TD inf/120 m

1st asc.: CHANTEAU/DEVILLEL, summer 1984

These slabs mostly face East. Climb a vague pillar to the right of the blank wall bordering the waterfall on the left-hand side.

fixed: pitons + bolts
descent: same as B.

B: VINGT MILLE LIEUES SOUS LA NEIGE: D sup/250 m/Ao/V

1st asc.: G. GHILINI/M. PIOLA, 26/9/1983

A pleasant and varied route.
From the left corner of the big lower terrace climb up the obvious crack left of the big roof.

fixed: pitons + 15 bolts
descent: rappel down "Une sale affaire" or walk down the trail of Envers des Aiguilles hut.

"Trois et Trois font quatre"

"Voie Georges"

"Une sale affaire de sexe et de crime"

lower terrace

Montenvers
1 h. 30
1 h. 00

EAST FACE OF TOUR ROUGE – A: MARCHAND DE SABLE, 1983 · B: HASTA-LUEGO, 1983 · C: TENTATIVE DE COUP D'ETHIQUE, 1984 · D: ATTENDS-TOI A LA PUDEUR, 1984 – Photo: M. Piola.

LOWER SLABS OF ENVERS DES AIGUILLES
2406 m

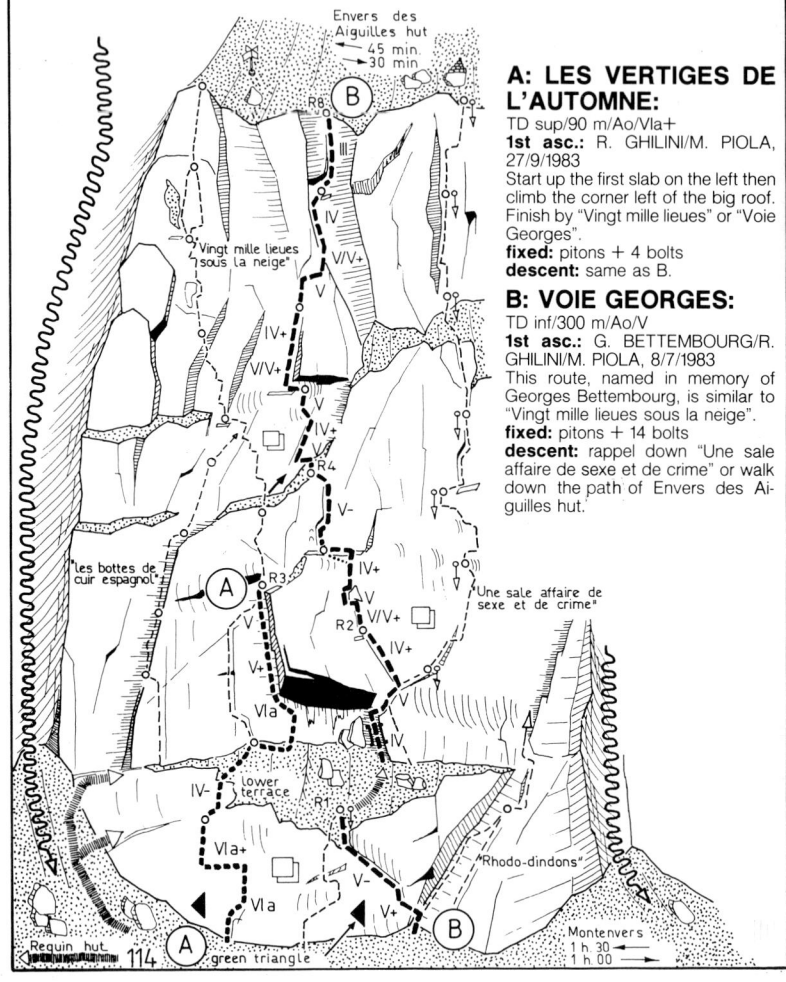

A: LES VERTIGES DE L'AUTOMNE:

TD sup/90 m/Ao/VIa+
1st asc.: R. GHILINI/M. PIOLA, 27/9/1983
Start up the first slab on the left then climb the corner left of the big roof. Finish by "Vingt mille lieues" or "Voie Georges".
fixed: pitons + 4 bolts
descent: same as B.

B: VOIE GEORGES:

TD inf/300 m/Ao/V
1st asc.: G. BETTEMBOURG/R. GHILINI/M. PIOLA, 8/7/1983
This route, named in memory of Georges Bettembourg, is similar to "Vingt mille lieues sous la neige".
fixed: pitons + 14 bolts
descent: rappel down "Une sale affaire de sexe et de crime" or walk down the path of Envers des Aiguilles hut.

STARTING UNE SALE AFFAIRE DE SEXE ET DE CRIME (VIIa), ON THE LOWER SLABS OF ENVERS DES AIGUILLES – Photo: M. Piola.

LOWER SLABS OF ENVERS DES AIGUILLES
2406 m

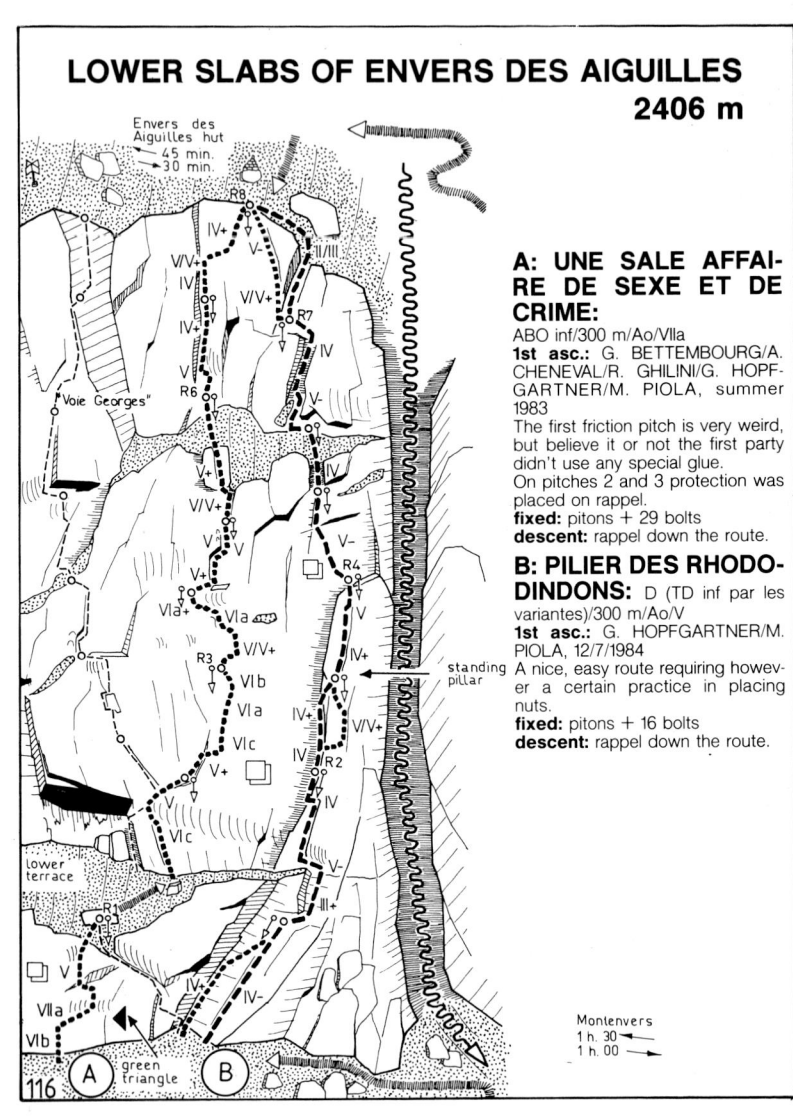

Envers des
Aiguilles hut
← 45 min.
→ 30 min.

R8

IV+

V/V+

IV

V/V+

II/III

R7

IV

V

R6

V-

"Voie Georges"

V+

V/V+

V-

V+

R4

Vla+

Vla

V

V/V+

IV+

R3

V/V+

Vlb

Vla

IV+

IV

Vlc

R2

V+

IV

IV/V+

standing
pillar

V

Vlc

IV

Lower
terrace

R1

III+

V

IV+

Vlla

IV-

Vlb

A

green
triangle

B

116

A: UNE SALE AFFAIRE DE SEXE ET DE CRIME:

ABO inf/300 m/Ao/VIIa
1st asc.: G. BETTEMBOURG/A. CHENEVAL/R. GHILINI/G. HOPFGARTNER/M. PIOLA, summer 1983
The first friction pitch is very weird, but believe it or not the first party didn't use any special glue.
On pitches 2 and 3 protection was placed on rappel.
fixed: pitons + 29 bolts
descent: rappel down the route.

B: PILIER DES RHODODINDONS:
D (TD inf par les variantes)/300 m/Ao/V
1st asc.: G. HOPFGARTNER/M. PIOLA, 12/7/1984
A nice, easy route requiring however a certain practice in placing nuts.
fixed: pitons + 16 bolts
descent: rappel down the route.

Montenvers
1 h. 30 →
1 h. 00 →

AREA n° 7

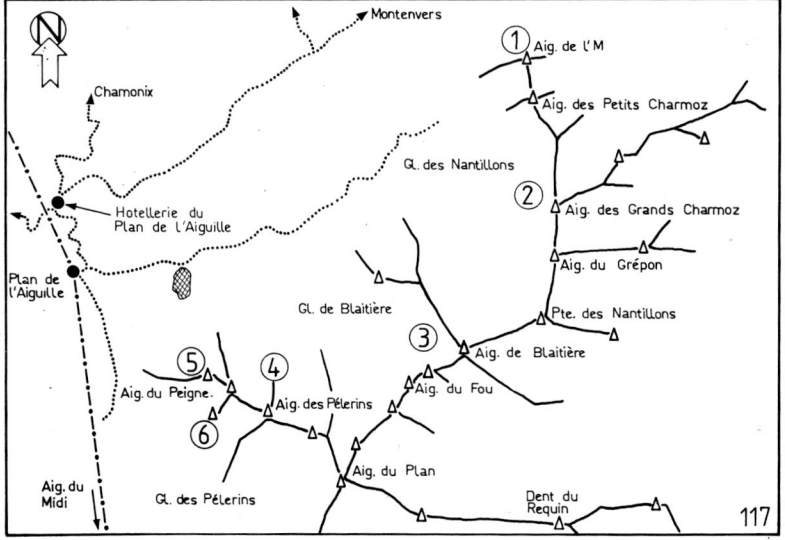

N

Chamonix

Montenvers

① Aig. de l'M

Aig. des Petits Charmoz

Gl. des Nantillons

② Aig. des Grands Charmoz

Aig. du Grépon

Hotellerie du
Plan de l'Aiguille

Plan de
l'Aiguille

Pte. des Nantillons

Gl. de Blaitière

③ Aig. de Blaitière

⑤ ④

Aig. du Peigne. Aig. des Pélerins

Aig. du Fou

⑥

Aig. du Plan

Aig. du
Midi

Gl. des Pélerins

Dent du
Requin

AREA N. 7   LES AIGUILLES DE CHAMONIX

This is the "valley" side of the Aiguilles of Chamonix with a width stretching up to 2.5 kilometers. Even though not so sunny (most cliffs face West or even North) this area is very popular because of its moderate altitude and easy approach. And late starters will indeed enjoy the afternoon sun.

Plan de l'Aiguille (2310 m)
This is the intermediate téléphérique station from Aiguille du Midi. There are no lodging facilities but the nearby meadows provide great camping spots. Free water at the Plan de l'Aiguille lake.

"Hôtellerie du Plan de l'Aiguille" (2233 m) No phone.
To reach this privately owned hut, follow a well worn trail towards Chamonix for 10 minutes.

Approaches to the cliffs:
1. North-west and North North-east sides of Aiguille de l'M
From Plan de l'Aiguille follow the path to the lake and go up the moraine to cross the glacier of Blaitière and then that of Nantillons. Go down diagonally and walk up the grassy slopes to the pass beneath Aig. de l'M (between Pointe 2503 m and Pic Albert). On the other side reach the base of l'M's North-west face and further its North North-east ridge.

2. West face of Grands Charmoz
Same way as 1 up to the Nantillons glacier. Walk up its lower part to the base of the cliff.

3. West side of Aiguille de Blaitière
Same way as 1 up to the other side of Blaitière glacier. Follow the moraine ridge to a snow slope beneath Blaitière's North-west ridge, that leads to a small pass on the right. On the other side follow easy but sometimes snow covered ledges to the start of the routes (see topo "Pilier Rouge de l'Aig. de Blaitière").

4. North Buttress of "Aiguille des Pélerins"
Same as 1 but before crossing Blaitière's glacier which you follow to the base of the cliff.

5. Lower upper North-west side of "Aiguille du Peigne"
From "Plan de l'Aiguille" up the grassy slopes below the Peigne's West ridge ("Papillons" ridge) then left to reach a little snowfield. Scramble to the base of the North-west slabs below Gendarme 3009 m.

6. East side of Gendarme 3068 m on "Aig. du Peigne"
From "Plan de l'Aiguille" follow the trail towards Pélerins glacier. Walk up the moraine and a short snowfield to the base of the cliff.

NORTH NORTH EAST SIDE OF AIGUILLE DE L'M
2844 m

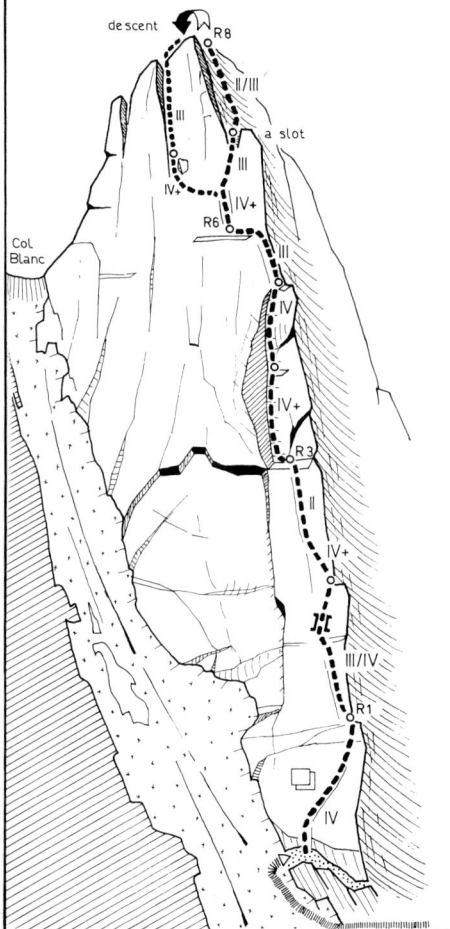

NORTH NORTH-EAST RIDGE: D inf/200 m

1st asc.: Mme A. DAMESNE/F. BA-TIER/M. DAMESNE/J. MORIN, 28/8/1945

A short interesting climb with an amazing view on the Drus and Verte area.

From the snow gully move right onto the ridge by a steep step that leads to a fractured slab.

fixed: pitons

descent: from the top scramble down the South side (II/III) to the Bûche pass (between Aig. de l'M and Petits Charmoz). Hike down the West side of the gully (ladders on the left at the end) back to the Nantillons glacier.

NORTH WEST SIDE OF AIGUILLE DE L'M 2844 m

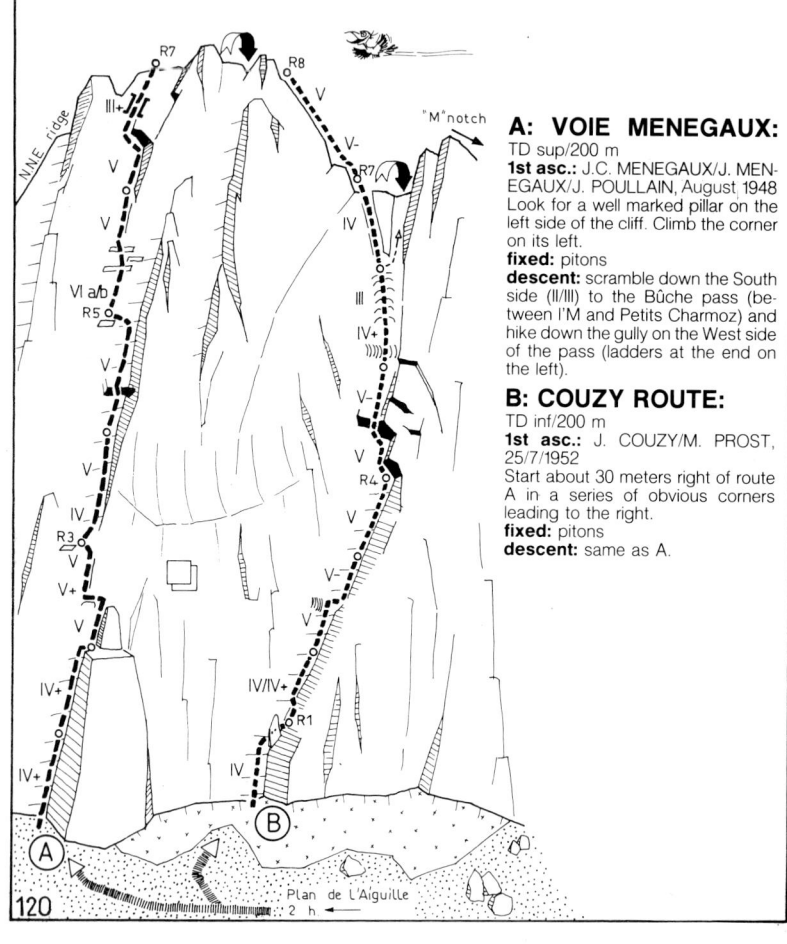

A: VOIE MENEGAUX:

TD sup/200 m

1st asc.: J.C. MENEGAUX/J. MEN-EGAUX/J. POULLAIN, August, 1948
Look for a well marked pillar on the left side of the cliff. Climb the corner on its left.

fixed: pitons

descent: scramble down the South side (II/III) to the Bûche pass (between I'M and Petits Charmoz) and hike down the gully on the West side of the pass (ladders at the end on the left).

B: COUZY ROUTE:

TD inf/200 m

1st asc.: J. COUZY/M. PROST, 25/7/1952
Start about 30 meters right of route A in a series of obvious corners leading to the right.

fixed: pitons

descent: same as A.

WEST FACE OF GRANDS CHARMOZ 3445 m

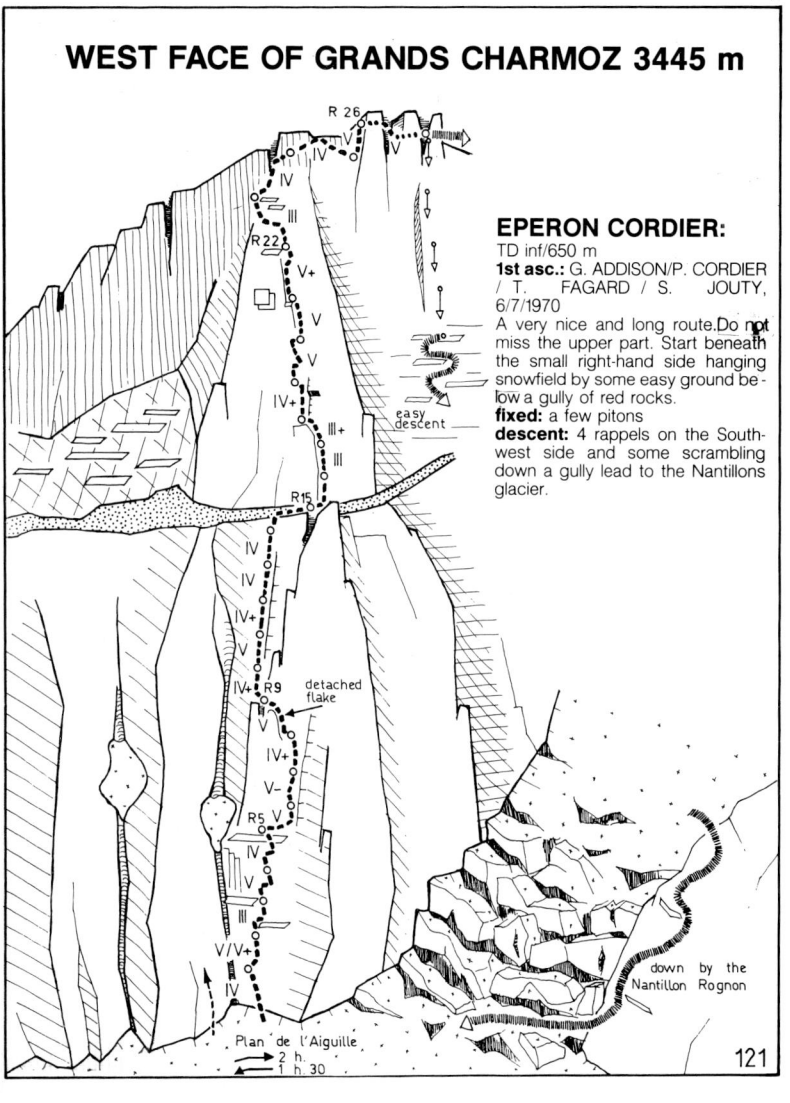

EPERON CORDIER:

TD inf/650 m

1st asc.: G. ADDISON/P. CORDIER / T. FAGARD / S. JOUTY, 6/7/1970

A very nice and long route. Do not miss the upper part. Start beneath the small right-hand side hanging snowfield by some easy ground below a gully of red rocks.

fixed: a few pitons

descent: 4 rappels on the South-west side and some scrambling down a gully lead to the Nantillons glacier.

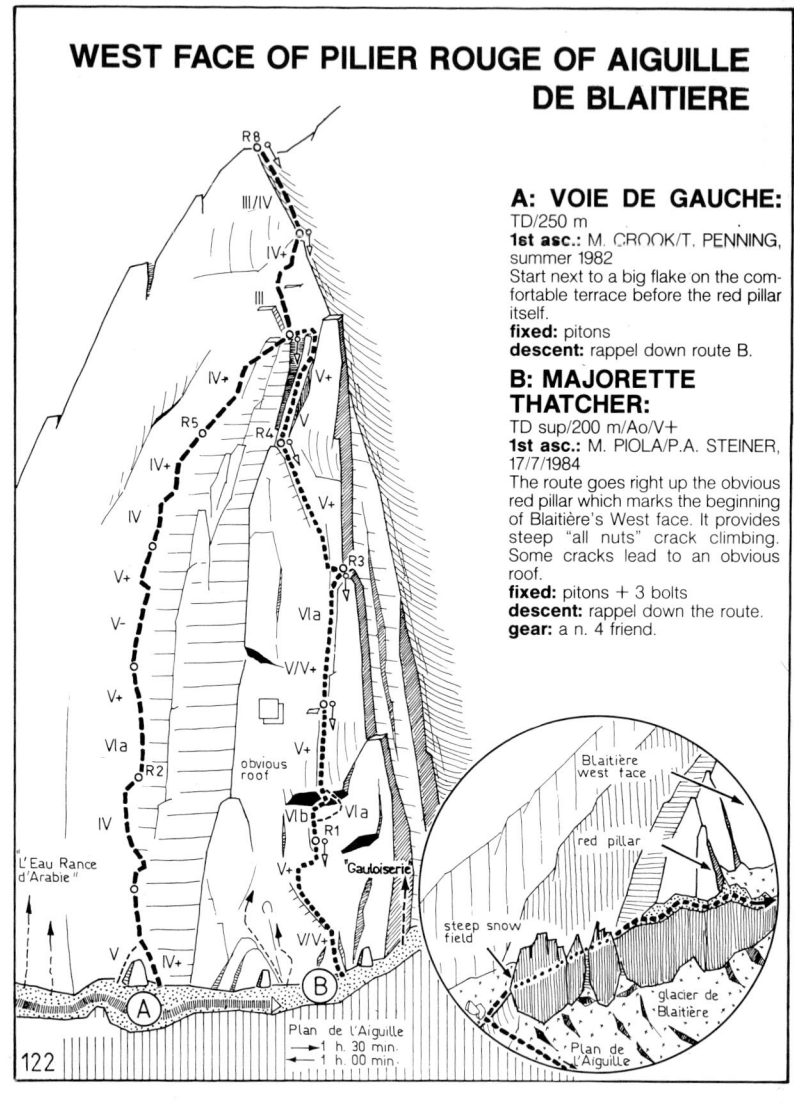

WEST FACE OF PILIER ROUGE OF AIGUILLE DE BLAITIERE

R8

III/IV

IV+

III

IV+   V+

R5   V

R4   V

IV+

IV

V+   V+

V+   R3

V-   VIa

V+   V/V+

VIa   V+

R2

IV   obvious roof

VIb   VIa

R1

"L'Eau Rance d'Arabie"

V+

'Gauloiserie'

V   IV+

V/V+

A   B

Plan de l'Aiguille
→ 1 h. 30 min.
→ 1 h. 00 min.

A: VOIE DE GAUCHE:

TD/250 m
1st asc.: M. CROOK/T. PENNING, summer 1982
Start next to a big flake on the comfortable terrace before the red pillar itself.
fixed: pitons
descent: rappel down route B.

B: MAJORETTE THATCHER:

TD sup/200 m/Ao/V+
1st asc.: M. PIOLA/P.A. STEINER, 17/7/1984
The route goes right up the obvious red pillar which marks the beginning of Blaitière's West face. It provides steep "all nuts" crack climbing. Some cracks lead to an obvious roof.
fixed: pitons + 3 bolts
descent: rappel down the route.
gear: a n. 4 friend.

Blaitière west face

red pillar

steep snow field

glacier de Blaitière

Plan de l'Aiguille

WEST FACE OF AIGUILLE DE BLAITIERE – A: MAJORETTE THATCHER, 1984 - B: FIDEL FIASCO, 1984 - C: WILLIAMINE DADA, 1983 - D: FACE OUEST CLASSIQUE, 1954 – Photo: J. Winkler.

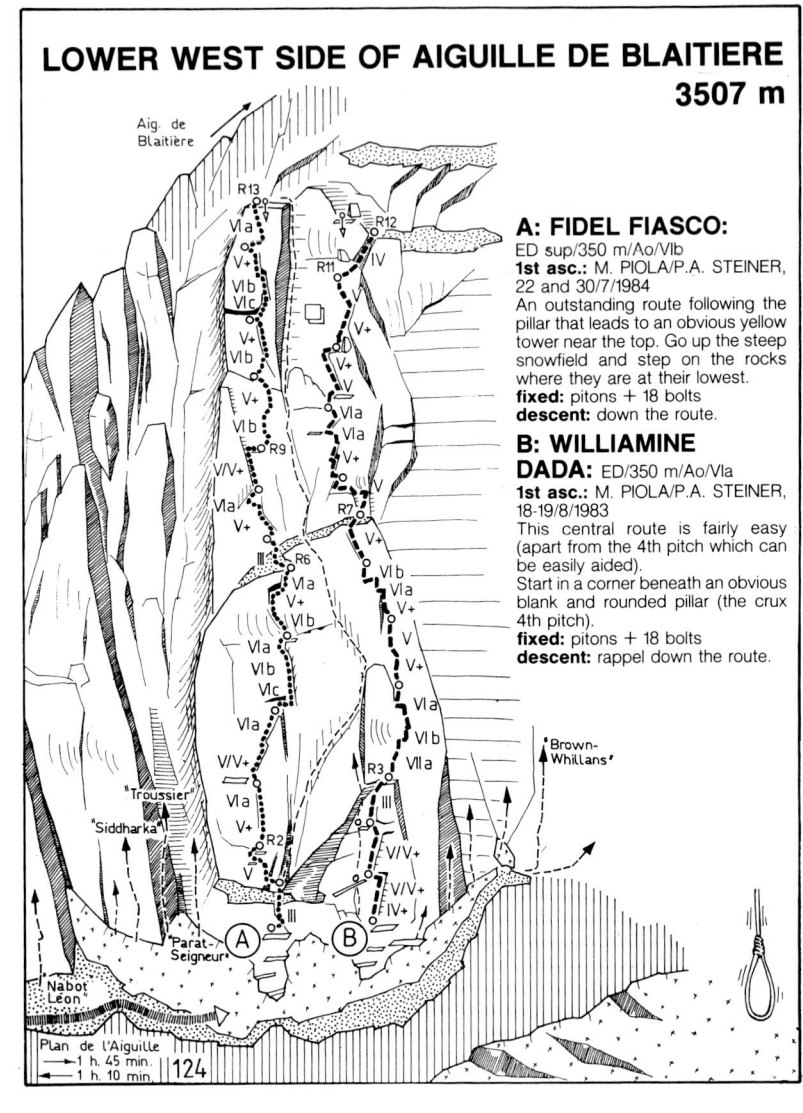

LOWER WEST SIDE OF AIGUILLE DE BLAITIERE
3507 m

A: FIDEL FIASCO:
ED sup/350 m/Ao/VIb
1st asc.: M. PIOLA/P.A. STEINER,
22 and 30/7/1984
An outstanding route following the
pillar that leads to an obvious yellow
tower near the top. Go up the steep
snowfield and step on the rocks
where they are at their lowest.
fixed: pitons + 18 bolts
descent: down the route.

B: WILLIAMINE
DADA: ED/350 m/Ao/VIa
1st asc.: M. PIOLA/P.A. STEINER,
18-19/8/1983
This central route is fairly easy
(apart from the 4th pitch which can
be easily aided).
Start in a corner beneath an obvious
blank and rounded pillar (the crux
4th pitch).
fixed: pitons + 18 bolts
descent: rappel down the route.

LOWER WEST SIDE OF AIGUILLE DE BLAITIERE
3507 m

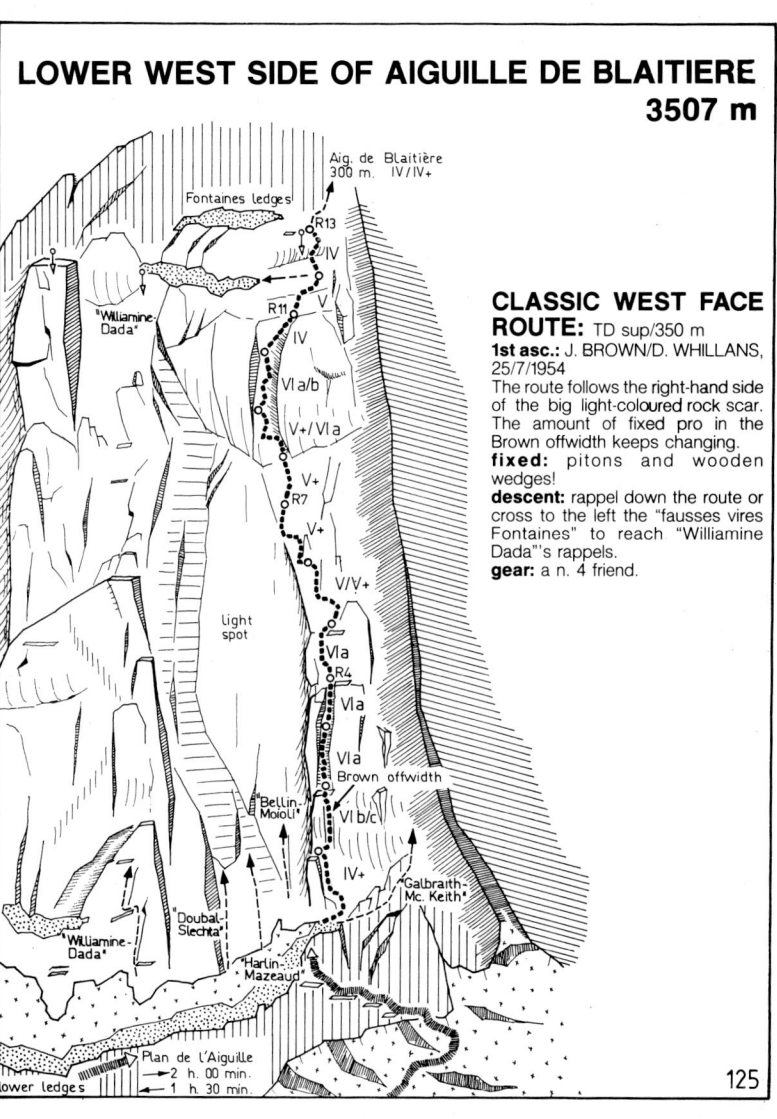

Aig. de Blaitière
300 m. IV/IV+

Fontaines ledges

R13

IV

"Williamine Dada"

R11

V

IV

VIa/b

V+/VIa

V+

R7

V+

V/V+

Light spot

VIa

R4

VIa

VIa

Brown offwidth

"Bellin-Moioli"

VI b/c

IV+

Galbraith-Mc.Keith"

"Doubal-Slechta"

"Williamine Dada"

"Harlin-Mazeaud"

Plan de l'Aiguille
→ 2 h. 00 min.
← 1 h. 30 min.

lower ledges

CLASSIC WEST FACE

ROUTE: TD sup/350 m
1st asc.: J. BROWN/D. WHILLANS, 25/7/1954
The route follows the right-hand side of the big light-coloured rock scar. The amount of fixed pro in the Brown offwidth keeps changing.
fixed: pitons and wooden wedges!
descent: rappel down the route or cross to the left the "fausses vires Fontaines" to reach "Williamine Dada"'s rappels.
gear: a n. 4 friend.

NORTH BUTTRESS OF AIGUILLE DES PELERINS

3318 m

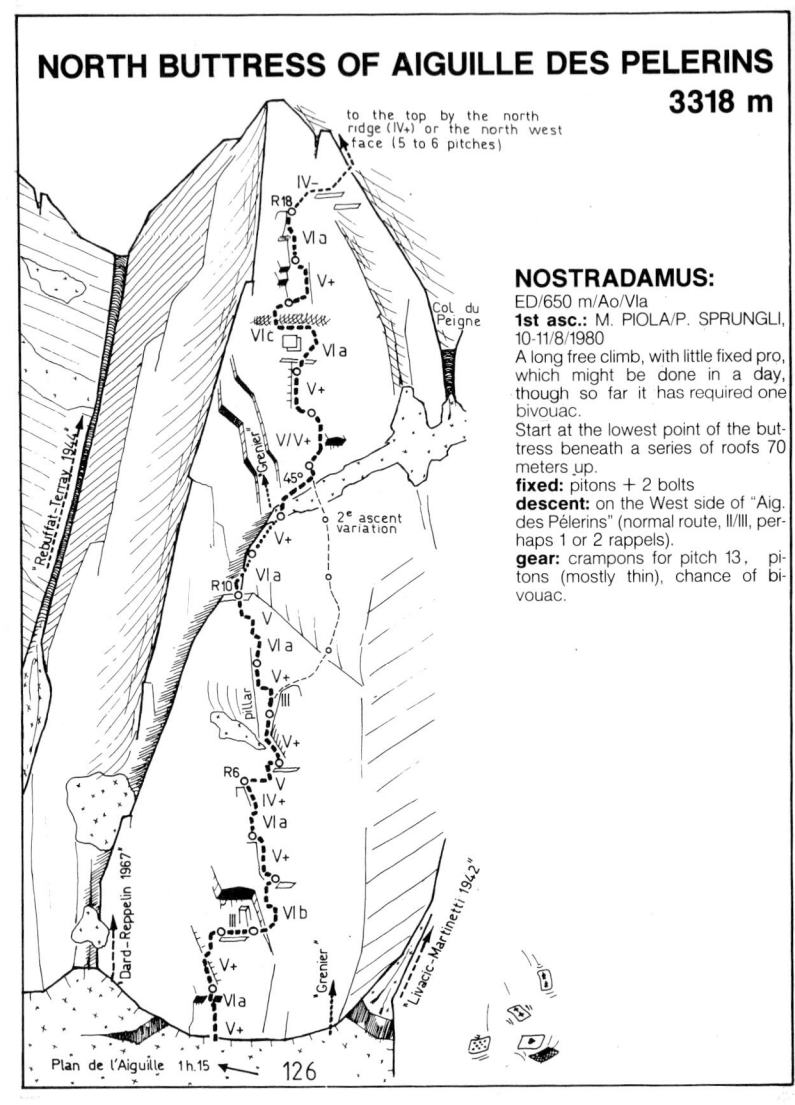

to the top by the north ridge (IV+) or the north west face (5 to 6 pitches)

IV−
R18
VIa
V+
VIc
VIa
V+
V/V+
45°
2e ascent variation
V+
VIa
R10
V
VIa
V+
III
V+
V
IV+
R6
VIa
V+
VIb
V+
VIa
V+

Col du Peigne
"Rebuffat-Terray 1944"
"Grenier"
pillar
"Dard-Reppelin 1967"
"Grenier"
"Livacic-Martinetti 1942"

Plan de l'Aiguille 1 h.15

NOSTRADAMUS:

ED/650 m/Ao/VIa

1st asc.: M. PIOLA/P. SPRUNGLI, 10-11/8/1980

A long free climb, with little fixed pro, which might be done in a day, though so far it has required one bivouac.

Start at the lowest point of the buttress beneath a series of roofs 70 meters up.

fixed: pitons + 2 bolts

descent: on the West side of "Aig. des Pélerins" (normal route, II/III, perhaps 1 or 2 rappels).

gear: crampons for pitch 13, pitons (mostly thin), chance of bivouac.

NORTH WEST SLABS OF GENDARME 3009 m

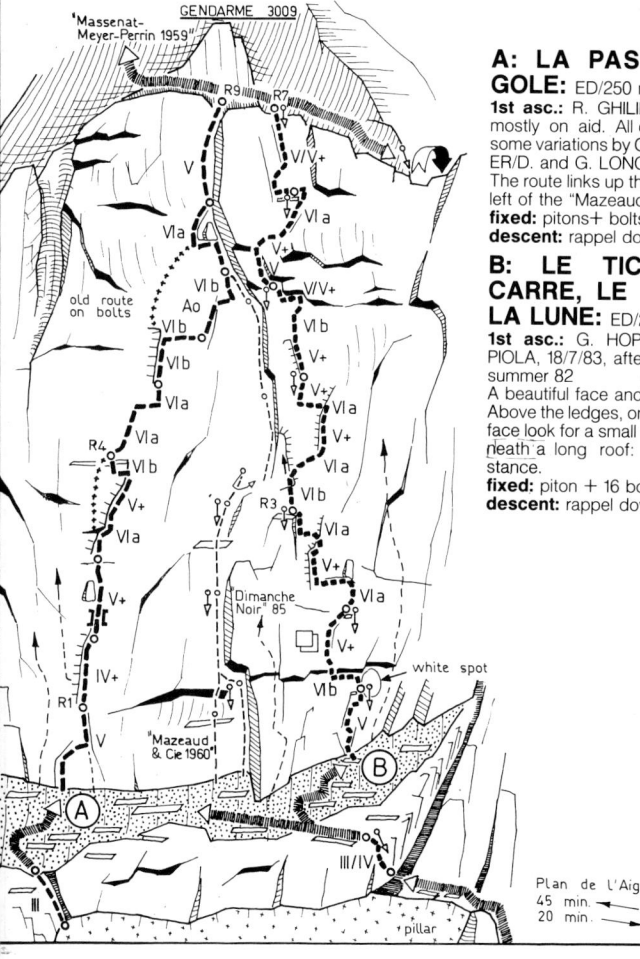

A: LA PASSE MON-GOLE: ED/250 m/Ao/VIb

1st asc.: R. GHILINI and a friend mostly on aid. All done free with some variations by G. and R. VOGLER/D. and G. LONG, 5/7/1982
The route links up the arches on the left of the "Mazeaud route".
fixed: pitons+ bolts
descent: rappel down route B.

B: LE TICKET, LE CARRE, LE ROND ET LA LUNE: ED/250 m/Ao/VIb

1st asc.: G. HOPFGARTNER/M. PIOLA, 18/7/83, after some work in summer 82
A beautiful face and slab climb. Above the ledges, on the right of the face look for a small white spot beneath a long roof: it is the first stance.
fixed: piton + 16 bolts
descent: rappel down the route.

Plan de L'Aiguille
45 min. ◄—
20 min. —►

UPPER NORTH WEST FACE OF AIGUILLE DU PEIGNE 3192 m

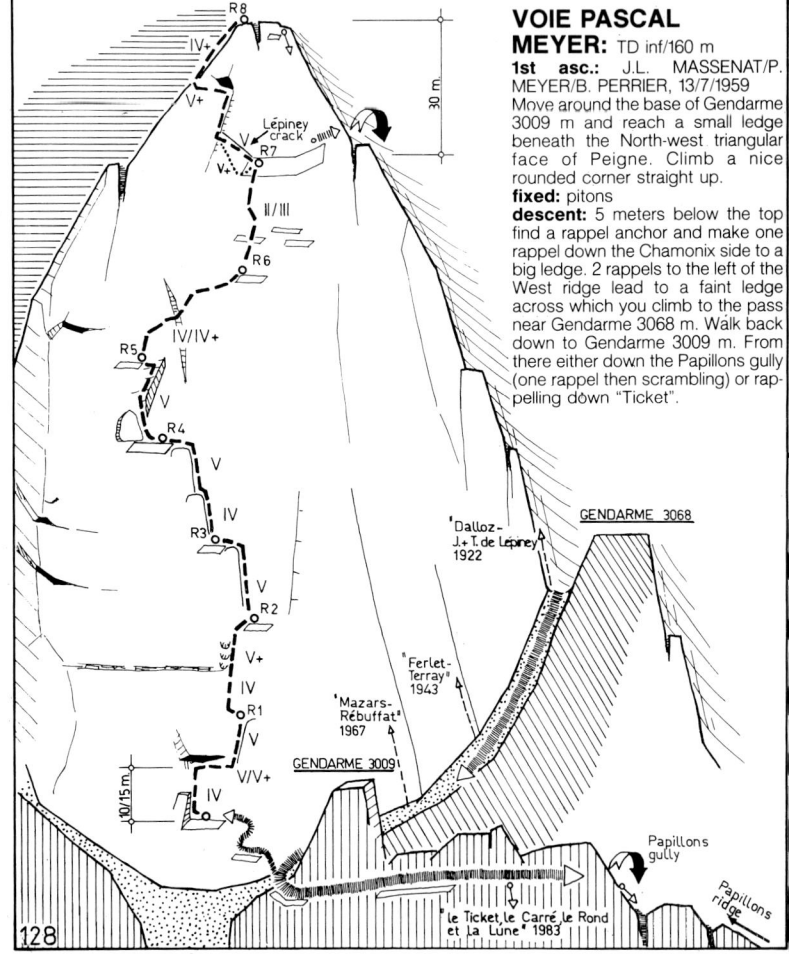

VOIE PASCAL MEYER: TD inf/160 m

1st asc.: J.L. MASSENAT/P. MEYER/B. PERRIER, 13/7/1959

Move around the base of Gendarme 3009 m and reach a small ledge beneath the North-west triangular face of Peigne. Climb a nice rounded corner straight up.

fixed: pitons

descent: 5 meters below the top find a rappel anchor and make one rappel down the Chamonix side to a big ledge. 2 rappels to the left of the West ridge lead to a faint ledge across which you climb to the pass near Gendarme 3068 m. Walk back down to Gendarme 3009 m. From there either down the Papillons gully (one rappel then scrambling) or rappelling down "Ticket".

AIGUILLE DU PEIGNE - EAST FACE OF GENDARME 3068 m

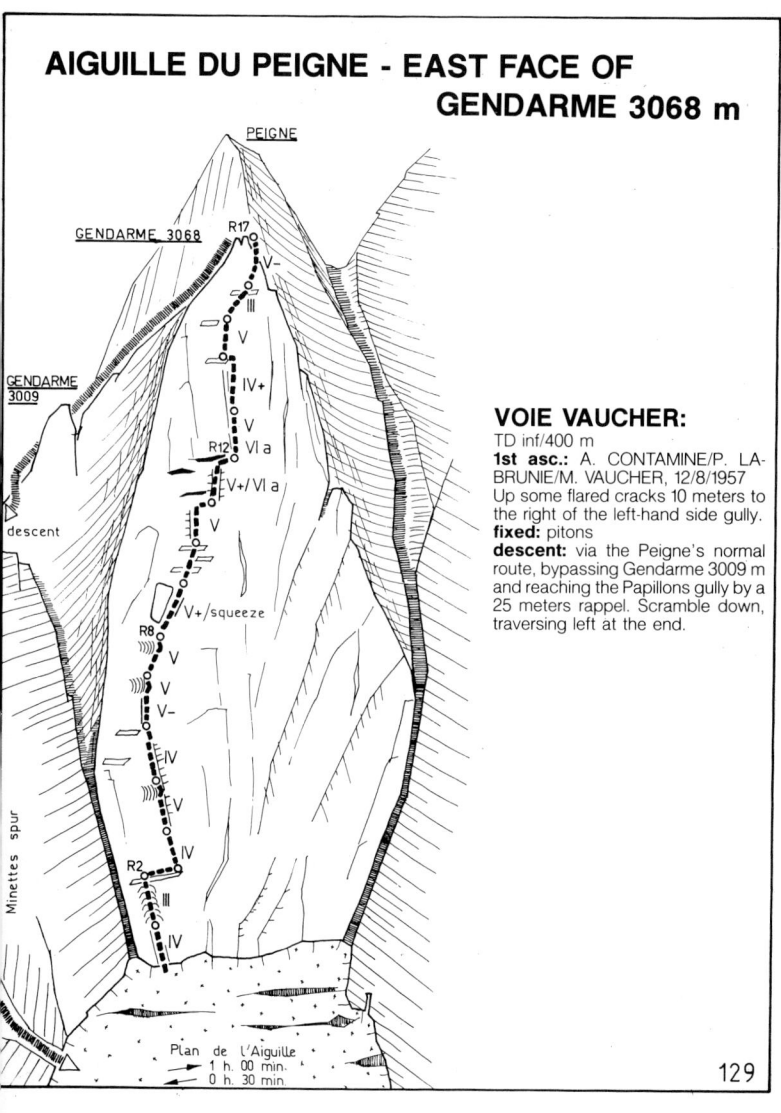

VOIE VAUCHER:

TD inf/400 m

1st asc.: A. CONTAMINE/P. LA-BRUNIE/M. VAUCHER, 12/8/1957
Up some flared cracks 10 meters to the right of the left-hand side gully.
fixed: pitons
descent: via the Peigne's normal route, bypassing Gendarme 3009 m and reaching the Papillons gully by a 25 meters rappel. Scramble down, traversing left at the end.

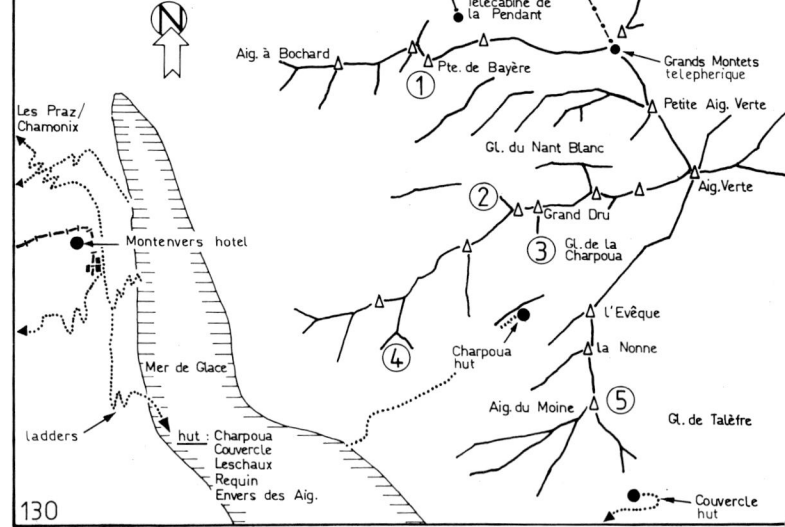

Télécabine de la Pendant

Aig. à Bochard

Pte. de Bayère
①

Grands Montets telepherique

Petite Aig. Verte

Les Praz/ Chamonix

Gl. du Nant Blanc

② Grand Dru

Aig. Verte

③ Gl. de la Charpoua

Montenvers hotel

Charpoua hut

④

L'Evêque

la Nonne

Mer de Glace

Aig. du Moine ⑤

Gl. de Talèfre

ladders

hut : Charpoua
Couvercle
Leschaux
Requin
Envers des Aig.

Couvercle hut

130

AREA N. 8   THE DRUS

Who in the Chamonix valley has not dreamt of scaling this perfect granite spire rising from the timberline? The Dru, wild and jagged, is definitely the landmark of this eighth area.

Montenvers hotel (1909) Phone: (50) 53.00.33
Sleeping there once is a must for whoever enjoys a romantic "turn of the century" atmosphere. Can be reached by the Montenvers train or various trails.

Charpoua hut (2841 m) No phone.
From Montenvers reach the "Mer de Glace" (ladders) and cross the first crevassed area. Move left towards the moraine coming down from the Charpoua and walk up it on a faint path (3 hours).

Couvercle hut (2687 m) Phone: (50) 53.16.94
From Montenvers reach the "Mer de Glace" (ladders) and follow it to the junction of the Tacul and Leschaux glaciers. At the corner on the left step onto the Egralets rocks and climb up some ladders. A good path then leads to the hut (3 to 4 hours).

Upper téléphérique station of Grands Montets (3237 m)
Even though this station is the starting point for numerous climbs there is no acommodation and no water either. For the West face routes on Petit Dru it is best to bivouac on the Rognon du Dru at the foot of the West face.

Approaches to the cliffs:
1. South face of Pointe Bayère
From the Grands Montets go down to the west along the Grands Montets glacier. Keep close to the wall to reach the big ledge at the base.
2. West side of Petit Dru (Passage Cardiaque and Directe Américaine)
From the Grands Montets go up the first slope of "Petite Aig. Verte" (about 40 meters of vertical rise) to a rocky ridge. Start going down on the West side on some loose rocks and cross the upper part of a snow slope to reach a small gully facing the Nant Blanc side of Aig. Verte. Go down the steep narrow gully (45 degrees), step on the glacier and traverse it, going slightly up, to walk beneath the North face of "Pic sans nom". Continue under Petit Dru's North face (up for a shortwhile) and reach the Rognon du Dru, which can also be reached from the Montenvers (long walk).
2 bis. West side of Petit Dru
("Directissime américaine + française" et "Pilier Bonatti")
From Charpoua hut go up the Rognon's ridge to its end, then up the glacier and cross left as soon as possible to reach the ledges below the Grand Dru's pillars. Wander up some easy rocks and ledges to reach the ridge of "Flammes de Pierre" to the South-west of Pointe 3361 m. Good bivy spots. Rappel down the steep rock spur to the left of the North-west gully. One can also climb up that gully from the Rognon du Dru (rockfalls).
3. South side of Grand Dru
Same as 2 but stop at the base of the Grand Dru's pillars.
4. South face of Triangle des Flammes de Pierre
From the moraine leading to the Charpoua hut cross left (North) just beneath the glacier.
5. East face of Aiguille du Moine
From Couvercle hut up Talèfre glacier to the cliff's base.

SOUTH FACE OF POINTE DE BAYERE

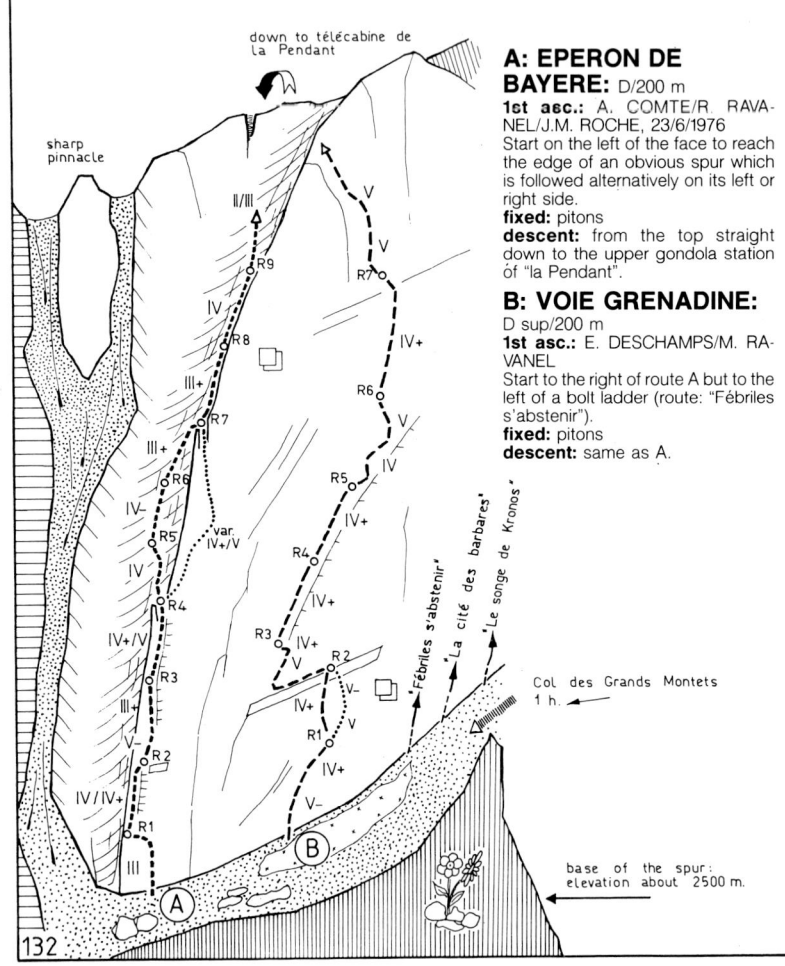

down to télécabine de
la Pendant

sharp
pinnacle

II/III

R9

V

V

R7

IV

R8

III+

R7

IV+

III+

R6

R6

IV-

R5

var.
IV+/V

IV

R5

R4

IV+

IV

R4

IV+

R3

R3

IV+

III+

R2

R2

V

IV+/V

V-

IV+

R2

R1

v

IV/IV+

IV+

R1

V-

III

A

B

"Fébriles s'abstenir"

"La cité des barbares"

"Le songe de Kronos"

Col des Grands Montets
1 h.

base of the spur:
elevation about 2500 m.

A: EPERON DE BAYERE: D/200 m

1st asc.: A. COMTE/R. RAVA-NEL/J.M. ROCHE, 23/6/1976
Start on the left of the face to reach the edge of an obvious spur which is followed alternatively on its left or right side.

fixed: pitons

descent: from the top straight down to the upper gondola station of "la Pendant".

B: VOIE GRENADINE:
D sup/200 m

1st asc.: E. DESCHAMPS/M. RA-VANEL
Start to the right of route A but to the left of a bolt ladder (route: "Fébriles s'abstenir").

fixed: pitons

descent: same as A.

SOUTH FACE OF POINTE DE BAYERE

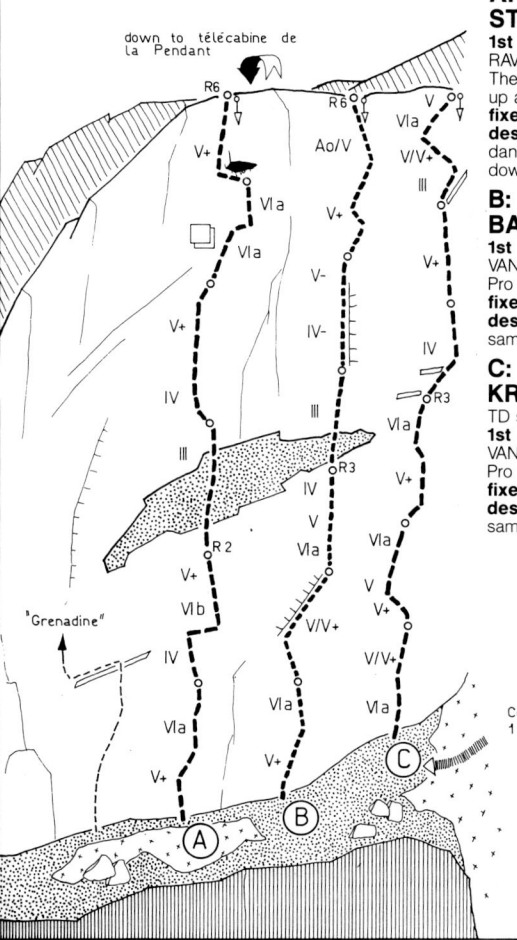

down to télécabine de la Pendant

"Grenadine"

Col des Grands Montets 1 h.

A: FEBRILES D'ABSTENIR: ED inf/200 m/Ao/VIb
1st asc.: E. ARBEZ-GINDRE/M. RAVANEL, 7/3/1984
The pro was placed on rappel. Start up a bolted slab.
fixed: pitons + bolts
descent: walk down to "la Pendant" gondola station or rappel down the route.

B: CITE DES BARBARES: TD sup/200 m/Ao/V+
1st asc.: E. DESCHAMPS/M. RAVANEL, 16/7/1984
Pro placed on rappel.
fixed: pitons + bolts
descent: rappel down the route or same as A.

C: LE SONGE DE KRONOS:
TD sup/200 m/Ao/VIa
1st asc.: E. DESCHAMPS/M. RAVANEL, 19/7/1984
Pro placed on rappel.
fixed: pitons + bolts
descent: rappel down the route or same as A.

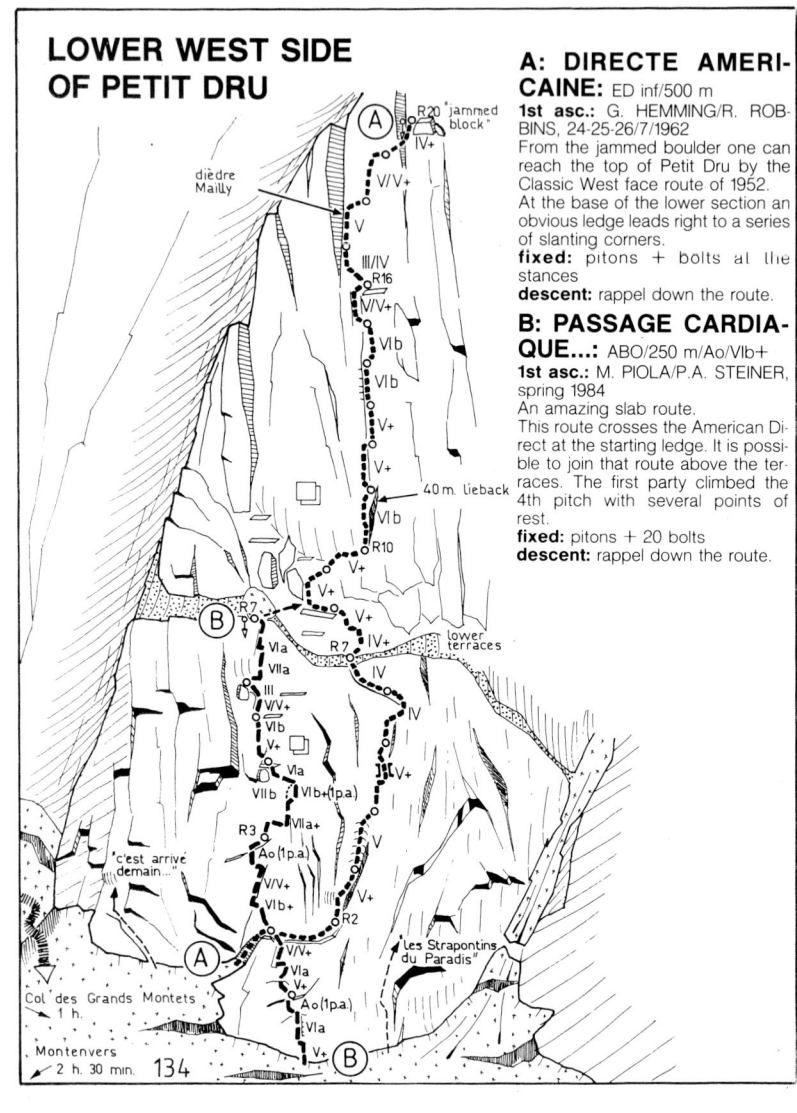

LOWER WEST SIDE OF PETIT DRU

A: DIRECTE AMERICAINE: ED inf/500 m

1st asc.: G. HEMMING/R. ROBBINS, 24-25-26/7/1962

From the jammed boulder one can reach the top of Petit Dru by the Classic West face route of 1952.

At the base of the lower section an obvious ledge leads right to a series of slanting corners.

fixed: pitons + bolts at the stances

descent: rappel down the route.

B: PASSAGE CARDIAQUE...: ABO/250 m/Ao/VIb+

1st asc.: M. PIOLA/P.A. STEINER, spring 1984

An amazing slab route.

This route crosses the American Direct at the starting ledge. It is possible to join that route above the terraces. The first party climbed the 4th pitch with several points of rest.

fixed: pitons + 20 bolts
descent: rappel down the route.

Labels on topo:
- R20 'jammed block' — IV+
- diédre Mailly
- V/V+
- V
- III/IV — R16
- V/V+
- VIb
- VIb
- V+
- V+
- 40 m. lieback
- VIb
- R10
- V+
- V+
- V+
- R7
- VIa
- VIIa
- R7 — IV+
- III — IV
- V/V+
- VIb
- V+
- VIa
- lower terraces
- V+
- VIIb — VIb+(1p.a.)
- VIIa+
- R3 — Ao(1p.a.)
- V/V+
- VIb+
- R2
- V+
- "c'est arrive demain..."
- V/V+
- VIa
- V+
- Ao(1p.a.)
- VIa
- "les Strapontins du Paradis"
- V+
- Col des Grands Montets 1 h.
- Montenvers 2 h. 30 min.
- A
- B

134

UPPER WEST SIDE OF PETIT DRU 3733 m

GRAND DRU

PETIT DRU

notch:
down the
south side

R15

hole joining the
south face

IV

IV+

V+

shoulder

snow covered ledge

V

IV+/V

R10

V

IV+/V

VIa

V

IV+

V

V/V+

V/V+

R4 the Germans
Ledge

V+

VIc

VIa

VIc

V/V+

R1

IV+

VIb

V

jammed
block

Directe
Américaine

classic west
face route

variation:
E. + R. Escoffier/C. Profit
(2.9.81)

CLASSIC ROUTE - UPPER PART: ED inf/500 m

1st asc.: L. BERARDINI/A. DAGORY/M. LAINE/G. MAGNONE, 17-18-19/7/1952

The jammed boulder at the base of the 90 m corner can be reached from the "Classic West face", "Genevois route", "Strapontins du paradis" or "American Direct".

fixed: pitons

descent: on the South side of Petit Dru down to the ridge of Flammes de Pierre, and then the Charpoua valley.

DOWN ON THE SOUTH SIDE OF PETIT DRU'S NOTCH

PETIT
DRU

notch
45m

IV   15m

25m   45m

15m   30m

45m

45m

40m   shoulder

20m

45m

Flammes de
Pierres   45m

135

WEST SIDE OF PETIT DRU 3733 m

DIRECTISSIME AMERI-CAINE:

ABO/600 m/VIc or A3

1st asc.: J. HARLIN/R. ROBBINS, 10-11-12-13/8/1965

One of the hardest and most sustained free climbs of the area. Mostly up cracks with a few dangerous sections on loose rock. Same approach as Bonatti pillar but go further down (3 rappels) and follow the Classic West face route to the upper terraces.

fixed: pitons

descent: from the shoulder rappel down (one diagonal rappel) and cross towards the Petit Dru normal route.

From the notch below Petit Dru by the normal route (topo "Classic West face route").

gear: n. 4 friend, chance of bivouac.

DOWN FROM THE BONATTI PILLAR SHOULDER

136

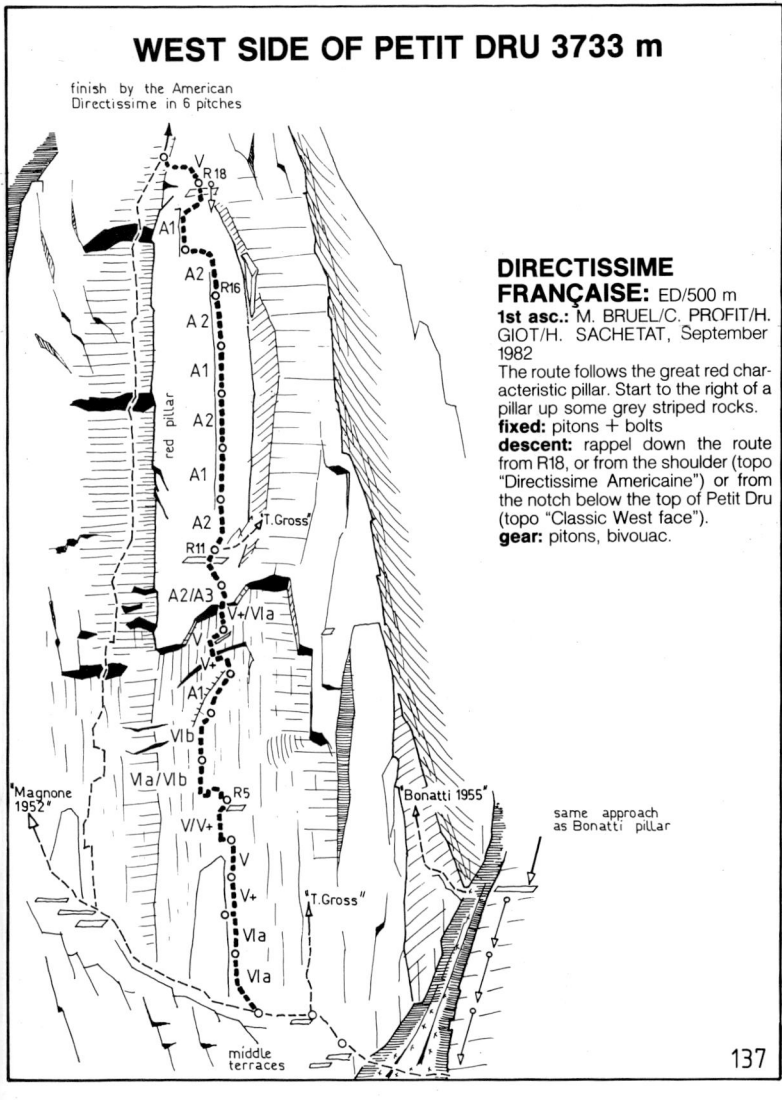

WEST SIDE OF PETIT DRU 3733 m

finish by the American
Directissime in 6 pitches

V R 18

A1

A2 R16

A 2

A 1

A 2

A 1

A 2

"T.Gross"

R11

A2/A3

V+/VIa

V

V+

A1

VIb

VIa/VIb

R5

"Magnone 1952"

V/V+

V

V+

"T.Gross"

VIa

VIa

red pillar

"Bonatti 1955"

same approach
as Bonatti pillar

middle
terraces

DIRECTISSIME FRANÇAISE: ED/500 m

1st asc.: M. BRUEL/C. PROFIT/H. GIOT/H. SACHETAT, September 1982

The route follows the great red characteristic pillar. Start to the right of a pillar up some grey striped rocks.

fixed: pitons + bolts

descent: rappel down the route from R18, or from the shoulder (topo "Directissime Americaine") or from the notch below the top of Petit Dru (topo "Classic West face").

gear: pitons, bivouac.

SOUTH WEST PILLAR OF PETIT DRU 3733 m

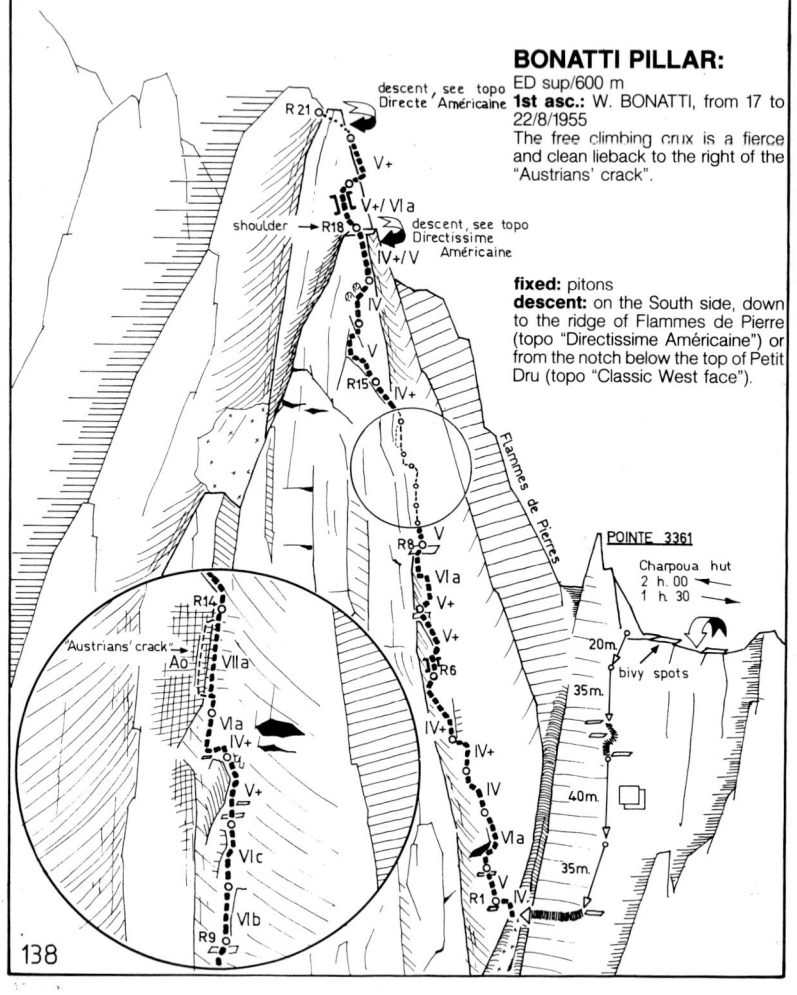

BONATTI PILLAR:

ED sup/600 m

1st asc.: W. BONATTI, from 17 to 22/8/1955

The free climbing crux is a fierce and clean lieback to the right of the "Austrians' crack".

fixed: pitons

descent: on the South side, down to the ridge of Flammes de Pierre (topo "Directissime Américaine") or from the notch below the top of Petit Dru (topo "Classic West face").

descent, see topo
Directe Américaine
R 21

V+

V+/ VI a

shoulder → R18

descent, see topo
Directissime Américaine

IV+/ V

IV

V

R15 IV+

V R8

VI a

V+

V+

R6

IV+

IV+ IV

IV

VI a

V

R1 IV

R14

"Austrians' crack" Ao VII a

VI a IV+

V+

VI c

VI b R9

Flammes de Pierres

POINTE 3361

Charpoua hut
2 h. 00
1 h. 30

20m. bivy spots

35m.

40m.

35m.

138

SOUTH SIDE OF GRAND DRU
3754 m

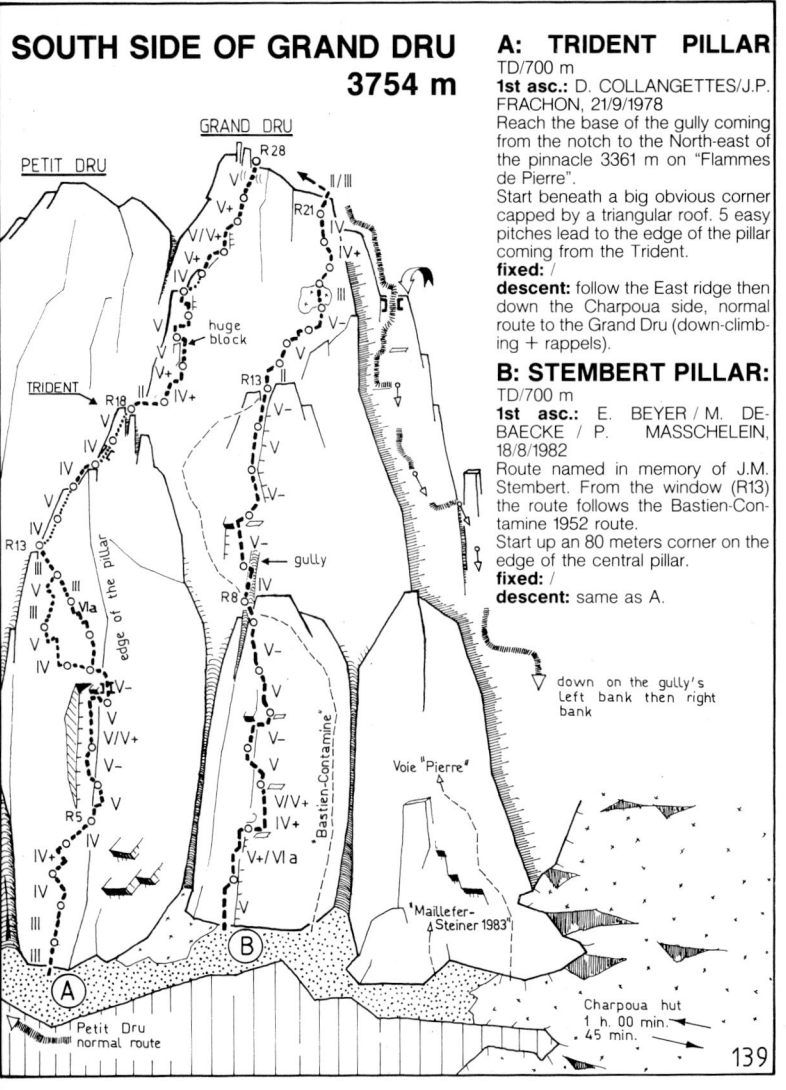

GRAND DRU

PETIT DRU

TRIDENT

R 28

R 21

R 18

R 13

R 8

R 13

R 5

huge block

edge of the pillar

gully

"Bastien-Contamine"

Voie "Pierre"

"Maillefer-Steiner 1983"

Petit Dru normal route

down on the gully's left bank then right bank

Charpoua hut
1 h. 00 min.
45 min.

A: TRIDENT PILLAR

TD/700 m

1st asc.: D. COLLANGETTES/J.P. FRACHON, 21/9/1978

Reach the base of the gully coming from the notch to the North-east of the pinnacle 3361 m on "Flammes de Pierre".

Start beneath a big obvious corner capped by a triangular roof. 5 easy pitches lead to the edge of the pillar coming from the Trident.

fixed: /

descent: follow the East ridge then down the Charpoua side, normal route to the Grand Dru (down-climbing + rappels).

B: STEMBERT PILLAR:

TD/700 m

1st asc.: E. BEYER / M. DE-BAECKE / P. MASSCHELEIN, 18/8/1982

Route named in memory of J.M. Stembert. From the window (R13) the route follows the Bastien-Contamine 1952 route.

Start up an 80 meters corner on the edge of the central pillar.

fixed: /

descent: same as A.

139

SOUTH FACE OF TRIANGLE DES FLAMMES DE PIERRE 2699 m

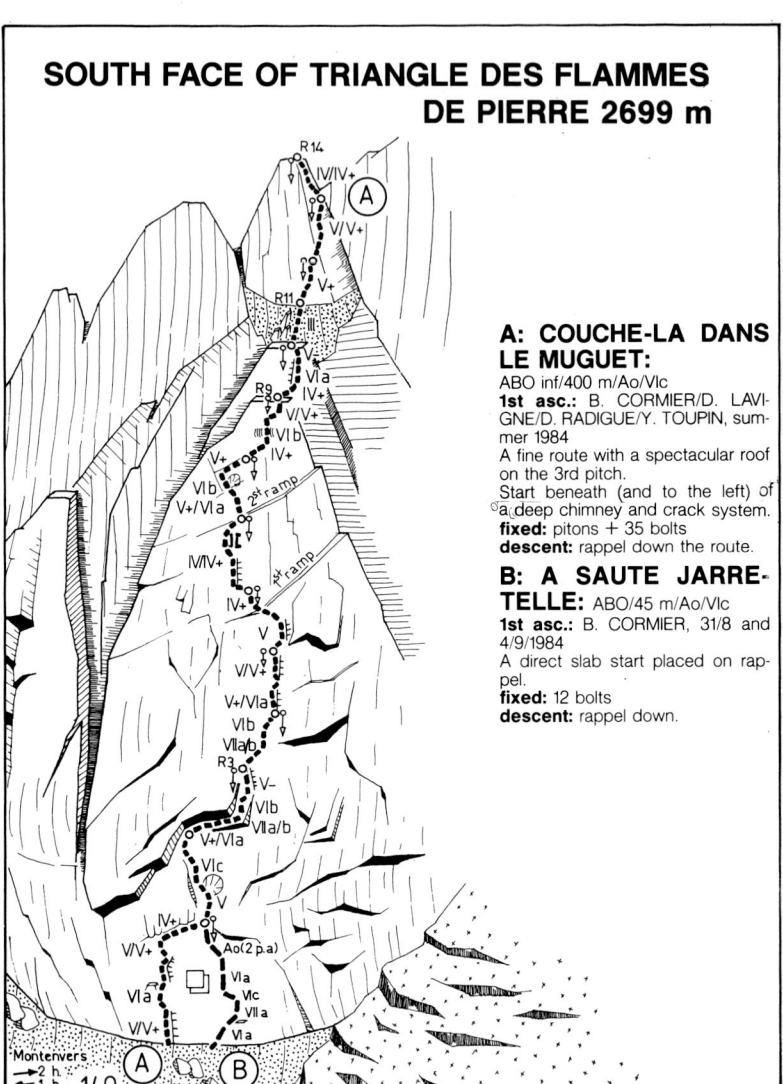

A: COUCHE-LA DANS LE MUGUET:

ABO inf/400 m/Ao/VIc
1st asc.: B. CORMIER/D. LAVIGNE/D. RADIGUE/Y. TOUPIN, summer 1984
A fine route with a spectacular roof on the 3rd pitch.
Start beneath (and to the left) of a deep chimney and crack system.
fixed: pitons + 35 bolts
descent: rappel down the route.

B: A SAUTE JARRETELLE: ABO/45 m/Ao/VIc

1st asc.: B. CORMIER, 31/8 and 4/9/1984
A direct slab start placed on rappel.
fixed: 12 bolts
descent: rappel down.

EAST FACE OF AIGUILLE DU MOINE 3412 m

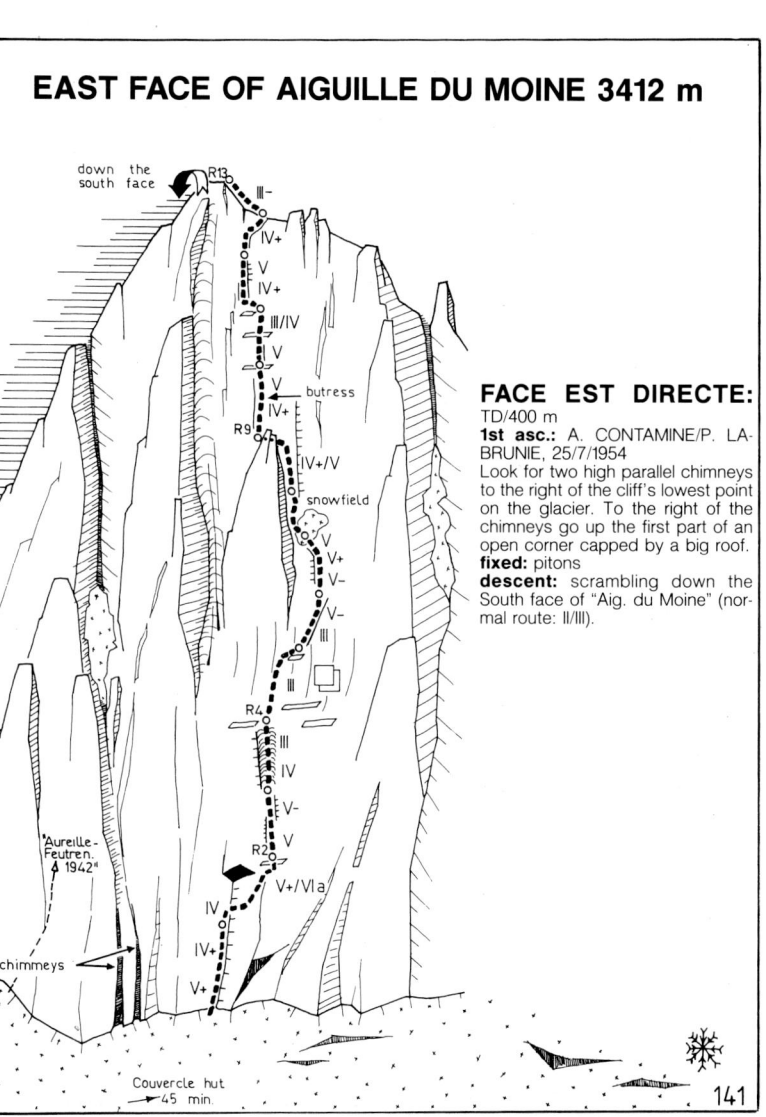

FACE EST DIRECTE:

TD/400 m

1st asc.: A. CONTAMINE/P. LA-BRUNIE, 25/7/1954

Look for two high parallel chimneys to the right of the cliff's lowest point on the glacier. To the right of the chimneys go up the first part of an open corner capped by a big roof.

fixed: pitons

descent: scrambling down the South face of "Aig. du Moine" (normal route: II/III).

AREA n° 9

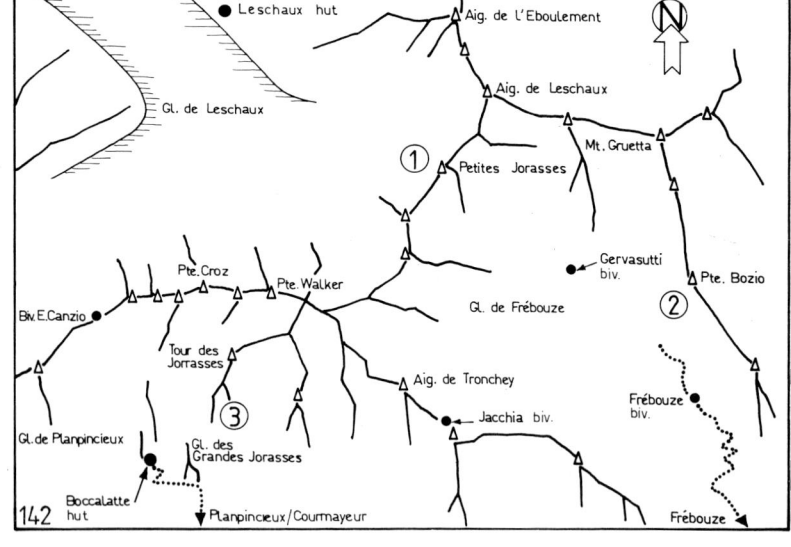

Leschaux hut

Aig. de L'Eboulement

Aig. de Leschaux

Gl. de Leschaux

Mt. Gruetta

① Petites Jorasses

Pte. Croz

Pte. Walker

Gervasutti biv.

Pte. Bozio

②

Biv. E. Canzio

Gl. de Frébouze

Tour des Jorrasses

Aig. de Tronchey

③

Jacchia biv.

Frébouze biv.

Gl. de Planpincieux

Gl. des Grandes Jorasses

142

Boccalatte hut

Planpincieux/Courmayeur

Frébouze

N

AREA N. 9   THE JORASSES

This mountain ridge along the French-Italian border is one of the wildest and most remote areas around Mont Blanc.

Leschaux hut (2431 m) No phone.
From Montenvers reach the "Mer de Glace" glacier and follow it up until the junction between the Leschaux and Tacul glaciers. Go up left on the Leschaux glacier towards the Petites and Grandes Jorasses up to an altitude of about 2380 m and step left off the glacier to reach the hut (3 to 4 hours).

Frébouze shelter (2363 m) No phone.
This shelter, shaped like half of a barrel, can fit a maximum of 3 to 4 people. From Frébouze (Italian Val Ferret, next to "La Vachey Chalet-hôtel") walk up the South-east slopes beneath Frébouze glacier and move right across a rocky ridge (cables) to reach the shelter (2 h 30 min).

Boccalatte or Grandes Jorasses hut (2804 m) No phone.
From the Chapel of Planpincieux glacier, climb a steep rocky section on the right and follow a moraine leading to a rock spur (altitude approximate 2600 m). Cross left and go up the steep slopes to the hut perched on a rocky ridge (3 to 4 hours).

Approaches to the cliffs:
1. West face of Petites Jorasses
From Leschaux hut step back on the glacier and follow it, soon moving left and up the slopes to the cliff's base.
2. South-west face of Pointe Bosio
From Frébouze shelter follow the path to the first snowfields and move right to the cliff's base.
3. South face of Tour des Jorasses
From Boccalatte hut walk back down the path to the top of the moraine beneath the rock spur (altitude of about 2600 m) and go up the Grandes Jorasses glacier to the North-east avoiding the first spur coming down from the "Tour des Jorasses".

WEST FACE OF PETITES JORASSES 3649 m

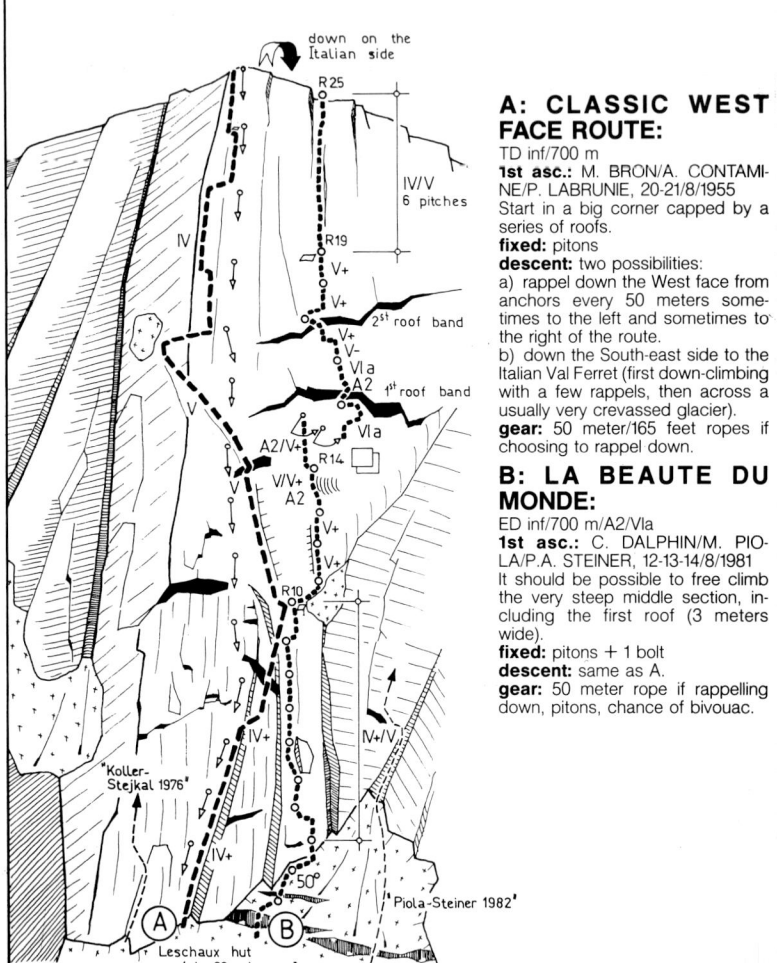

down on the Italian side

R 25

IV/V
6 pitches

R 19

V+
V+

2st roof band

V+
V–
VIa
A2

1st roof band

VIa

A2/V+
R 14

V/V+
A2

V+

V+

R 10

IV+

IV+/V

IV+

50°

"Koller-Stejkal 1976"

Piola-Steiner 1982

Leschaux hut
1 h. 30 min.
45 min

Ⓐ Ⓑ

A: CLASSIC WEST FACE ROUTE:

TD inf/700 m

1st asc.: M. BRON/A. CONTAMINE/P. LABRUNIE, 20-21/8/1955

Start in a big corner capped by a series of roofs.

fixed: pitons

descent: two possibilities:

a) rappel down the West face from anchors every 50 meters sometimes to the left and sometimes to the right of the route.

b) down the South-east side to the Italian Val Ferret (first down-climbing with a few rappels, then across a usually very crevassed glacier).

gear: 50 meter/165 feet ropes if choosing to rappel down.

B: LA BEAUTE DU MONDE:

ED inf/700 m/A2/VIa

1st asc.: C. DALPHIN/M. PIOLA/P.A. STEINER, 12-13-14/8/1981

It should be possible to free climb the very steep middle section, including the first roof (3 meters wide).

fixed: pitons + 1 bolt

descent: same as A.

gear: 50 meter rope if rappelling down, pitons, chance of bivouac.

144

WEST FACE OF PETITES JORASSES – A: FACE OUEST CLASSIQUE, 1955 - B: LA BEAUTE DU MONDE, 1981 – Photo: J. Winkler.

PETIT GRUETTA 3226 m
SOUTH WEST FACE OF POINTE BOSIO

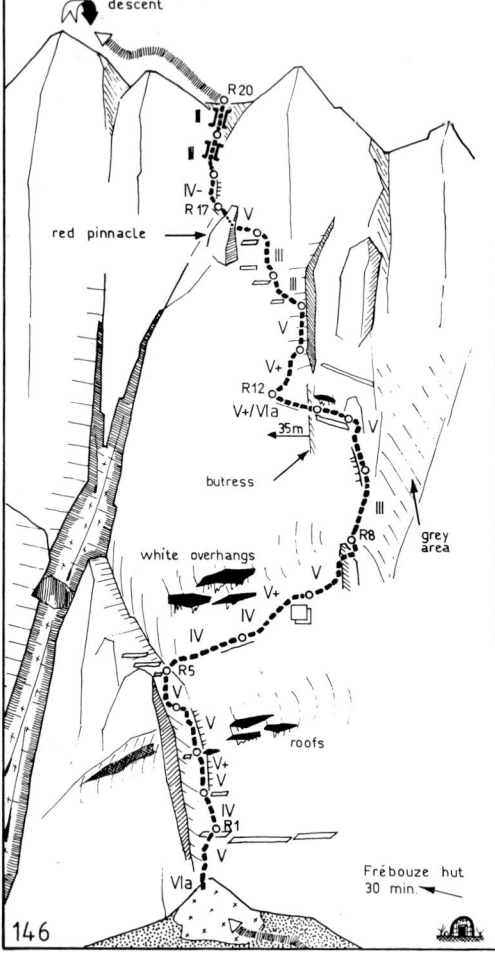

descent

R 20

IV-
R 17

red pinnacle ➤

V

III

III

V

V+

R12

V+/VIa

35m ➤

V

butress ➤

white overhangs

V

III

R8

grey
area

V+

IV

V

IV

R5

V

V

roofs

V+
V

IV
R1

V

VIa

Frébouze hut
30 min. ◄

146

SOUTH WEST FACE:
TD/700 m/Ao/V+
1st asc.: M. BARTHASSAT/J. EMERY, 5-6/8/1976
The descent is rather tricky.
Start on top of a small triangular snowfield at the base of a big obvious corner beneath the huge red pinnacle near the top of the cliff.
fixed: pitons
descent: down the East side: from the top go down crossing several rocky ridges (resisting the temptation of going straight down the gullies on the Gruetta side).
Cross to the right to reach a clear cut little pass at the base of the South-east ridge of Pointe Bosio. This pass can be seen from the Frébouze shelter (4 to 5 hours from the top back to the shelter).
gear: a few pitons.

SOUTH FACE OF TOUR DES JORASSES 3813 m

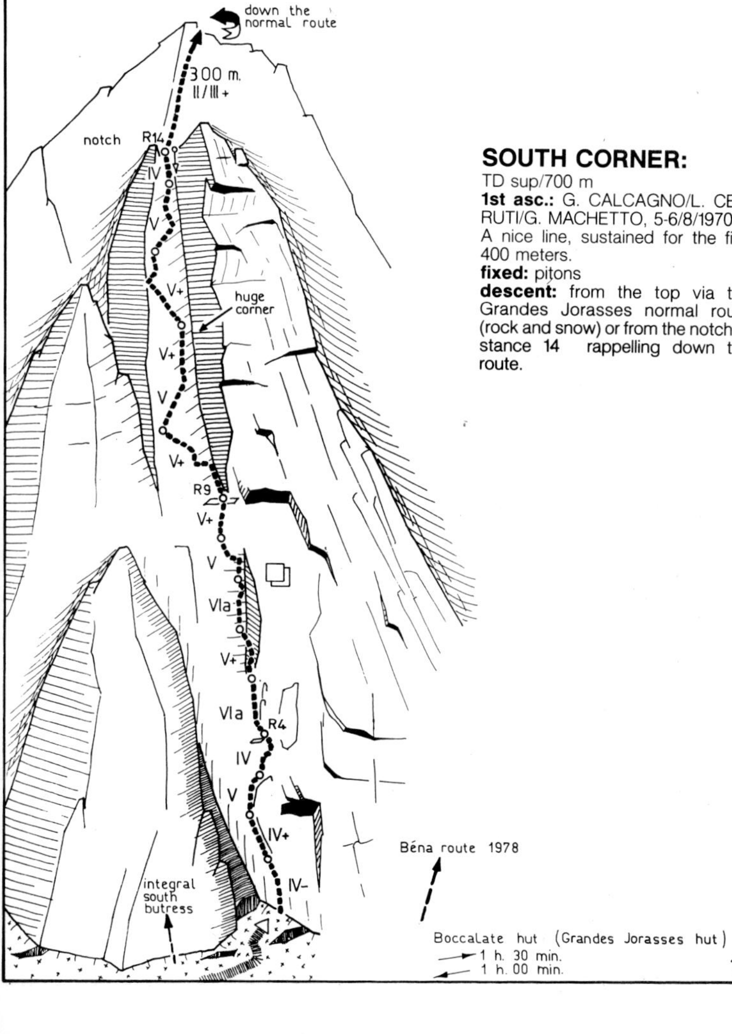

down the
normal route

300 m.
II / III +

notch

R14

IV

V+

huge
corner

V+

V

V+

R9

V+

V

VIa

V+

VIa

R4

IV

V

IV+

IV−

integral
south
butress

SOUTH CORNER:
TD sup/700 m
1st asc.: G. CALCAGNO/L. CER-
RUTI/G. MACHETTO, 5-6/8/1970
A nice line, sustained for the first
400 meters.
fixed: pitons
descent: from the top via the
Grandes Jorasses normal route
(rock and snow) or from the notch of
stance 14 rappelling down the
route.

Béna route 1978

Boccalate hut (Grandes Jorasses hut)
→ 1 h. 30 min.
→ 1 h. 00 min.

147

AREA n° 10

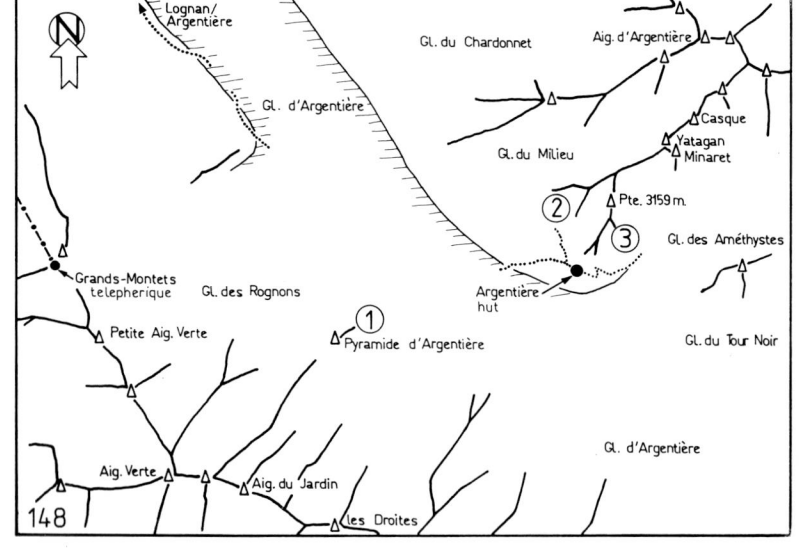

N

Lognan/
Argentière

Gl. du Chardonnet

Aig. d'Argentière

Gl. d'Argentière

Gl. du Milieu

Casque

Yatagan
Minaret

Pte. 3159 m.

② ③

Gl. des Améthystes

Grands-Montets
telepherique

Gl. des Rognons

Argentière
hut

Petite Aig. Verte

① Pyramide d'Argentière

Gl. du Tour Noir

Gl. d'Argentière

Aig. Verte

Aig. du Jardin

148

les Droites

AREA N. 10   THE ARGENTIERE GLACIER

Better known for its great ice routes or as the first stop on the "Haute Route" ski tour, the area around the Argentière hut has nonetheless, much potential for rock climbing.

Argentière hut (2771 m) Phone: (50) 53.16.92
a) From Croix de Lognan (intermediate téléphérique station of Grands Montets) follow the path East towards the old hostel and move right to walk up the moraine on the right of the Argentière glacier. At 2250 m reach the glacier and go up, sometimes staying on the glacier itself, sometimes on its side (red point marks). Continue towards the "Pyramide d'Argentière" and then traverse to the other side of the glacier and up to the hut which can't be missed (3h 30 min).
b) From the upper téléphérique station of Grands Montets walk down on the North east side of the Grands Montets pass, on the Rognons glacier. Move right to reach a flat part on the Argentière glacier and then same as a) (1h 30 min).

Approaches to the cliffs:
1. East face of Pyramide d'Argentière
a) From the téléphérique of Grands Montets follow the way to the Argentière hut to the base of the Pyramide, which is a characteristic rock buttress and the first part of the Grande Rocheuse North-east buttress.
b) From Argentière hut go back down to the glacier and cross it to the West South-west.
2. South-west face of lower Plateau on "l'Aig. d'Argentière"
From Argentière hut follow a small track leading to the moraine on the right of the Milieu glacier.
3. "Antécime sud de la Pointe 3159 m" on the "Plateau du Jardin d'Argentière"
From Argentière hut, follow a good path to the moraine on the right bank of the Améthystes glacier, avoiding the first buttress coming from the Jardin ridge and then moving left to reach the cliff's base.

EAST FACE OF PYRAMIDE D'ARGENTIERE
POINTE 2866 m

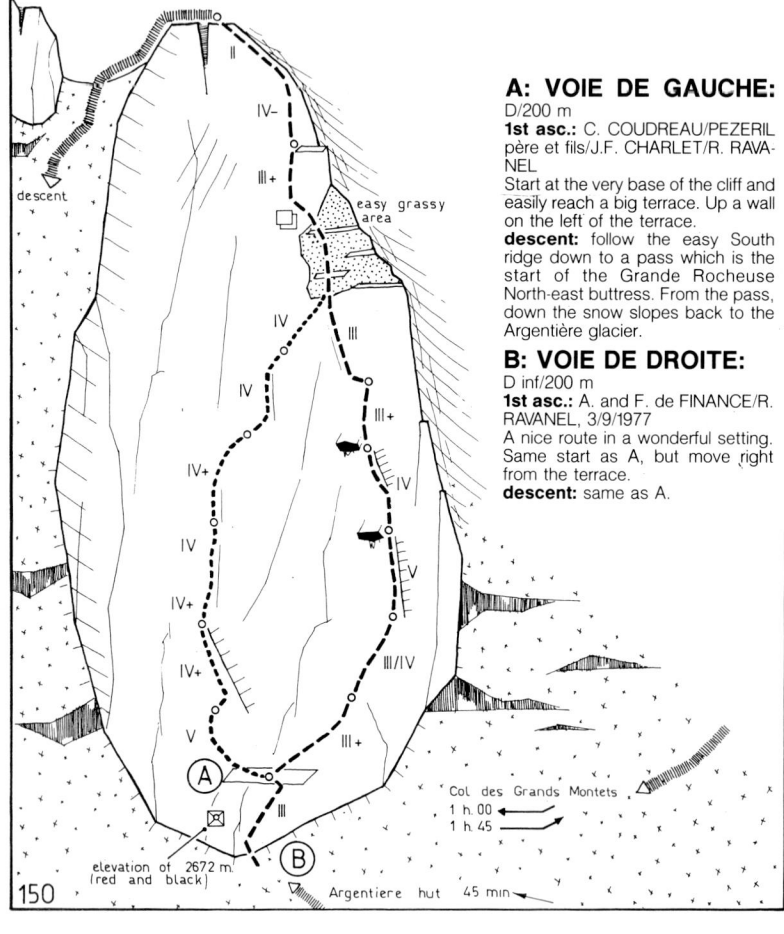

A: VOIE DE GAUCHE:
D/200 m

1st asc.: C. COUDREAU/PEZERIL père et fils/J.F. CHARLET/R. RAVANEL

Start at the very base of the cliff and easily reach a big terrace. Up a wall on the left of the terrace.

descent: follow the easy South ridge down to a pass which is the start of the Grande Rocheuse North-east buttress. From the pass, down the snow slopes back to the Argentière glacier.

B: VOIE DE DROITE:
D inf/200 m

1st asc.: A. and F. de FINANCE/R. RAVANEL, 3/9/1977

A nice route in a wonderful setting. Same start as A, but move right from the terrace.

descent: same as A.

AIGUILLE D'ARGENTIERE
SOUTH WEST FACE OF LOWER PLATEAU

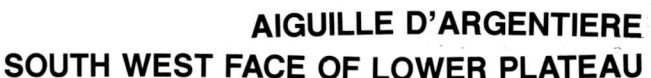

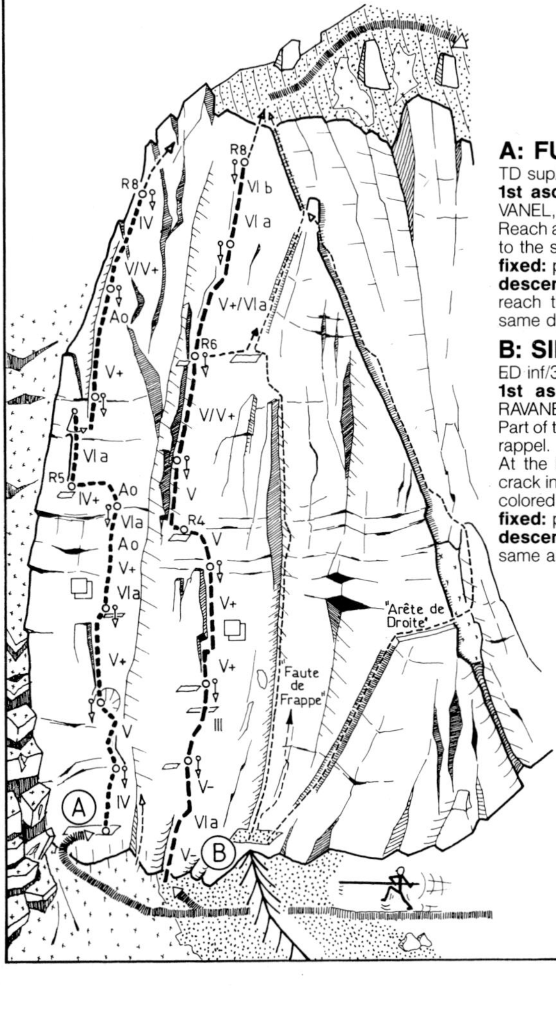

Argentière hut
15 min ←
10 min →

A: FUREUR DE VIVRE:

TD sup/300 m
1st asc.: E. DESCHAMPS/M. RAVANEL, 30/7/1984
Reach a ledge on the left, very close to the seracs.
fixed: pitons + bolts
descent: rappel down the route or reach the lower Plateau and then same descent as "Dièdre central".

B: SINGE BLEU:

ED inf/300 m/Ao/VIa
1st asc.: E. ARBEZ-GINDRE/M. RAVANEL, 11/3/1984
Part of the protection was placed on rappel.
At the base of the cliff, look for a crack in between two rounded light-colored pillars. Go up the crack.
fixed: pitons
descent: rappel down the route or same as "Dièdre central".

AIGUILLE D'ARGENTIERE
SOUTH WEST FACE OF LOWER PLATEAU

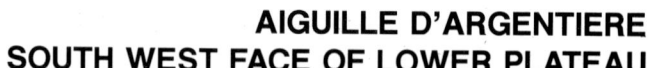

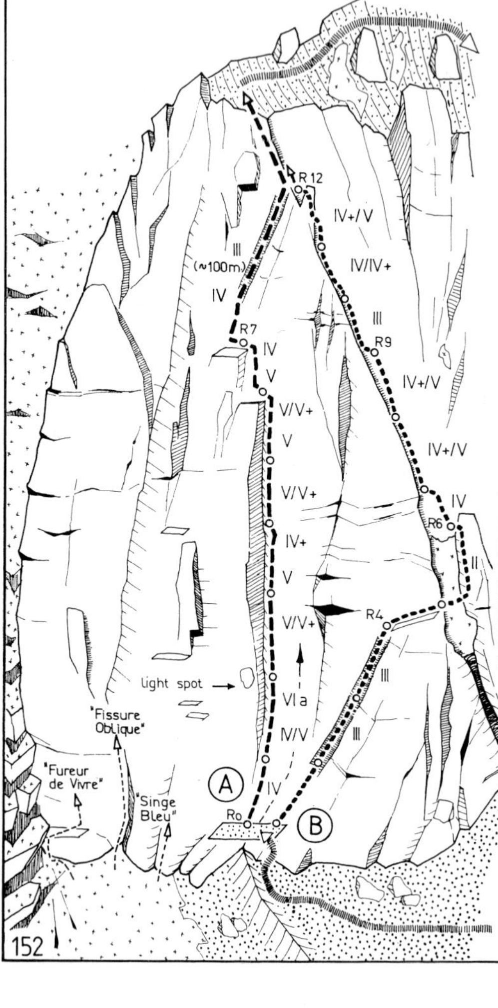

R 12
IV+/V
III
(≈100m)
IV/IV+
IV
III
R7
IV
R9
V
IV+/V
V/V+
V
IV+/V
V/V+
IV
R6
IV+
II
V
V/V+
R4
III
light spot
VI a
III
"Fissure Oblique"
IV/V
"Fureur de Vivre"
A
IV
"Singe Bleu"
Ro
B
Argentière hut
15 min.
10 min.

A: LE DIEDRE CENTRAL: TD/300 m

1st asc.: R. RAVANEL/F. SIMATOS, august 1972

An obvious line up the main central corner. The VIa crux as well as the other moves can be easily backed up with nuts. Right above the moraine easily reach a terrace beneath the corner.

fixed: pitons, wooden wedges!

descent: move East and go down an easy chimney on the Améthystes side. To the right follow some big pinkish slabs and easily move back to a notch which leads on its East side to the moraine from Améthystes glacier, and then to the hut (40 min).

B: RIGHT-HAND SIDE RIDGE: D sup/300 m

1st asc.: H. FESSNER/R. RAVANEL, 18/8/1974

From the terrace move diagonally to the right up some easy ground.

fixed: pitons

descent: same as A.

ANTECIME SUD OF POINTE 3159 m ON THE PLATEAU DU JARDIN

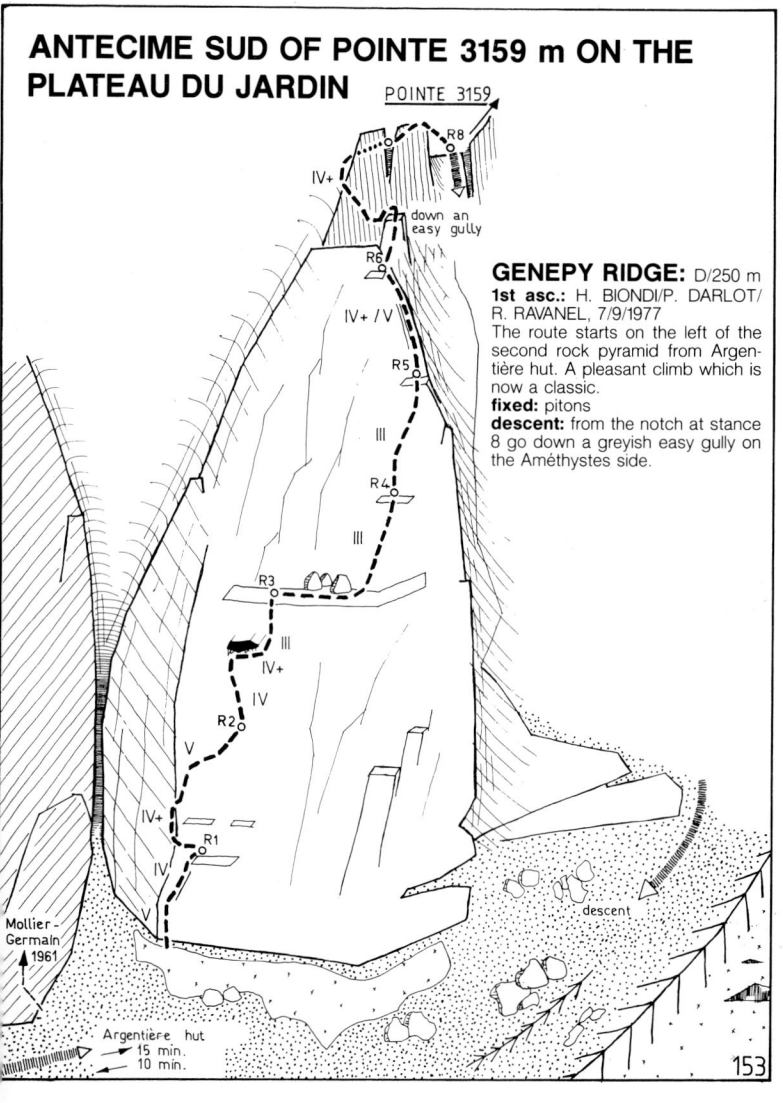

POINTE 3159

GENEPY RIDGE: D/250 m
1st asc.: H. BIONDI/P. DARLOT/ R. RAVANEL, 7/9/1977
The route starts on the left of the second rock pyramid from Argentière hut. A pleasant climb which is now a classic.
fixed: pitons
descent: from the notch at stance 8 go down a greyish easy gully on the Améthystes side.

IV+

R8

down an easy gully

R6

IV+ / V

R5

III

R4

III

R3

III

IV+

IV

R2

V

IV+

R1

IV

V

Mollier-Germain
1961

descent

Argentière hut
15 min.
10 min.

AREA n° 11

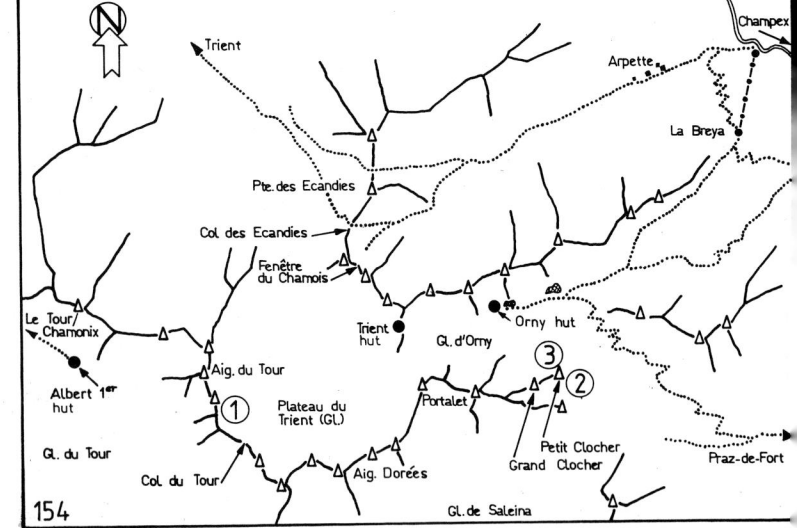

Trient

Champex

Arpette

La Breya

Pte. des Ecandies

Col des Ecandies

Fenêtre
du Chamois

Orny hut

Le Tour/
Chamonix

Trient
hut

Gl. d'Orny

Albert 1er
hut

Aig. du Tour

① ③ ②

Plateau du
Trient (GL)

Portalet

Petit Clocher
Grand Clocher

Praz-de-Fort

Gl. du Tour

Col du Tour

Aig. Dorées

Gl. de Saleina

AREA N. 11   THE TRIENT PLATEAU

None of the summits from this French and Swiss area can be seen from the Chamonix valley. Thus this intricate area is little known but well worth a visit.

Albert Premier hut (2702 m) Phone: (50) 54.06.20
a) From Tour follow the path next to the skilift towards the lower part of the Tour glacier. Reach the moraine on the glacier's right bank and follow it up to the hut (2 h 30 min).
b) From the intermediate gondola station of Tour (Charmillon) follow a path that goes beneath Charmillon lake and then moves South around the Bec du Picheu ridge. A steep track (cables) leads to the moraine on the Tour glacier's right bank which is followed to the hut (2 hours).
c) From the upper gondola station of Tour (Balme) follow the path to South that goes beneath Charmillon lake and then same as b).

Trient hut (3170 m) Phone: (026) 4.14.38
a) From Orny hut walk up the left bank of the Orny glacier to the Orny pass and move right (or, before the pass, follow some red marks up the rocks on the right) (1 hour).
b) From Trient follow the path to the Ecandies pass, cross it, go down its East side and up to the "Fenêtre des Chamois", to reach the Trient plateau and then the hut (5 to 6 hours).
c) From Champex, up to the "Chalets d'Arpette" and follow "Val d'Arpette". Walk up the valley beneath the Ecandies pass and move left to cross the "Fenêtre des Chamois" (5 to 6 hours).

Orny hut (2686 m) Phone: (026) 4.18.87
a) From the upper chairlift station of Breya, follow the path crossing at the same level the South-East side of the Orny valley-Walk up this valley and then the left bank of the Orny glacier to the hut (2h 30 min).
b) From Praz-de-Fort follow the path up the Saleina Val d'Arpette and reach a) on the left bank of the moraine of the Orny glacier (4 hours).

Approaches to the cliffs:
1. Aiguille Purtscheller
a) From Albert Premier hut go up the Tour glacier and cross the Tour pass to reach the Trient Plateau.
b) From Trient hut simply cross the Trient plateau towards the South ridge.
2. South-east ridge of Petit Clocher du Portalet
From Orny hut, cross the Orny glacier above its lowest point; cross the moraine on the glacier's right bank; move up beneath the Petit Clocher's North face and bypass the East face on the left by a ledge, in order to reach the start of the South-east ridge.
3. North face of Petit Clocher du Portalet
Same as 2 until beneath the North face.

AIGUILLE PURTSCHELLER 3478 m

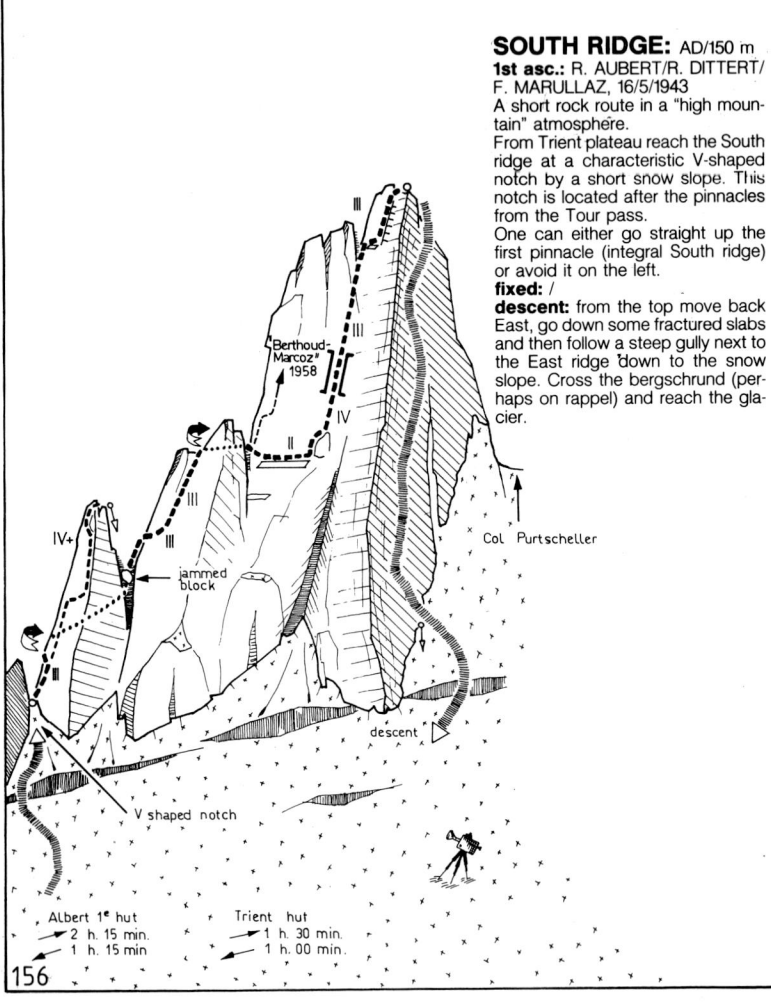

SOUTH RIDGE: AD/150 m
1st asc.: R. AUBERT/R. DITTERT/
F. MARULLAZ, 16/5/1943
A short rock route in a "high mountain" atmosphere.
From Trient plateau reach the South ridge at a characteristic V-shaped notch by a short snow slope. This notch is located after the pinnacles from the Tour pass.
One can either go straight up the first pinnacle (integral South ridge) or avoid it on the left.
fixed: /
descent: from the top move back East, go down some fractured slabs and then follow a steep gully next to the East ridge down to the snow slope. Cross the bergschrund (perhaps on rappel) and reach the glacier.

III

III

III

Berthoud-
Marcoz
1958

IV

II

III

IV+

III

jammed
block

II

Col Purtscheller

descent

V shaped notch

Albert 1ᵉ hut
2 h. 15 min.
1 h. 15 min.

Trient hut
1 h. 30 min.
1 h. 00 min.

SOUTH EAST RIDGE OF PETIT CLOCHER DU PORTALET 2823 m

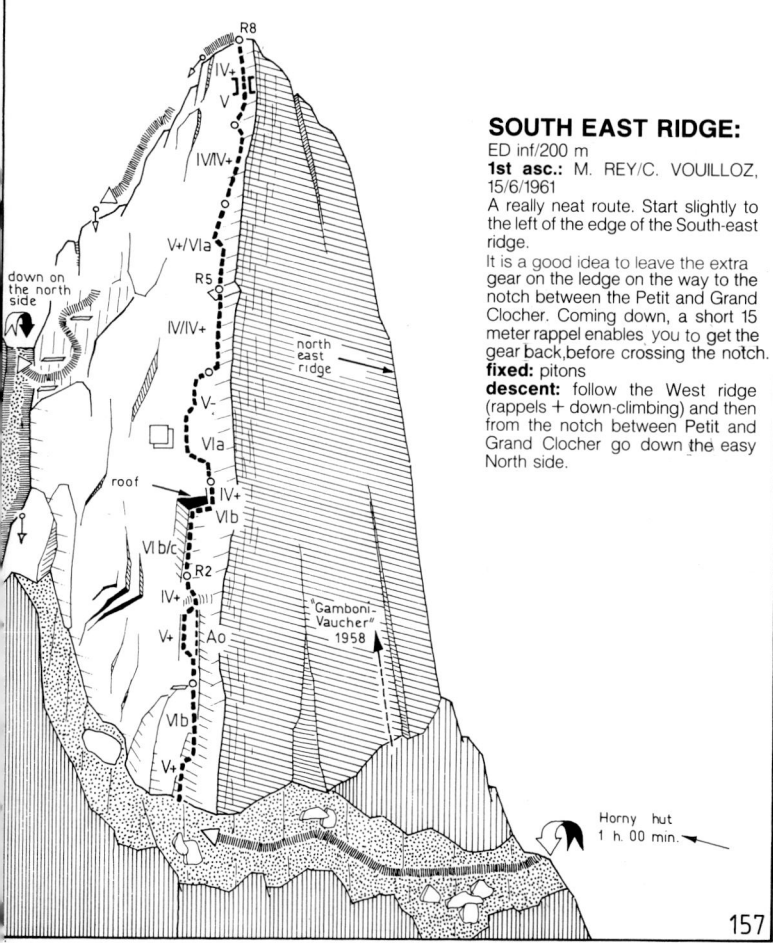

SOUTH EAST RIDGE:
ED inf/200 m

1st asc.: M. REY/C. VOUILLOZ, 15/6/1961

A really neat route. Start slightly to the left of the edge of the South-east ridge.

It is a good idea to leave the extra gear on the ledge on the way to the notch between the Petit and Grand Clocher. Coming down, a short 15 meter rappel enables you to get the gear back, before crossing the notch.
fixed: pitons
descent: follow the West ridge (rappels + down-climbing) and then from the notch between Petit and Grand Clocher go down the easy North side.

R8
IV+
V
IV/IV+
V+/VIa
R5
IV/IV+
V-
VIa
roof
IV+
VIb
VI b/c.
R2
IV+
V+ Ao
VIb
V+

down on the north side

north east ridge

"Gamboni-Vaucher" 1958

Horny hut
1 h. 00 min.

NORTH FACE OF PETIT CLOCHER DU PORTALET 2823 m

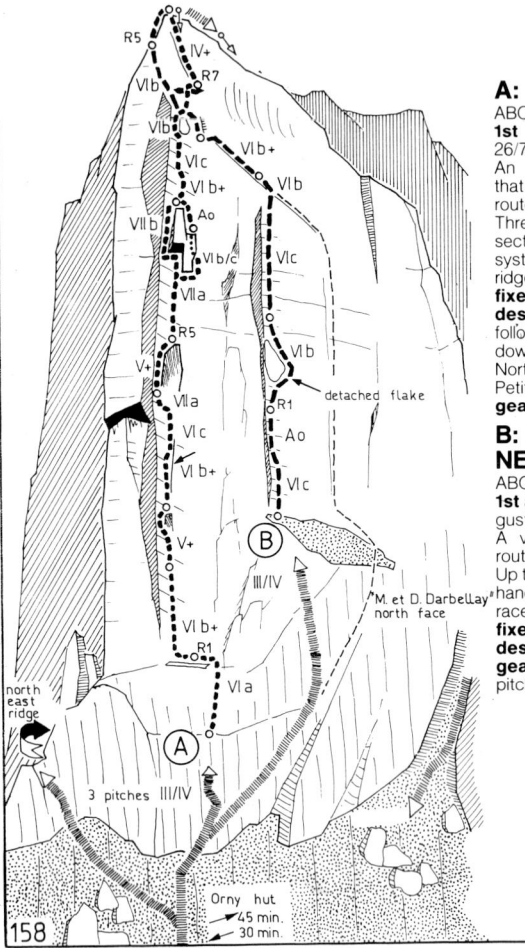

A: ETAT DE CHOC:

ABO inf/200 m/Ao/VIb+
1st asc.: C. REMY/Y. REMY, 25-26/7/1983
An amazing and strenuous climb that matches the best Yosemite routes.
Three easy pitches up the lower section lead to the obvious crack system to the right of the East ridge.
fixed: pitons + 6 bolts
descent: rappel down the route or follow the West ridge (rappels + down-climbing) and then down the North side of the notch between Petit and Grand Clocher.
gear: n. 4 friend, a few large nuts.

B: LA GUERRE DES NERFS:

ABO inf/150 m/Ao/VIb
1st asc.: L. ABBET/F. RODUIT, August 1983
A very strenuous and sustained route up wide cracks.
Up the easy lower section to the left-hand side corner of a wide terrace.
fixed: pitons
descent: same as A.
gear: 4 n. 4 friends for the third pitch.

boreal

FIRÉ

Jhon Bachar, Ron Kauk,
Wolfgang Gullich, Jerry
Moffat, Kim Carrigan...